Strategic Crisis Communication

Addressing 21st-century issues, threats, and opportunities with time-tested principles, this book empowers corporate communications professionals to protect, inspire, and energize organizations in the face of a crisis. Whether due to an external incident or an internal misstep, every major company or institution will find itself scrutinized, its normal operations disrupted, and its reputation and business continuity threatened at some point – and how it prepares for, and reacts to, a crisis can make a critical difference in the ultimate outcome of events. This book focuses on strategic crisis communication as a function of three elements: (1) crisis preparation – establishing a robust and nimble infrastructure and plans, in advance of any crisis, (2) crisis management – rapidly gathering information, activating and adjusting plans, making decisions, and relentlessly monitoring outcomes, (3) crisis communication – reaching multiple audiences, on multiple platforms, with clear, consistent, and purposeful messages that tell the truth and defend the organization. Bringing together best practices gleaned from hundreds of recent case studies, this book is an unmatched resource enabling corporate communications and PR professionals, and the organizations that employ them, to understand how to weather any reputational storm that may threaten their enterprise.

James Scofield O'Rourke, IV is an American rhetorician and professor of management with a global reputation in business education. He has taught for more than 30 years at the University of Notre Dame, pursuing research specialties in crisis management, change communication, and reputation management. He is the author of numerous academic texts and trade books and is directing editor of more than 400 business school case studies.

Jeffrey A. Smith leads Strategic Corporate Communications, providing counsel on crisis management, employee communications, and professional staffing. Formerly Vice President, North American Corporate Communications, at American Honda Motor Co., Inc., he was a trade association executive and senior staff member in the United States Congress. He holds a bachelor of arts degree from Georgetown University.

Strategic Crisis Communication

James S. O'Rourke, IV
and Jeffrey A. Smith

 Routledge
Taylor & Francis Group

NEW YORK AND LONDON

Designed cover image: Getty Images

First published 2023
by Routledge
605 Third Avenue, New York, NY 10158

and by Routledge
4 Park Square, Milton Park, Abingdon, Oxon, OX14 4RN

Routledge is an imprint of the Taylor & Francis Group, an informa business

Library of Congress Cataloging-in-Publication Data
Names: O'Rourke, James S., 1946– author. | Smith, Jeffrey A.
   (Crisis communication expert), author.
Title: Strategic crisis communication / James S. O'Rourke IV,
   Jeffrey Smith.
Description: New York, NY : Routledge, 2023. | Includes
   bibliographical references and index.
Identifiers: LCCN 2022060822 (print) | LCCN 2022060823 (ebook) |
   ISBN 9781032342610 (hardback) | ISBN 9781032342580 (paperback) |
   ISBN 9781003322849 (ebook)
Subjects: LCSH: Crisis management. | Communication in
   management. | Communication in organizations.
Classification: LCC HD49 .O76 2023 (print) | LCC HD49 (ebook) |
   DDC 658.4/056—dc23/eng/20230118
LC record available at https://lccn.loc.gov/2022060822
LC ebook record available at https://lccn.loc.gov/2022060823

ISBN: 978-1-032-34261-0 (hbk)
ISBN: 978-1-032-34258-0 (pbk)
ISBN: 978-1-003-32284-9 (ebk)

DOI: 10.4324/9781003322849

Typeset in Bembo
by Apex CoVantage, LLC

James S. O'Rourke, IV: This is dedicated to my wife, best friend, and lifelong companion, Pamela Spencer O'Rourke. And, alongside her, our daughters Colleen, Molly, and Kathleen. Extended family includes Jay, Cianan, Ty, Kristen, and Justin. Absent you in my life, this merry jig is all for naught.

Jeffrey A. Smith: Dedicated to Susan, my beautiful wife and superb editor, and to Bevin, Conor, Teague, Ashley and Austen.

Contents

Foreword

The trust landscape has changed profoundly in the past five years. Today, business is the most trusted institution and the last retaining wall for a functioning society. Our annual *Trust Barometer* points to competence being the key differentiator between business and government, with business ranking 50 points higher on that metric because it delivers on its goals. There has also been an evolution of trust in the workplace, which has become hyper-localized to "my CEO," a company's newsletter, or work colleagues. This inverted shift from top-down messages from authority figures to bottom-up messages from belief-driven employees and consumers has put new demands on corporate leaders to lead from the front on a broader set of issues that extend far beyond the bottom line.

These shifts in trust are magnified and complicated by a vigorous Battle for Truth, in which facts are easily replaced by fiction or opinion. Expressed across a fragmented ecosystem of both online and offline news, the battle lines themselves are often blurred. Mainstream media has become, in many instances, polarized. A quarter of people in our annual survey shared that they have altogether stopped consuming news media because it is too disturbing or too depressing. Those who do read and watch news media often get stuck in a silo of sameness reinforced each day by the consumption of information that is wholly consistent with their own world view while ignoring the rest. In this environment, fake news has been able to thrive and is challenged less – and worse, it is shared ten times more frequently than the truth.

Set against this backdrop and in a world of partial attention, a domino of crises sent tremors through already challenged institutions. The Me Too movement ignited employee activism, with mass walkouts from large companies that forced many to revisit, reeducate, and reform gender parity policies. The murder of George Floyd spurred a long overdue racial reckoning, with insistence on diverse audiences in positions of power and inclusion in the supply chain. The recognition at COP 26 that governments were at loggerheads while the planet continued to warm pushed the private sector to step up commitments to zero carbon by 2040. COVID caused scrutiny and growing mistrust of the scientific community, particularly those who work in government, as changing data patterns, inconsistent public health messages, and vaccine disbursement debacles made people believe science itself was negotiable. Most recently, the Russian invasion of Ukraine demonstrated on a global stage how fragile and perilous a brokered peace can be, with 1,300 companies exiting Russia, further fracturing the global economy. As the last institution with a fragile trust, business must decide how to navigate across these issues at scale and at speed.

Edelman's *Connected Crisis* study indicates that the vast majority of c-suites and board rooms alike admit that the growing number of risks affiliated with their business will likely result in a crisis in the next three years. However, they also admit that they feel woefully understaffed, underprepared, and underfunded to inoculate themselves against what is likely to come. There is new urgency spawned from these macro crises to better understand how they should lead their respective companies through these events – and those that have yet to occur.

We have helped our clients during these moments and worked to prepare them for what lies ahead. We create tools and provide resources so that they can see issues as they begin to percolate across their stakeholder set, and, based on insights gathered from data, we advise them on when to engage directly and when others who may be better suited will do so on their behalf. We deliver risk assessments on a wide range of challenges our clients face that may have a detrimental impact on their brand and reputation. And we help them better understand societal issues and the impact they will have on their employee base, supply chain, third parties, and customers and consumers of their products and services.

Yet when a crisis strikes, the reputational playing field is anew. The prologue of the past may inform decisions, but the stakes, nuances, and stakeholder set require renewed, if not fresh, thinking. Tools and plans are critical, and they need to be coupled with judgment to be deployed properly.

Strategic Crisis Communication by James S. O'Rourke, IV and Jeffrey A. Smith lays a foundation for leaders, communicators, and companies more broadly on how to get it right, how to move faster, and how to begin thinking ahead about crisis events on the horizon. Each chapter outlines not just the theory but real examples of how companies have faced their challenges head on, many requiring systemic changes, modifications of their business practices, or a complete reset of how to operate differently in the future.

While every crisis has its own unique set of circumstances and challenges, there are some universal truths that emerge in this book. The companies who got it right made tough decisions that usually meant taking actions that would have at least a short-term financial toll. They spoke to their issues and went about solving them openly and transparently. Those who got it wrong tried to short-circuit a response, failed to identify the right sets of challenges, and often delivered a solution that failed to meet stakeholder expectations.

The need for the corporate voice to be heard has never been more paramount. In a world of distrust and compounding crises, business leaders must be ready, resilient, and able to respond when their license to operate is put into question.

Whether a crisis has struck inside corporate walls or is hammering at the front door to enter, if there was ever a time for business to lead and for business leaders to solve, it is now. Communication needs to be predicated with action to rebuild trust, especially in a crisis. The fundamentals of when, how, and who should step forward to communicate about how a company is managing, mitigating, and responding to a crisis are outlined in the chapters that follow.

Richard Edelman
CEO of Edelman
New York, NY
November 1, 2022

Acknowledgments

James S. O'Rourke, IV: Acknowledgments to my Fanning Center colleagues, along with my friends and colleagues in the Arthur W. Page Society. You are an endless font of good ideas and sincere support. Finally, a heartfelt acknowledgment to my Mendoza College of Business students at Notre Dame. Your tireless work and boundless curiosity in producing copyrighted Notre Dame case studies have given me and our readers new and valuable insights into the ways business managers deal with crises of many sorts. My sincere thanks to all.

Jeffrey A. Smith: Sincere thanks to Brandon Borrman, Michael Fanning, Zenia Mucha, and Rick Schostek, the corporate communications executives and business leaders who provided invaluable insights on how organizations should best prepare for, manage, and communicate during a crisis. I am also indebted to veteran journalists Charles Duhigg, Jayne O'Donnell, Alan Ohnsman, Bill Koenig, Doron Levin, and E. Scott Reckard for their views about crisis communication from the other side of the looking glass, that of the vital lens through which society judges all organizations during a crisis – the news media.

Many experts enriched this book, and I am grateful to them for sharing their valuable time and knowledge: Mark Bernheimer, on media training; Ed Cohen, on the role of government relations in a crisis; Amy Edmondson, PhD on leadership's role in employee engagement; Ann Handley, on expressing empathy in social media; Stephen J. Newman, Esq., on the banking industry; Bevin Smith, on cross-selling as a business practice; Donald B. Smith, Esq., on the role of a legal team in a crisis; and Sayandro Versteylen, MSc, on the technology behind genetically modified organisms (GMO).

Introduction

Every major enterprise will find itself under the magnifying glass, examined by a dubious public, and judged by a skeptical news media concerning actions or inactions for which it may (or may not) be responsible. An external event or an internal misstep may disrupt the organization's day-to-day operations and pitch it into a crisis that threatens both reputation and continuity. The actions that an organization should or should not take, the words it should or should not write, and the things it should or should not say during a crisis are suggested in these pages.

This book is not only about managing communications for the crisis at hand, but also about how society will view and judge your organization well into the future. It is not about clever spin and how to get out of trouble. On the contrary, we are suggesting a fact-based, responsive, transparent approach – centered on responsibly telling the truth when times get tough, with principles anchored to ethics and institutional integrity.

As authors, we pooled our separate experiences gained from more than 80 combined years of extensive know-how in the discipline of crisis communication. As a senior academic and author at an elite American business school and as a recently retired senior executive at a global *Fortune 50* automotive company, we have merged our academic and real-world perspectives into a distinctive volume we believe the reader will find immensely helpful and instructive.

Strategic Crisis Communication is a function of three elements: (1) crisis preparation, (2) crisis management, and (3) crisis communication. Crisis preparation establishes a robust and nimble infrastructure and a plan to deal with multiple possible crisis scenarios and, then, communicates that plan throughout the company. Crisis management quickly gathers information, activates the plan, convenes the Crisis Communication Team for quick decision-making, and monitors both media and stakeholders. Crisis communication reaches multiple audiences, on various platforms, with clear and purposeful messages that tell the truth and defend the organization.

Best practices, gleaned from hundreds of case studies researched and written in the Fanning Center for Business Communication at the University of Notre Dame's Mendoza College of Business and from numerous crises in today's

DOI: 10.4324/9781003322849-1

headlines, provide an unmatched resource. Instructive examples, cautionary tales, time-tested principles, and innovative solutions are on offer here. To this, we add the voices of several nationally recognized corporate communication leaders, prominent journalists, and dedicated academics, who add their experience, perspective, and insights to inform our analysis.

Executives, corporate communication professionals, public relations firms, NGOs, and other public and private organizations will find the communication tools and processes to weather any novel circumstances that may threaten their revenue, financial stability, brand value, and corporate reputation.

Ask any chief communication officer of a major corporation for the definition of a "crisis," and they will probably recite something like United States Supreme Court Justice Potter Stewart's 1964 decision that attempted to define hard-core pornography: "I know it when I see it." But will CEOs, CFOs, and other C-suite and B-suite leaders know a crisis when they see one as well?

On a slow news morning, an email from a wire service lands in the media relations division of a household brand, seeking comment on alleged illegal practices by the human resources (HR) department. Surprised, the comms professionals make frantic phone calls and are instructed by the legal department to offer a "no comment." Early the same day, a class action lawsuit is filed against the company. Teary-eyed plaintiffs, all former employees, appear on the local morning news. Claiming to be victims, they offer accounts of the illicit conduct and describe a cover-up.

By noon, the local affiliate has fed the accusations to its network, and by midafternoon, the yet-unanswered charges become national headlines. A wire service locates a current employee anonymously claiming that "everybody knew about that." Twitter and Facebook blow up with sensational charges by the plaintiffs' attorney. Satellite trucks surround the corporate headquarters.

Law enforcement tells the media it is "not ruling out" possible criminal activity. A worried advertising agency advises the company to cancel the new campaign. A congressman calls for a hearing. On social media, a consumer boycott gains traction. The stock price drops. Betting on the public's short attention span, company leadership hunkers down. The fretful communication team sticks to its "no comment" posture, praying that the toxic attention will shift to someone else and the thing will blow over, which it might. But likely it will not and with grim consequences for the company.

A crisis can come from within or from without. It can emerge slowly or explosively. Some crises reach the level of national or global news. Some are more local but no less threatening. Most crises come out of nowhere, the result of a so-called trigger event, and rapidly escalate. No one expected the bitterly cold weather in February 2021 that triggered mass blackouts across Texas and led to chemical plant shutdowns, disrupting global supply chains and causing a shortage of raw materials and microchips for tech companies, automakers, home builders, and countless other businesses. Other crises are self-imposed, the result of poor judgment or bad behavior, despite good organizations' strong compliance programs, consistent ethics training, and solid codes of conduct.

The intense media and public scrutiny that crises bring is disruptive to an organization's normal flow of operations. Leadership is distracted. Existing business plans vanish, replaced by time pressure to make decisions, issue media statements, communicate with customers, and juggle stakeholders. Funds and time are inefficiently reallocated to stop the bleeding. Relentless news media and social media exposure can embarrass and mortally threaten the reputation of a respected brand or enterprise that has been built over decades.

Strategic Crisis Communication is a broad and practical examination of the strategic value of communication in preparing for and managing an organization's response to a crisis. The effectiveness of an organization's communication can make a critical difference in the ultimate outcome of events in this age of disrupted manufacturing, a persistent pandemic, chaotic supply chains, widespread social disorder, unrelenting climate change, and other seemingly uncontrollable forces disrupting commerce, trade, innovation, and business stability worldwide.

Our examples and conclusions are authentic because we have lived with them and through them. Our goal is to provide the tools and processes that equip readers to protect, inspire, and energize their organizations. It is our sincere hope we have succeeded.

Crisis Preparation

Chapter 1

A Few Important Distinctions

Businesses and organizations of all types and sizes will eventually be caught up in a crisis of some sort. Very few executives want to believe that, of course, thinking that if they properly manage their enterprise, none of the issues they deal with will become critical. Most managers believe they have a playbook ready for nearly anything and, in the unlikely event of an unusual business failure or calamity, their years of experience and managerial skill will save the day.

The plain fact is, of course, not all crises can be accurately predicted, and even those that are in the playbook will include unusual threats and features the company has never seen before.

Richard G. Starmann, retired senior executive at McDonald's Corporation once said, "We do not have a crisis plan because, when a real crisis occurs, we just won't have time to get out a snap-ring binder and begin reading." When asked how the company would respond to a crisis, he said, "We find six of the smartest people in the building, sit down, and work out a solution. Our collective experience will point us in the right direction."

That perspective changed on July 18, 1984, when James Oliver Huberty walked into a McDonald's restaurant in San Ysidro, California, with three firearms, including a semiautomatic 9mm Uzi. He fatally shot 21 people, wounding 19 others before being killed by police. At the time, the event was the deadliest mass shooting by a lone gunman in U.S. history.[1]

"It was the most horrific scene I have ever witnessed," Starmann said. As a Green Beret infantry officer in Vietnam, he thought he'd seen it all. The challenge for him and for McDonald's was that virtually all senior executives of the company were away from the headquarters: "The CEO was in China; the C-suite officers were either on vacation, or working in one of our retail regions." Starmann was on his own.

"I commandeered the corporate jet, brought two assistants with me, and headed for San Diego," he recalled. "By the time we arrived, the dead and wounded had been evacuated. The restaurant was a crime scene." The McDonald's Senior Vice President for Corporate Communication, known to

DOI: 10.4324/9781003322849-3

friends and colleagues as Dick, met with the owner-operator of the San Ysidro restaurant and worked out a plan. "The company owns the land beneath each McDonald's store," he explained. "The franchisee owns the building and equipment."

"My instincts told me that we could never make this right. If we tried to clean this up, re-decorate, and somehow re-open the store, every newspaper account, every TV story would be about the shooting. Neither the franchisee nor the brand would ever escape the horror of that Wednesday evening." Starmann concluded that the only way to resolve the issue would be to buy the store and equipment from the operator. "I wrote him a personal check for a very large sum of money. McDonald's legal helped work out the details," he said. "Then, of course, I called my bank and told them to expect the biggest personal check they'd ever seen."

In a whirlwind of just a few days, Starmann received permission from local police to have the structure destroyed, shoveled into a truck, and hauled away. "In those days," he said, "Southern California still had lawns, so we arranged for turf, trees, shrubbery, and sidewalks." He paused to gather himself. "We turned over the entire property to the City of San Ysidro department of parks and recreation. It now belongs to the people of San Ysidro."

Starmann spent the next five days conducting serial media interviews, explaining what had happened and what McDonald's Corporation did in response, including the establishment of a memorial fund for the victims' relatives and securing a new franchise for the operator of that restaurant. "Because my back hurt," he added, "I did a number of those media interviews lying on my desk." It was at that point, he said he thought to himself, "We need a better way to do this. We need a plan."

McDonald's Corporation now has a world-class crisis preparation and management plan, complete with delegation of responsibilities, contingency funding, and regular exercises ranging from tabletop checklists to all-hands-onboard, full-scale simulations. "Somehow," he said, "it took an event that horrific to convince me that we could no longer depend on experience and managerial skill. We had to have a plan."[2]

Preparation for the Next Crisis

"A crisis," according to professor Lawrence Barton of Penn State University, "is a major, unpredictable event that has potentially negative results. The event and its aftermath may significantly damage an organization and its employees, products, services, financial condition, and reputation."[3]

The stubborn fact about the vast majority of crises is that, while you cannot predict with any accuracy when they will occur or even how they will develop, you know with certainty they are coming. To be ready for that moment, an understanding of three concepts will be helpful.

Crisis Preparedness

It is possible to prepare for a crisis, even though you don't know when it will occur or what will happen. In fact, the better prepared a business organization and its people are, the greater their chances of survival and recovery. That usually begins with a crisis plan and extends through regular, routine exercises.

Ray Day, former Group Vice President for Global Communications at Ford Motor Company, said: "We exercise our crisis management plan every day." Every day? How is that possible? "We take some particular aspect of the plan and ask one or more of our staff to examine it," he replied. "Are those phone numbers still valid? Does anyone pick up the phone? Are the locations correct? Are the names of key officials up to date? If we request certain actions or responses, do we get what we need?"[4]

When asked if he runs such exercises on Christmas Day or Easter Sunday, he said simply, "Yes." What about Rosh Hashanah or Yom Kippur? "Yes." Federal holidays? "Of course." But why? "We learned in 2000, when Firestone Wilderness and Wilderness ATX tires began delaminating on Ford Explorers, that you cannot make up a response on the spot." That calamity resulted in the death of 62 people and injury to more than 100 others in the U.S. An additional 46 people were killed in Venezuela. Ford and Firestone recalled more than 14.4 million tires.[5] Financial damage to Bridgestone-Firestone amounted $1.67 billion. The company's shareprice dropped by 50 percent. Ford recorded a loss of $5.5 billion in 2001. Executives resigned or were fired. Firestone closed the Decatur, Illinois, plant where the tires were made, resulting in a $210 million write-down and the loss of hundreds of union jobs.[6]

"We shut down production at three truck assembly plants," Day said, "including the F-150 line, to redirect 70,000 tires to our dealers in the south and west. Then, we set up a team to scour the free world for new tires." It was a calamity neither Ford nor Firestone anticipated, but one that convinced Day that a crisis plan is only as good as the people who write, exercise, and revise key portions every day. "The tire crisis didn't take down the company, but we were fortunate to manage as well as we did. That was the moment I was convinced our plan had to be more robust and in action every day."[7]

Crisis Management

Managing a crisis becomes far simpler if you've planned properly. A good plan will assign actions, rank order their importance, offer a timeline for implementation, and specify metrics for assessing whether you've succeeded.

In many organizations, an Issues Management Team is designated to examine and work through everything from operational issues to supply chain disruption to customer experience with products and services. That same team is often identified as the core of the organization's crisis management team should an issue go wrong or something unexpected occur. They're often well-positioned to understand everything from product ingredients to manufacturing processes and can readily assist the executives and senior managers designated to quickly stand up a crisis response team.

We'll talk later in Chapter 3 about setting up a Rapid Response Team and in Chapters 3 and 4 about how to organize, equip, and manage those who will be responsible for seeing the organization through a crisis.

Crisis Communication

Communication is your primary tool in any crisis. That's because a key crisis management goal is to get "permission" to solve the problem. That means securing the confidence and approval of everyone involved from law enforcement to state and federal regulators, from victims and their families to elected officials. The business enterprise involved and its executives must convince all with a stake in the outcome that the company has their best interest at heart and is capable of finding and implementing a solution that will work.

As it happens, organizational credibility and legitimacy are central to obtaining that permission, and they can only be established by effective, truthful, and frequent communication. If experience is a guide, organizations that assume responsibility for solving the problem early gain credibility. Organizations seen to be avoiding what is thought of as their responsibility will lose credibility. If you lose credibility, you lose legitimacy. Once that's gone, the problem is no longer yours to solve.

A notable example of such a loss occurred in April 2010, when the Deepwater Horizon oil rig experienced a catastrophic blowout, leading to explosions, fire, and critical damage to the platform operated by Transocean. By the time U.S. Coast Guard helicopters arrived, 11 men were missing. None of them survived.

The firm supervising the oil extraction from an exploratory well, known as the Macondo Prospect, was the global petroleum giant BP. Formerly doing business as British Petroleum, the $250 billion company chose to blame the subcontractor for all that went wrong, even though Transocean was operating under BP's direction and following the oil company's procedures.

Tony Hayward, CEO of BP, said in an April 30, 2010, press statement that the company "assumes full responsibility for the spill."[8]

Then, on May 2, Hayward appeared on the NBC Television Network's *Today* show remarking: "It's not our accident." He then went on to say that, although BP was not responsible for the incident, it would play a direct role in containing the oil spill. The first few days following the incident were certainly marred by confusion and contradiction on BP's part.[9] Hayward, in an attempt to apologize to Gulf residents, said, "There's no one who wants this thing to be over more than me. I'd like my life back."[10] He made that statement just three days before releasing a print advertisement headlined "We will make this right." Many Gulf residents felt the comment was incredibly insensitive, considering the fact that 11 men *actually* had lost their lives in the incident. Two weeks before that statement,

Hayward was spotted at an exclusive yacht race off the coast of England, apparently on holiday with his son.

The result? Hayward lost his job as CEO of the company, and, perhaps more importantly, President Barack Obama removed Hayward and BP from the well-capping, remediation, and cleanup effort. In his place, Homeland Security Secretary Janet Napolitano announced that Coast Guard Admiral Thad Allen would become National Incident Commander, effectively handing responsibility to the U.S. government. Ineffective, confusing, and often insulting communication from BP cost the company and its CEO both legitimacy and credibility. It was no longer BP's problem to solve.

In Chapter 3 of this book, we'll talk at length about how to manage communication and how to know whether it's working. For now, please know that it is your central tool in establishing credibility, restoring confidence, and protecting the reputations of all who are involved.

The Reality of Dealing With a Crisis

What happens in a crisis? According to Washington, D. C. consultant Eric Dezenhall,

> The reality is absolute chaos. Nobody knows what the facts are. The lawyers are trying to get the PR consultants fired and the PR consultants are criticizing the lawyers. Everyone despises each other. It's a totally unimaginable situation. A corporation in crisis is not a corporation. It is a collection of individuals motivated by self-preservation.[11]

In a slightly more cynical observation, Raymond O'Rourke, Managing Director of Corporate Affairs at Morgan Stanley, once said: "A crisis exists when the news media intervene prematurely in a situation management is already aware of and is dealing with."[12] To understand just how to begin planning for, managing, and communicating in a crisis, it is often helpful to know just what type of crisis you are facing. Included in that understanding is the source of the problem and the speed at which it develops.

Internal Crises

These are problems you have created yourself. The issue began in your own organization, and, whether because of neglect or catalyst circumstance, it's grown and spun well out of your control. Your CEO may have chosen to backdate the stock options he was granted as compensation in his contract. A small change in the expiration date or striking price for the shares he is entitled to purchase and . . . voila! The problem of an underwater shareprice is solved. The real problem, of course, is that the action is illegal until it is approved by the company's board of directors, the Securities and Exchange Commission (SEC) is notified, and an SEC Form 8-K is filed to notify investors.

In another example, the ingredients in your packaged goods have somehow been contaminated. That has happened to hundreds of food service manufacturers, including Odwalla, a super-premium juice producer, in October 1996. When demand for the company's *unpasteurized* apple juice soared, CEO Greg Steltenpohl elected to move beyond the West Coast apple growers he had known for years and begin purchasing fruit from a broker. That meant he was bottling his product with apples from people he'd never met and didn't know. *E.coli* 0157-H7 had migrated into those apples, and, because the juice had never been pasteurized, consumers were unprotected. As a result, 16-month-old Anna Grace Gimmestad of Evans, Colorado, was poisoned. Despite the best efforts of doctors and a helicopter transport team, she died within days.[13] This crisis, which resulted in the sale of the company, was entirely avoidable.

External Crises

Circumstances that begin outside of an organization are sometimes called "oppositional crises," often because individuals or groups opposed to a company's business model, products, or practices choose to come after the business. Attacks, lawsuits, denigration in the press, and sometimes vandalism or physical confrontation are the result.

A notable example of this occurred in August 2004, when Baltimore activist Lorig Charkoudian organized a group of young mothers to stage a "nurse-in" at a Silver Spring, Maryland, Starbucks coffee shop. Their aim was to get the company to change its policy regarding public breastfeeding. Charkoudian's group targeted Starbucks precisely because the company is both wealthy and ubiquitous. If corporate policy in that firm could be changed to promote public acceptance of the practice, then surely all or most others would follow. As a Starbucks company spokesperson noted, however, its baristas were neither equipped nor trained to intervene in customer disputes over whether a nursing mother should "cover up" or carry on. Compounding the problem was the fact that each U.S. state had drafted its own legislation, either encouraging public breastfeeding or forbidding it under public indecency statutes. At the time, a number of states had no legislation on the issue of any sort. Starbucks executives, still trying to figure out coffee and food, were flummoxed.[14]

Slowly Emerging Crises

Some unfortunate situations can be seen a mile off. In these circumstances, early notice of a problem can breed indecision, complacency, and dithering. Dow Corning Corporation faced anger, backlash, and litigation over claims that silicone breast implants the company manufactured had caused illness, disease, or disability. This case did not involve claims of product failure (rupture, dissection, or leaking). The claims were that the implantation of the devices themselves led to horrible outcomes, including muscular dystrophy, scleroderma, lupus erythematosus, and more. Despite numerous independent clinical studies showing no connection to such disorders, plaintiffs' bar lawyers enthusiastically took up the cause and sued the company.

The litigation dragged on for 30 years, eventually taking Dow Corning into receivership and a $3.2 billion settlement. Despite the fact that breast implants, whether used for cosmetic or reconstructive purposes, accounted for less than 1 percent of Dow Corning's revenues, the claims – never proven in court – nearly took the company down. The litigation, in the eyes of most who followed the case, was won largely through clever public relations and talk show sympathy.[15] Dow Corning eventually left the implant market, unwilling to risk future exposure to claims that its products brought harm to people.

Explosive Crises

Other situations happen with literally no notice. On the evening of March 4, 1993, Jeff Bernel, Chairman and Chief Executive Officer of American Rubber Products (ARP), received a phone call from Mark Dilley, his EVP and Chief Operating Officer: "Jeff," he said, "there appears to have been an accident at work. Some kind of explosion. We have to get there."[16] When Bernel arrived at the LaPorte, Indiana, headquarters of ARP, a tier-one supplier to the auto industry, he was certainly unprepared for what he saw: fire trucks, ambulances, rescue vehicles, police cars, chaos, and considerable confusion.

Sheriff's Deputy Greg Bell, a friend from Bernel's church, knocked on the car window and said, "You've had a boiler explosion, Mr. Bernel. You have two fatalities." The news was stunning. In 20 years of business experience and 6 years of submarine duty in the Navy, Jeff had never experienced anything like this. A Morrison tube boiler, regularly maintained, certified by the State of Indiana, and about halfway through its expected lifecycle, had launched from its concrete moorings, gone through a brick wall, and landed 30 meters out, on the Conrail tracks.

Some 20,000 pounds of water, heated to 400 degrees Celsius, vented to atmosphere and killed a 32-year-old mother of two and an 18-year-old woman hired earlier in the week as a temporary employee. Six others were injured but survived. Bernel quickly realized that he couldn't even access his own property: it was now a crime scene, taped off by the local police. The electrical power and gas had been shut off. He was unable to reach his office or his computer. His only assets were a partially charged cell phone and a warm automobile.

Ultimately, a state-led investigation proved that neither Bernel nor his company had done anything wrong. A licensed repair firm from St. Louis, Missouri, had reassembled a freshly cleaned and repaired boiler with the wrong bolts. They became plastic under the boiler's tremendous heat and fractured when they cooled. It wouldn't be long before they failed. Still, as Bernel said in an interview: "Despite our best efforts, two people died and six others were injured. I had no way to intervene and no idea what do to. The press were hounding me for a statement – or perhaps a confession – and none of us really knew what just happened." He paused and said to a colleague, "You still want to be a CEO?"[17]

Knowing the source of the problem, along with the timeline over which it develops, will be helpful in devising a solution that will satisfy most, if not all, of the stakeholders. It's useful, as well, to understand just how managing and communicating in a crisis is different from the day-to-day task of running a business.

How Crises Are Different From Simply Running a Business

Most crises distinguish themselves from the mundane, though sometimes exciting, activities involved in running a business in eight specific ways.

Surprise

The very fact that an event is unexpected is a problem in itself. Business operates with a calendrical rhythm that is entirely predictable and for which managers and hourly employees can plan. Such routine, anticipated events make their way into the budget, the sales and marketing plans, and people's vacation schedules. Crises operate on their own schedule and create problems that many, if not most, in the organization have never seen.

Insufficient Information

Like Jeff Bernel of American Rubber Products, many managers will receive conflicting statements, unproven evidence, or false claims, leaving them to guess which part of what they know is actually true. Gathering current, accurate, useful information becomes a priority. Ensuring people make decisions based on fact rather than rumor is essential.

Intense Time Pressure

In a genuine emergency, everyone seems to want the problem solved quickly. Today, if possible. If managers responsible for a solution don't entirely know what's gone wrong or how to fix it, those with a stake in the outcome grow impatient, angry, and resentful. Without a playbook or checklist to apply, managers are often pressured to try ideas they have no idea will work.

Escalating Flow of Events

Nothing seems to remain constant in a crisis. With a steady flow of oil from the floor of the Gulf of Mexico, things grew worse by the day for BP and for those whose livelihood came from the Gulf waters. Small errors compound themselves, increasing damage and costs begin to mount, and a cascading series of events can appear unstoppable.

No Precedents to Work From

Managers who plan for and deal with critical situations will often say, "History repeats itself, but never in quite the same way." If you think you've seen this problem before, think again. Situations that imperil a business, its customers, and reputation can appear similar to previous problems, but inevitably they aren't. Stakeholders are angry that this is the second or third such occurrence and you've done nothing to stop it. Working with a dated template or from approaches based on prior events may be of little help.

Intense Scrutiny From the Outside

Unsurprisingly, everyone seems to have an interest in what's happening. Many have unworkable suggestions and, perhaps, a few outrageous demands. The press, who are never true stakeholders in a crisis, will be there to cover events and report what's happened to the world. With the aid of wire services, digital cameras, and the internet, it seems everyone is paying attention. You cannot simply lock the front gate and wait until this blows over.

Loss of Control

For most managers, who are problem-solvers at heart, the idea that they are not in complete control is anathema. It's not how they were raised or trained in business school. Most executives work very hard to stay calm. Cool heads think best. But, if your best ideas and most basic instincts don't seem to be working, what's the best approach?

Panic

You don't have to be a control freak to panic at the idea that you not only have no influence over events, you don't even know for sure what's going on. How can you produce a result that true stakeholders – those with something to win or lose, depending on how you act – will appreciate and applaud when this is something you've never seen before and simply do not know how to respond to?

As we move on to Chapter 2, we'll encourage you to be strategic in your thinking. Many people have yet to reach that level of cognition, though, believing tactics alone will solve the problem and save the day.

References

1. San Ysidro McDonald's Massacre. *Wikipedia*. Retrieved online: February 3, 2022. https://en.wikipedia.org/wiki/San_Ysidro_McDonald%27s_massacre
2. Personal interview. Richard G. Starmann, Senior Vice President for Corporate Communication, McDonald's Corporation. March 21, 1997. McDonald's Corporation Headquarters, Oak Brook, IL.

3. Barton, L. *Crisis in Organizations: Managing and Communicating in the Heat of Chaos.* Cincinnati, OH: South-Western Publishing Company, 1993, p. 2.
4. Telephone Interview. Ray Day, Group Vice President, Global Communications, Ford Motor Company, Dearborn, MI. May 12, 2014.
5. Pries, J. and Lagueux, M. *Bridgestone/Firestone, Inc. and Ford Motor Company: Crisis Management and Product Recall.* Notre Dame, IN: Eugene D. Fanning Center for Business Communication, Mendoza College of Business, University of Notre Dame, 2001.
6. Firestone and Ford Tire Controversy. *Wikipedia.* Retrieved online: February 3, 2022: https://en.wikipedia.org/wiki/Firestone_and_Ford_tire_controversy
7. Personal interview. Raymond Day, Group Vice President, Global Communications, Ford Motor Company. April 12, 2012. By telephone.
8. *The Today Show,* Interview with Tony Hayward, May 2, 2010. *TPM Muckraker,* May 4, 2010. http://tpmmuckraker.talkingpointsmemo.com/2010/05/bp_chief_claims_oil_spill_wasnt_our_accident.php
9. Marques, D., Kim, J. and Mikols, J. *BP and the Gulf Oil Spill (A).* Notre Dame, IN: Eugene D. Fanning Center for Business Communication, Mendoza College of Business, University of Notre Dame, 2011.
10. *The Today Show,* May 30, 2010 available from YouTube, "BP CEO Tony Hayward: 'I'd Like My Life Back.'" Retrieved online: October 1, 2010.
11. Dezenhall, E. Nail. *Em: Confronting High Profile Attacks on Celebrities & Businesses.* Amherst, NY: Prometheus Books, 2003.
12. Personal interview by telephone. Raymond O'Rourke, Managing Director of Corporate Affairs, Morgan Stanley. February 27, 2004. New York, NY.
13. Halverson, S., Rake, K. and Gallagher, J. *Odwalla, Inc. (A).* Notre Dame, IN: Eugene D. Fanning Center for Business Communication, Mendoza College of Business, University of Notre Dame, 1999.
14. Bailey, J., Ranier, S. and McHale, C. *Starbucks Coffee Company: Can Customers Breastfeed in a Coffee Shop?* Notre Dame, IN: Eugene D. Fanning Center for Business Communication, Mendoza College of Business, University of Notre Dame, 2005.
15. Schleiter, K. Silicone Breast Implant Litigation, *AMA Journal of Ethics,* 2010; 12(5):389–394. doi: 10.1001/virtualmentor.2010.12.5.hlaw1-1005. Retrieved online: https://journalofethics.ama-assn.org/article/silicone-breast-implant-litigation/2010-05.
16. O'Rourke, J. S. *American Rubber Products.* A Notre Dame case study, 1998.
17. O'Rourke, J. S. *American Rubber Products Company (A).* Notre Dame, IN: Eugene D. Fanning Center for Business Communication, Mendoza College of Business, University of Notre Dame, 1999.

Chapter 2

Be Strategic in Your Planning

Planning, both strategic and tactical, is an indispensable tool for prevailing over any crisis. While no blueprint crisis communications plan will automatically avert a crisis, both strong and flexible plans and actions taken in advance will better prepare organizations to withstand any unforeseen trigger event or unnerving situation that threatens an enterprise.

Crises are inevitable. You cannot fully control or avoid them. But you can control how prepared you are. A strong strategic planning approach to crisis management and crisis communications will give an embattled organization a key focal point against which to constantly check and evaluate its day-to-day actions. Such an overarching set of long-term strategic goals is the North Star during any given crisis that will help keep the organization on course, help keep it from becoming distracted, and help maintain consistency and evenness in the tactics it chooses to deploy.

The ride-sharing firm Uber was clearly operating without a strategic crisis plan when its brand fell from universally esteemed to widely unloved following a series of missteps. In 2017, news reports revealed that CEO Travis Kalanick was serving on President Trump's economic advisory council, news of which gave birth to the hashtag #DeleteUber, which would haunt the company. The hashtag reappeared when Uber continued its operations and lifted surge pricing at JFK International Airport, despite a strike by taxi drivers protesting President Trump's immigration ban on citizens from several majority-Muslim countries.[1]

The troublesome hashtag resurfaced once again amid allegations of sexual harassment and HR wrongdoing at the ride-sharing company. #DeleteUber went viral once a video revealed Kalanick arguing with a driver over a pay cut. Kalanick released a statement saying, "I must fundamentally change as a leader and grow up." The company, however, had lurched from problem to problem without any apparent guiding principle or plan. For hundreds of thousands of Uber customers, due to the company's constant fumbles and lack of transparency about how it was fixing them, the damage was done.[2]

Jill Hazelbaker, who joined the company in 2015 as Senior Vice President of Marketing and Public Affairs when the company was under scrutiny for sexual harassment and discrimination, began to right the ship with a more strategic and

DOI: 10.4324/9781003322849-4

transparent approach. Under her leadership, Uber published its first *Safety Report* in 2019 and has committed to updating it every two years. "There is no question that things happened in the company that were not OK," Hazelbaker told *The New York Times*. "We needed to get our house in order internally and then fix it externally."[3]

Compare this with how JetBlue strategically handled communications when its operations buckled after a massive ice storm hit the East Coast of the U.S. in 2007, resulting in 1,000 cancelled flights over five days. The airline clearly had an advance strategic plan for managing such a catastrophe, and while it still received tremendous backlash, with thousands of passengers stranded in airports, the brand survived to fly another day.

Why? Advance planning combined with transparency and accountability to customers were embedded as JetBlue's strategic principles. Founder and CEO David Neeleman did not blame the bad weather, and the company was as straightforward and forthcoming as possible. No hiding and hoping it would all go away. Neeleman published a widely circulated letter of apology to JetBlue customers. He established a JetBlue customer's bill of rights and provided an itemized list of actions the company would take to help the affected passengers – including monetary compensation.

By being open and forthcoming in the following weeks, JetBlue managed to quell much of the furor. As part of JetBlue's strategic plan, an exhausted-looking Neeleman appeared on a corporately produced YouTube video to apologize and admit that his company had been "overwhelmed." He told NBC's *Today* show, "We had a weakness in the system" that caused "horrifying" inconveniences to passengers. "We had a problem and we had a defining moment and a painful lesson," he said. Appearing on *Late Night with David Letterman*, and *Anderson Cooper 360*o, he did not plead his case or attempt to place blame but apologized for his company's faults and pledged that such problems would never happen again. Neeleman's presence, candor, and personal accountability were crucial because of the airline's focus on its distinctive brand of customer service. While JetBlue sustained much reputational damage, its comeback from this catastrophe has been remarkable.[4]

The Distinction Between Strategic and Tactical Planning

The terms *strategic* and *tactical* are frequently used interchangeably, and often incorrectly so. They are similar and complementary, depending on context. But they are not synonymous. Confusing the two terms can result in a murky mess at the onset of a crisis. Simply stated, strategy is a set of overarching, long-term goals toward which the organization advances. In Steven Covey's *Seven Habits of Highly Effective People*, he tells us to "begin with the end in mind."[5] Strategy is determining where you want to be when the dust finally settles.

Tactics, on the other hand, are the specific steps or actions you deploy to achieve your strategy. Tactics are the tasks and activities that, coin-by-coin, fill your strategic war chest. For example, in a crisis involving a potentially fatal defect found in a company product, a good communication strategy may be to "maintain the trust of our customers." The supporting tactics you might consider could include a strong legacy media presence that puts executives out front on the airwaves, promising to make things right with customers. Or, depending on resources, you may deploy relatively inexpensive Facebook advertising that can help you find people who fit your customer profile, allowing your customer relations team to join the conversation about your product. Or, you might decide to publish a series of corporate ads in newspapers where your markets are strong, explaining your actions to do the right thing by your customers. Perhaps all of these tactics and more, to "maintain the trust of our customers."

Paint the Devil on the Wall

In crisis communication, it is unquestionable that confidence, enthusiasm, and optimism are critically important to success. Expect the best of yourself and others, and when a crisis is looming, maintaining hopefulness and a positive outlook will create a tide that lifts everyone's spirits.

As corporate communicators, however, when you are preparing to confront a crisis that may affect your organization, you will want to abide by the old Irish adage to "paint the devil on the wall." In other words, think through the problems and challenges you may face in the future with a logical, realistic vision of every possible bad scenario and angle. Examine the complexities of potential future problems, understand each component for what it is, and, especially, where it may lead. Then, relentlessly game each one with a set of potential countermeasures.

The stakes are critically high for your organization if you are unprepared at the onset of a crisis that threatens your company's reputation, brand, and, perhaps, its existence. Even though we have encouraged you to be optimistic, overconfidence is your enemy. A crisis in your organization is a matter of *when*, not *if*. According to the *PWC Global Crisis Surveys* of 2019 and 2021, fully 95 percent of the companies responding to the surveys expect to be involved in a crisis.[6]

A healthy measure of analytic pessimism, worst-case thinking, and advance planning will help you produce a more effective strategic communication plan for the long run. Every preemptive and proactive step you can take in advance to intercept and prevent that reputational damage will benefit your company once a crisis materializes. And, as the PWC data indicate, it *will* happen.

Content Moderation at Facebook

Facebook was hoping for a positive outcome when they hired Accenture, the world's largest public management consulting firm, to perform content moderation for the social media giant, primarily outside the United States. But did

Facebook "paint the devil on the wall"? Content moderation is the practice of using human beings to monitor social media's most noxious posts. While about 90 percent of inappropriate content is identified and deleted using artificial intelligence (AI) software and machine learning programs, the remaining content, including images and videos of suicides, beheadings, and child pornography, must be manually scanned and rated.[7]

Cleaning up the internet is repugnant work, to say the least, and many content moderators, often located overseas, quickly trained, and not well-paid, say they suffer from anxiety, depression, paranoia, and insomnia. Facebook pays Accenture handsomely to keep this darkest corner of its business at arm's length – an estimated $500 million annually. They honestly expected that the consulting firm would be able to handle the problem, and, with the help of improvements in content review algorithms, it would be mostly resolved. The problem, unfortunately, has grown increasingly worse by the day.

Facebook has been criticized for trying to distance itself from workplace issues raised by Accenture content moderators, claiming that the workers were Accenture's, not Facebook's. A class action lawsuit which ensued brought a $52 million settlement for current and former moderators. Cognizant, another content moderator for Facebook, has cancelled its contract following investigations of horrible working conditions for its employees. While Accenture's leadership has discussed the advisability of continuing in this line of work, it may be too lucrative to resist.[8]

The Value of a Plan

No crisis communications plan is infallible, simply because we cannot predict the future with any accuracy. Once a crisis lands on your doorstep, things will start to go wrong. Extreme events or unlucky timing may overtake even the most resilient plan. But plan you must. Writing in the *Harvard Business Review*, Graham Kenny explains the strategic planning approach taken by 9th-century Prussian Field Marshal Helmuth von Moltke the Elder, who famously said of advance planning, "No plan of operations extends with certainty beyond the first encounter with the enemy's main strength." Today, this assertion is often stated as "no plan survives first contact with the enemy."[9]

Field Marshal von Moltke was not in business and he left the planet long ago, but his advice that organizations should develop a series of strategic options, rather than a single plan, applies directly to crisis communications. You must create a robust plan, both offensive and defensive, accounting for as many contingencies as possible, and then work that plan. Do so with the knowledge that the plan will be imperfect once a crisis arrives and that it will require both speed and flexibility to overcome unexpected obstacles. As Kenny notes, "Moltke the Elder wasn't advocating *not* having a plan to start with but that the plan itself and the planners needed to be flexible because it generates preparedness."

A Proactive Framework for Advance Planning

In subsequent sections of this chapter, you will find specific proactive measures you can take in advance of a crisis to help your organization be well-prepared. Much more than a simple checklist, these recommendations are drawn both from best practices in the corporate communications profession and from the hard-won and real-world experience of the authors.

Develop a Generic Crisis Communications Team Template

The benefit of using a teamwork approach to crisis communication is well-tested and inarguable. But it does not mean just gathering a few smart people to figure out what happened and then devising a solution. The corporate dustbin is filled with the logos of organizations that took just such an approach.

Prior to any crisis, a generic Crisis Communications Team template should be developed that is not specific to a potential threat, whether operational, technical, human capital, legal, or otherwise. Such a framework should be comprehensive enough to cover all potential areas of future need and flexible enough to adapt to any situation that may arise. The generic Crisis Communications Team template should include all the company stakeholders that may be affected by a crisis as well as all functional areas responsible for formulating, analyzing, and deploying the organization's crisis response.

The template should not contain anyone's name because employees change frequently. The functionality of the construct should be re-evaluated and refreshed at least annually. If thoughtfully executed, a generic Crisis Communications Team template will provide lasting value to an organization, inspiring confidence in the communications team that developed it, and providing year-over-year readiness and awareness throughout the enterprise. A typical generic Crisis Communications Team template might look like Figure 2.1.

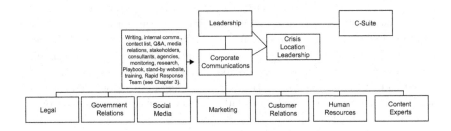

Crisis Communications Team Template

Figure 2.1 Crisis Communications Team Template

Potential Crisis Communications Team Members

In your organizational template for crisis communications, here are some useful functions you may want to position, in advance, for action. These sample roles are based on a company of about 50,000 employees. If such an expansive team seems cumbersome due to the size of your organization, you will want to consolidate some of these roles. These roles are described in greater detail in Chapter 7, "Activate the Crisis Communications Team."

- **Leadership**. A senior leader who holds the final decision-making authority.
- **Corporate Communications**. Coordinates the crisis communications response.
- **Social Media**. Leads and monitors the organization's social media outreach.
- **Marketing**. Coordinates local and national print, digital, and broadcast advertising.
- **Customer Relations**. Interacts directly with customers and reports customer sentiment.
- **Legal**. Approves all public company statements and counsels company leadership.
- **Government Relations**. Represents the company to local and national public officials.
- **Human Resources.** Leads employee relations and conducts sensing of employee attitudes.
- **Content Experts**. Provides expert information, depending on the nature of the crisis.

Predetermine a Clear Chain of Command

A chain of command exists in most businesses to allocate decision-making authority, clarify responsibilities, maintain stability, and strengthen communication.

Based on the need for speed, crisis communication requires a separate chain of command distinct from the overall organization's daily processes. For crisis planning, predetermine a chain of command within the various Crisis Communications Team functions and with senior executive management. For example, within the corporate communications function on a crisis team, everyone involved on that team should have a clear understanding of their roles and expectations, approval levels, and who has the authority to release copy, graphics, or other materials to the final approver.

Once the chain has been determined within corporate communications, that function must also establish reporting relationships with other members of the larger team, such as social media, customer relations, and legal. No confusion in this respect is acceptable. Executive leadership will and should expect rapid consensus from these various groups on public statements or other official public actions they are being asked to support.

Establish a Social Media Policy and Crisis Plan

In advance of any crisis, the social media team should develop and communicate an effective policy that clearly guides employees on their use of social media and protects company confidentiality. Such a policy is usually developed by collaboration among social media, corporate communications, human resources, and legal, and it should align with any use of social media by the customer relations group as well. Waiting until a crisis happens to develop a social media policy is dangerous; it may be impossible to rein in employees who are accustomed to speaking their minds about the company on social media. Several helpful resources are available to collect industry best practices for developing an effective social media policy.[10]

In addition to establishing an overall social media policy, the social media team will also need an advance plan of action specifically designed for crisis response. The team should establish a quick approval process for social media messaging. What would you do if a highly damaging YouTube video goes totally viral? How would you handle an orchestrated campaign on Twitter where thousands of customers are complaining? What is your tolerance level for negative posts? What is your threshold for differentiating a few negative comments from a true crisis? What type of crisis would merit direct individual engagement, and what type would merit a robust public comment from the organization? We'll have a more thorough discussion of social media during a crisis in Chapter 19, "Social Media Has Changed the Crisis Communications Landscape."

Create a Crisis Scenario Playbook With Draft Materials

In the context of your organization's annual risk assessment exercise (assuming you have one, and you should), identify all the potential types of crises that your business is likely to face and, then, rank them by probability, severity, potential for growth, and likely duration. For the most probable crisis scenarios that may affect your business, develop a crisis communications playbook containing prewritten and preapproved materials you can deploy at a moment's notice. Such a playbook is designed to help your organization get through the critical initial stages of a crisis when public perception is first being shaped.

Most larger organizations have operational plans in place that outline procedures for managing natural disasters like blizzards, floods, and earthquakes. Hardly anyone foresaw the global COVID pandemic, but health and safety protocols that include quarantine and employee treatment are now certainly in place in many organizations. Increasingly, companies are planning for crises related to financial performance, supply chain disruptions, labor union activity, product boycotts, cybercrime, negative social media campaigns, leadership misconduct, and many more, depending on the nature of the business. While communication is often a component of these operational plans, its critical importance may get lost in the whirlwind of operational details. A solid crisis communications playbook will help a beleaguered company get through the early hours or days of a crisis spreading across social media and network news and is every bit as valuable as an evacuation plan.

Once you determine the issues most likely to throw your organization into a crisis, decide on the draft materials you will want in your playbook for each potential threat. If a trigger event occurs, you can then modify the materials accordingly, but the playbook gives you a template for what you would potentially release and to whom.

Without a playbook, people under pressure often make bad decisions about what to communicate, to whom, and how, which can quickly make matters worse. Importantly, since the playbook materials are in draft form and involve speculation about the future, you will want to have the materials in your playbook thoroughly approved by your legal team and marked *Confidential: Attorney Client Privileged*. Some of the draft elements of your crisis communications playbook might include the following (not all will apply in each case):

- Designated spokesperson(s) on the topic.
- Basic media statement on the issue.
- Letter to employees providing background and facts about the situation and how you are addressing it.
- Talking points for managers.
- Contact information and letter providing background and facts about the situation and how you are trying to rectify it, to:
  - State, local, and federal officials, particularly in areas where your organization operates.
  - External stakeholders (societal, business, NGO) with whom your organization interacts.
  - Internal stakeholders (suppliers, business affiliates).
- Contact information and background on key journalists and social media influencers who cover the beat, with copies of their coverage of the topic.
- Contact information and background on key analysts who cover the topic and who may be consulted and quoted by media.
- Holding statement indicating that information is being gathered and updates will be provided.

- Holding statement indicating you are cooperating with authorities.
- Holding statement indicating that you are unable to provide information based on pending litigation.
- Holding statement expressing empathy and sympathy if appropriate.
- Biographies of key executives.
- Brief history of the organization.
- Brief history of each facility.

Create a Stand-By Website That Can Be Up and Running in an Instant

Among the most valuable instruments in any strategic crisis communication toolkit is a stand-by website: a premade, hidden website that is always at the ready and activated when a crisis occurs. In the same way that you prioritize your most probable crises and then develop a playbook for each, you should create a stand-by site for each major potential threat. The stand-by website content, written in advance and preapproved, should be capable of updating easily and quickly. Stand-by websites are standard practice in the airline industry for good reason.

Websites of this sort have several advantages in a crisis. As a crisis builds steam, stakeholders will turn to an embattled organization's website for information. Speed is key, and your stand-by site must be up and running at the touch of a button. Once up, it allows you to immediately control your messages and to speak to your audiences openly and in a transparent manner. As journalists, customers, stakeholders, and your employees converge on your site, they will see credible information, facts, and your company's perspective on the situation.

A standard approach for stand-by sites is for an organization to create a parallel site that operates separately from its existing main website. All traffic and questions about the crisis are directed to the stand-by site, but the main site remains accessible. In such cases, a button or banner is often placed on the main landing page that links directly to the stand-by site. This latter best practice is an important acknowledgment that the organization takes the matter seriously and has information readily available elsewhere.

Prior to the onset of the H1N1 (swine flu) virus, the Santa Clara, California, County public health department had joined forces with a team from Stanford University to develop a stand-by site. The idea was that the stand-by site would replace the department's existing website if it ever went down. And down it went. In April 2009, the health department was providing constant updates on its website about proliferating H1N1 cases. With alarming news reports coming out of Mexico, people flooded the public health website to learn more, and the website crashed. To make matters worse, the crash also disabled all other county web functions. The county health department and Stanford engineers were able to quickly load information relevant to H1N1 onto the new site and make it available to the public within hours.[11]

Given the importance of speed, a stand-by website should be simple, easy-to-update, and spartan in design. Establish criteria for when the site should be activated, and determine who will be responsible for updating details there. If marketing and an agency partner are responsible for managing the main site on a day-to-day basis (as is often the case), consider shifting those roles to corporate communication exclusively for the stand-by site. Information often changes fast in a crisis, and frequent updates should be made quickly and easily. There is no time for elaborate coding and exquisite photographs. You will also need a technical team to manage the interface between the main site and the stand-by site. The components of your stand-by website might include:

- **A basic statement about the crisis**. This statement should contain your organization's succinct and quotable position on the crisis. Lead with the point you want the public to understand. This is not the place for history or much background on the issue, which can be included further down in the site. A statement from a senior executive may be appropriate.
- **Countermeasures.** These are the detailed actions your organization is taking to mitigate the crisis for anyone affected by it. Add a timeline for resolution, if available.
- **Customer relations support**. If the crisis is consumer-related, this set of instructions will provide the means for customers to contact your organization on the channels you designate, such as social media, phone banks, or email.
- **Media contact information.** This is a list of designated spokespersons available globally, 24/7.
- **Active links.** These hypertext crosslinks will assist people in navigating between your stand-by site, main site, social media channels, and news releases. Let people know if you are providing updates via social media and how they can follow you.
- **Corporate social responsibility.** This section will explain charitable or other cause-related actions you may be taking in response to the crisis. Explain how the public can donate, if applicable.
- **Relevant background on the crisis.** This section contains useful narrative and factual background to help people understand in greater detail what happened and why. Resist using your basic statement for this purpose.
- **Company purpose, footprint, and history.** For those coming to the stand-by site who may not be familiar with your organization, this section should be straightforward and fairly brief. Avoid advertising jargon and self-praise. Link to your main site.

Designate and Equip a Situation Room

Call it a situation room, command center, HQ, operations center, or otherwise, the concept of a predetermined central gathering place from which to manage a crisis is a best practice, and one that continues to evolve due to new technologies and workplace practices. The old term, "war room" no longer seems appropriate or acceptable. The basic template for a classic situation room convenes the crisis team in a single place appropriate for confidential meetings and of sufficient size to accommodate the entire team. The room should be equipped with white-boards and markers, digital projector, printer, omnidirectional speaker phone, state-of-the-art Wi-Fi, and facility maps for all locations.

The advent of remote work and advanced videoconferencing platforms such as Zoom, Microsoft Teams, Webex, and Google Meets allow immediate international communication, and with features like chat, screen sharing, and recording, they have quickly made the virtual situation room a reality.

Whether in-person, virtual, or a hybrid of the two, the situation room concept shares one common requirement: make sure the right people are in the room and that they are decision makers and frontline participants, not delegates or notetakers. Situation room activity often results in immediate action, offering little time for subordinates to check with their supervisors to confirm if a course of action is acceptable. For additional detail, see Chapter 10, "Centralize Communication."

Plan for Dealing With Unplanned Media Visits

News media will unexpectedly arrive at your facilities for two likely reasons. First, an accident, injuries, spill, strike, protest, or other incident pitches you into crisis mode. The media will rush to capture compelling images and file the story then remain for updates. Second, media may come uninvited to your facility probing for an on-camera comment about an existing crisis in your organization, particularly if interviews had been refused in the past.

In this latter case, if no interviews are allowed, a simple and friendly lobby meeting is appropriate. A trained staff member can meet with the media, indicate that they are not authorized to speak on behalf of the company, provide the company's written statement, and politely ask the media to leave.

Whatever the reason for the sudden appearance of cameras on your campus, of primary importance is that you remain calm and create a nonconfrontational environment. Greet the media with a helpful smile. Captivating television images are fueled by conflict. For instance, by no means should you send your security team out to wave their hands in front of cameras to stop them recording and kick them off the property. YouTube is thick with such examples because this conflict-escalating behavior creates pure joy for TV news crews.

Not every facility has trained corporate communication staff on-site, but every facility should have someone trained in the rules and designated to work with the media when they arrive. Anyone designated to work with the news media face-to-face should be gracious and polite, above all else. A staff member can make clear to reporters that they are not authorized to speak for the organization, but they will try to be helpful and provide written statements and updates as they become available.

On-site media relations folks should never show up empty-handed. The news media, like nature, abhor a vacuum, and failure to provide information will lead reporters to speculate. A written-in-advance holding statement like, "We are assessing the situation and gathering facts and will provide details as soon as they are confirmed," is certainly preferable to an abrupt "no comment."

Train Your Spokespersons

If media show up on your doorstep and you decide that producing a live, local spokesperson is to your strategic advantage, without exception, make sure he or she has been properly trained in advance. Media training for spokespersons is expensive, time-consuming, hard work, but absolutely necessary. In other words, do not go on camera without it. Such training often includes several practice sessions in front of a camera, where a trainee learns to refine the message, as well as how to "block and bridge" in order to get past unconstructive questions and guarantee that the key messages are heard up front. These sessions will also help trainees recognize and avoid speculative "what if" questions. Above all, media training inspires self-confidence, which resonates through the camera.

Mark Bernheimer, a former CNN correspondent, has experienced the value of media training from both sides of the interview. As Founder and Principal of MediaWorks Resource Group in Los Angeles, California, Bernheimer has media trained spokespersons at all levels for many large corporations for more than two decades.

From his viewpoint as a former reporter, Bernheimer emphasizes, "Journalists are trained communicators – some better trained than others. They spend their careers honing their abilities to extract information and share it publicly."[12]

From the perspective of a corporate representative, he notes, "When spokespersons face off with a reporter in a crisis, they're at an automatic disadvantage. Trying to weather a serious PR crisis without foreknowledge and practice of the dos and don'ts is like removing your own wisdom teeth; it will be painful, bloody, and will probably lead to more problems than you had before."[13]

"Media training levels the playing field, helping communicators anticipate reporter behavior, develop key messages, and deliver those messages efficiently during the interview," he said. "The best coaches and consultants will not only help you develop and prioritize your messaging and predict tough questions, they will also help you decide which media interviews to grant and which ones are better to decline."[14]

According to Bernheimer, media training also has ancillary benefits not often considered by executives during a crisis: "Once you have the confidence to command a news media interview, your communication with investors, customers, regulators, lawmakers, and internal audiences almost always improves as well."[15]

We will look more deeply at the characteristics of an effective crisis spokesperson in Chapter 17, "Engaging with Legacy Media." The condensed version is that trained, on-site spokespersons should be fully familiar with the facility in question and the products manufactured, stored, transported, or sold there. They should explain the known facts with confidence and always maintain an appropriately positive expression. Although an interview may last 15 minutes or longer, only a few moments will likely end up in the news report. A hostile news editor may choose to show the spokesperson shifting his or her eyes or wiping his or her brow. But, if the spokesperson maintains a professional expression throughout, the editor has no choice but to include it.

For the most part, reporters will not be familiar with the facts and background on most facilities they are dispatched to cover. Prewritten fact sheets should be prepared and distributed by company staff prior to briefings or interviews so that the spokesperson can avoid answering these types of basic questions.

Maintain Up-to-Date Contact Information for Key Personnel

A crisis can emerge very quickly, set off by a single phone call from a wire service reporter on deadline or by some other unforeseen trigger. The corporate communications team will instantly scramble for answers and background, alert executives to the inquiry, dig up subject matter experts, notify international colleagues, and activate the predeveloped Crisis Communications Team.

A useful best practice in strategic crisis planning is to have crisply up-to-date contact information on hand, including email addresses and personal cell phone numbers for your key personnel. The contact list should include at least:

- Top executives.
- Their executive assistants.
- Designated Crisis Communications Team leader.
- Plant or facility top leadership.
- Chief engineers or scientists.
- Corporate security leadership.

- Risk management officer.
- IT leadership.
- Advertising leadership.
- PR agency account executive.
- All corporate communications staff.
- Prepositioned Crisis Communications Team members including leadership for:

  - Social media.
  - Marketing.
  - Customer relations.
  - Legal.
  - Government relations.
  - Human resources.

Communicate Your Plan Within the Organization

Your strategic crisis communications plan is only as strong as your organization's awareness of it. A customary perch for many crisis plan binders is on a dusty bookshelf, put aside and labeled "it will never happen to us." With a statistically high likelihood that your company will face some form of crisis in the future,[16] we advise that you take that binder off the shelf and transform it into an active, living, well-understood training module for anyone potentially involved in crisis communication.

By webinar or otherwise, roll the plan out to executives and other potential crisis team members and internal stakeholders, making sure that everyone knows their role should a crisis occur. If this training is not current practice in your organization, it ought to be. Prioritizing strategic crisis communication planning in your company is good business and is an opportunity for corporate communication to expand its strategic role.

Next, review and update the plan at least annually, including all the components detailed in this chapter (up-to-date contact information for key personnel should be revised at least quarterly). Your annual freshening of the plan should be consistent with the shifting landscape of potential threats you may face. The social and business climate changes rapidly, and today's windfall can become tomorrow's threat. Unprecedented developments emerge from nowhere. Each year, look within and review internal factors potentially affecting your company, such as how your organization was covered in the news, changes in employee treatment, diversity statistics, profitability, product line changes, and other emerging internal issues. Analyze external factors as well, such as the political landscape, societal trends, general news media climate, labor trends, financial markets, and the actions of your competitors. This annual checkup and adjustment to your overall plan will inform any changes you want make to your crisis communications playbook and stand-by websites.

Conduct Periodic Crisis Training

Once your plan has been adequately communicated within your organization, conduct periodic training exercises with the current employees who would be members of your Crisis Communications Team. As you read in Chapter 1, Ray Day, former Group Vice President for Global Communications at Ford Motor Company, said he learned from hard experience that "a crisis plan is only as good as the people who write, exercise, and revise key portions every day."[17]

Consider holding a mock crisis or a simulation to test your procedures and better prepare your team and its resources. Overnight delivery service FedEx regularly gathers its main communications forces for just such a crisis simulation. That often means a global exercise involving dozens of participants from FedEx's four operating companies in offices around the United States, Europe, Asia, Canada, and Latin America. FedEx and its partners at Ketchum, a public relations firm, have developed numerous potential crisis scenarios, including one involving a terrorist attack on the FedEx system, infecting employees around the globe with a deadly chemical warfare agent. In that exercise, FedEx communicators faced the possible shutdown of the entire system and the threat of serious damage to the company's reputation.[18]

Armed with nearly a hundred scripts that advanced the storyline, facilitators in seven cities role-played a variety of FedEx personnel, media outlets, and customer contacts to make the situation as real as possible for the players. After the exercise, facilitators addressed gaps that the simulation exposed and incorporated the best practices that emerged into all FedEx communicators' crisis processes. The company also made a commitment to testing its crisis preparedness annually.[19]

"Preparation really is the key," says Adaire Putnam, Director of Corporate Communications at the Kellogg Company in Battle Creek, Michigan, and formerly of Ketchum. "Simply expect the unexpected. The better prepared you are for the worst to happen, the more quickly and effectively you can respond. The best way to manage communications during a crisis truly is to plan for it in advance."[20]

On a much less elaborate scale than the FedEx example is the tabletop exercise, often called TTX, a facilitated exercise in which a hypothetical crisis scenario is presented and members of the crisis team practice developing a solution. Several companies provide TTX training, which can range from very intricate over a series of days, to very simple, in as little as a few hours. A company brought in to conduct TTX training should always involve employees in creating the various crisis scenarios in order to make them germane to the operations of the organization and more realistic.

References

1. Prater, M. "Crisis Management Examples: Learn from these Seven Brands." *Brandfolder.com*. Retrieved online: May 10, 2022. https://brandfolder.com/resources/crisis-management/
2. Ibid.
3. Vora, S. "Shifting Uber's Narrative from Crisis to Safety," *The New York Times*, March 7, 2022. Retrieved online: May 25, 2022. www.nytimes.com/2022/03/07/business/jill-hazelbaker-uber-safety.html
4. Bhasin, K. "9 PR Fiascos That Were Handled Brilliantly by Management," *Business Insider*. May 26, 2011. Retrieved online: May 10, 2022. www.businessinsider.com/pr-disasters-crisis-management-2011-5#jetblues-week-long-operational-breakdown-2007-6
5. Covey, S. *The Seven Habits of Highly Effective People: Restoring the Character Ethics*. New York: Simon and Schuster, 1989, p. 95
6. "Global Crisis Survey 2021: Building Resilience for the Future," *PWC Research*. March 2021. Retrieved online: January 26, 2022. www.pwc.com/gx/en/issues/crisis-solutions/global-crisis-survey.html
7. Clough, J., Watford, T. and Wray, A. *Accenture PLC: Profiting from Employee Trauma and the Reality of Content Moderation*. Notre Dame, IN: Eugene D. Fanning Center for Business Communication, Mendoza College of Business, University of Notre Dame, 2021.
8. Ibid.
9. Kenny, G. "Strategic Plans Are Less Important Than Strategic Planning," *Harvard Business Review*, June 21, 2016. Retrieved online: February 2, 2022. https://hbr.org/2016/06/strategic-plans-are-less-important-than-strategic-planning
10. Hirsh, S. "How to Create an Effective Social Media Policy," Society for Human Resources Management, March 18, 2021. Retrieved online: February 5, 2022. www.shrm.org/resourcesandtools/hr-topics/employee-relations/pages/how-to-create-an-effective-social-media-policy.aspx See also: Sehl, K. "How to Create Effective Social Media Guidelines for Your Business," Hootsuite, February 3, 2020. Retrieved online: February 1, 2022. https://blog.hootsuite.com/social-media-guidelines/
11. University of Minnesota Center for Infectious Disease Research and Policy. "Dark Site Stores Emergency Communications Until Crisis Occurs." Retrieved online: May 16, 2022. www.cidrap.umn.edu/practice/dark-site-stores-emergency-communications-until-crisis-occurs.
12. Personal interview. Mark Bernheimer, CNN Correspondent, June 1, 2022. By email.
13. Ibid.
14. Ibid.
15. Ibid.
16. *Global Crisis Survey 2021*. op. cit.
17. Personal interview. Raymond Day, Group Vice President, Global Communications, Ford Motor Company, April 12, 2012. By telephone.

18. O'Rourke, J. S. IV. *Management Communication: A Case-Analysis Approach*, 6th edition, Abingdon, Oxfordshire: Routledge, 2019, pp. 42–44.

19. Ibid.

20. Personal interview. Putnam, J. A. Director of Corporate Communications, The Kellogg Company, Battle Creek, MI. August 1, 2005, Chicago, IL. In person.

Chapter 3

Set Up a Rapid Response Team Process

Decades of practical experience among corporate communication professionals have shown that an early and effective tool in gathering and moving information is a Rapid Response Team. In this chapter, we will look at how others have used the concept and how you should think about this in preparing your own organization to confront the next crisis, whether anticipated or unexpected.

In November 2019, the U.S. Food & Drug Administration (FDA) deployed its 24 state-based Rapid Response Team process when romaine lettuce in supermarket salad kits was found to be contaminated with *E. coli* 0157-H7, sickening 167 people in 27 states. Fast analysis by Rapid Response Team members in Maryland and Wisconsin allowed the FDA to quickly isolate the contamination source to California's Salinas Valley. Romaine sourced from the valley was pulled from shelves, people stopped getting sick, and the FDA was able to avoid a nationwide ban on romaine lettuce prior to the Thanksgiving holiday.[1]

In hospitals everywhere, Rapid Response Teams of carefully identified clinicians react to a "Code Blue" or similar signal and rush to the bedsides of patients who show signs of imminent decline, "to immediately assess and treat the patient with the goal of preventing intensive care unit transfer, cardiac arrest, or death."[2]

The United States Army and United States Air Force jointly maintain an Immediate Response Force, capable of deploying worldwide within 18 hours.[3] In Quantico, Virginia, a Marine Corps Quick Reaction Force of about 145 specially trained Marines stands constantly ready to deploy in small teams at a moment's notice to protect American embassies anywhere in the world.[4] With the alarming spread of the COVID pandemic in 2020, sailors aboard the amphibious landing ship USS *Germantown* formed a COVID Rapid Response Team (CRRT) while underway in the Pacific. Supplementing the ship's small medical team, the CRRT quickly reviewed limited data and developed shipboard social distancing, sanitizing, and testing protocols, allowing the warship to remain COVID-free and continue its mission of supporting amphibious assaults.[5]

How does the Rapid Response Team concept apply to a business during a crisis? A common thread running through all forms of rapid response units is speed. Another is the team's distinctiveness from the larger organization it supports.

DOI: 10.4324/9781003322849-5

Once you have established a Crisis Communications Team template as discussed in Chapter 2, "Be Strategic in Your Planning," you can greatly strengthen the capabilities and effectiveness of your crisis response by setting up a Rapid Response Team (RRT) process as a strong adjunct to the larger team.

The RRT is designed to achieve speed and accuracy in your responses to the news media within the first moments of a news cycle. The bygone news cycle was certainly fast enough, when a reporter's story appeared in the morning paper the day following the first inquiry. The modern 24-hour news cycle compels media organizations to deliver the latest news instantly, in the most captivating fashion, and first, ahead of their competitors. Often originating on wire services, news is reported simultaneously on several television networks, cable channels, radio stations, blogs, and social media channels. A second wave soon expands the story by reporting on public, political, or other stakeholder reaction to the earlier news reports, further contracting the news cycle. Information released too late in this cycle by a company in crisis may be passed over, misunderstood, or ignored.

An Unaccountable Delay

On July 29, 2017, the credit reporting agency Equifax discovered a cybersecurity breach that affected approximately 143 million U.S. consumers. Cybercriminals exploited a vulnerability in the company's systems to gain access to customers' names, Social Security numbers, birth dates, addresses, and, in some cases, driver's license numbers. In addition, the thieves accessed the credit card numbers of approximately 209,000 U.S. consumers and personal information for some U.K. and Canadian residents. The incident was the single largest reported cyberbreach in history.[6]

Astonishingly, Equifax did not publicly announce the breach until September 7, 2017, six weeks after discovering it. A storm of criticism followed. The company chose not to individually contact affected consumers about the breach but, instead, directed bewildered and potentially vulnerable consumers to a website to learn if their data had been compromised. The company's website strained under the huge demand, did not work properly, and told people to come back later. Equifax's understaffed call center was also swamped. On September 8, a day after the breach was made public, U.S. Representative Maxine Waters (D-CA) ordered Equifax to divulge all the information related to the breach along with a comprehensive timeline. Finally, on September 13, Equifax CEO Richard Smith broke his silence. He apologized for the breach and acknowledged the complaints expressed by consumers and media about the services the company offered and the substandard operations of its call center and website.[7] Three weeks later, Smith abruptly retired but still faced hours of grilling before four separate congressional committees. In the end, Equifax settled with the Federal Trade Commission (FTC) for some $575 million, with $425 million earmarked to help people affected by the data breach.[8]

During Smith's October 3, 2017, congressional hearing, Chairman of the House Energy and Commerce Committee Rep. Greg Walden (R-OR) told Smith, "I don't think we can pass a law that . . . fixes stupid. I can't fix stupid."[9] While the data breach itself was enormous, Equifax's astounding six-week delay in announcing the breach severely complicated an already bad situation. When the breach was finally announced in a defensive and succinct news release, it contained no reference to consumer inconvenience or risk and certainly no hint of empathy or an apology. The six-week delay remained unexplained. Consumers and other stakeholders needed to hear from executives that the company owned the problem and was going to fix it. Furthermore, the company's crisis response systems had not been stress tested, and so they failed.

A Subgroup Built for Speed

If an organization in crisis wants its story told accurately, fairly, and completely, the blinding speed of today's news cycle often requires the organization to quickly inject its voice into the churning news stream. The job of the larger Crisis Communications Team is to set the strategy and tactics for managing the crisis at hand. But given the frequent need for swift reaction to an unexpected news media inquiry or other surprising development that requires a public response, a nimbler process is required. The full Crisis Communications Team and its experts are likely too cumbersome to efficiently deliberate over every company statement or every proposed comment by its spokespersons.

Yet, by abandoning the safety net of extensive internal review and approval, an organization may put itself at risk by making statements more quickly than it should. Public comments receive more scrutiny than usual during a crisis, and organizations under duress must choose their words with precision, often carefully nuanced, and free from any meaning or interpretation that could make matters worse. However, the news media wants your information immediately, right now, or it will proceed without you. At best, you may be thumped with "The company could not be reached for comment" or "The company did not return phone calls from the reporter" both of which imply potential uncooperativeness or secrecy on your part.

Enter the RRT, which should consist of a small, talented subset of writers drawn from the larger Crisis Communications Team. You want a small team because they will have to move fast and be ready to work long hours together. Five or six members should suffice, representing corporate communications, social media, legal, a content expert on the topic, the day-to-day spokesperson, and government relations, if the crisis has the attention of public officials. Good teamwork is essential within this lean and focused group, and attention to process and speed are the keys to its success. Do not include the crisis response senior leader or other final approvers, whose job it is to authorize public statements, not develop them. The RRT should be made up of your very best, most trusted, knowledgeable, and resourceful writers because their end product will have to be of the highest quality and will have little opportunity for revision.

The Utility of a Master Q-&-A

The RRT's very first and foundational task should be to develop a robust Master Q-&-A for internal use regarding the crisis. Having a Q-&-A on hand for any interaction with the news media is a best practice and a valuable tool in most circumstances.

- The Master Q-&-A should be comprehensive in that it contains not only all the known facts pertaining to the crisis but also includes carefully scrutinized and approved language, in a question-and-answer format, expressing the organization's point of view on all sides of the crisis.
- Divide the Master Q-&-A into sections by groups who will naturally have questions for the organization, including employees; internal stakeholders such as customer relations, suppliers, and business partners; external stakeholders such as public officials and interest groups; and, notably, the news media.
- Update it daily during a crisis and distribute it to the Crisis Communications Team and anyone else who might need it in any time zone. An out-of-date Master Q-&-A is worthless.
- Make it scrupulously honest and candid, including the very toughest, most uncomfortable questions imaginable. Striking an ugly or discomforting question from the Master Q-&-A because it may embarrass someone by having it in print may make everyone on the team feel more comfortable, but it will leave your spokespersons flat-footed when the distressing question ultimately gets asked. It's not a matter of *if*, it's a matter of *when*.
- Finally, be sure your legal team scrutinizes this document and labels it: *For Internal Use Only: Confidential Attorney Client Privileged*.

Involve the Entire Enterprise

Fan out the RRT within the organization and have it solicit every possible potential question that might be asked about the crisis, no matter how detailed or speculative. Stand in the shoes of journalists and formulate questions the way they would ask them. Then, frame follow-up questions, continuing to think like a journalist, and repeat the same question but in a different manner. Anticipate the questions your employees would ask. What would they want to know or need to know? The same goes for your customers, suppliers, public officials, and other stakeholders. What, from their perspective, is important information? An added benefit to the question-gathering process is that the RRT may uncover unforeseen angles, weaknesses, or gaps in your organization's stance on the crisis. Furthermore, as the RRT puts out feelers and makes inquiries throughout the enterprise, it will make contacts and develop resources and working relationships that will serve the company as the crisis persists.

Once all the questions are collected for the Master Q-&-A and the exceptional writers on your RRT have drafted as many answers as possible, give the entire

Master Q-&-A to the larger Crisis Communications Team for careful review and consensus on every point. Make sure the document is vetted at the highest levels. Express a sense of urgency to avoid delay. Are the facts airtight? Are all the right questions included? Are the tough questions answered? Once agreement is reached, the Master Q-&-A is no longer a draft and should be submitted to the senior crisis response leadership, including, perhaps, the CEO, for review and approval.

True unanimity at this point in the process is essential. Make it very clear to everyone on the Crisis Communications Team that, going forward, the approved language in your Master Q-&-A will be used word-for-word by your spokespersons to answer any question that appears in the document. There will be no time for internal second-guessing or tolerance for objections once agreed-upon language from the Master Q-&-A appears on the front page of *The Washington Post*.

Using the RRT Process

The Master Q-&-A is a powerful reference tool that will prevent your spokesperson from casting around for information and expertise when time is short. However, what happens when a new and unexpected issue surfaces related to your crisis that is not covered in the Master Q-&-A? Newly scheduled Congressional hearings? An indictment or arrest? An expanded product recall? A substance of concern found on company property? An FBI investigation? The media will unquestionably light up your telephones and email for an immediate reaction.

Here again, the RRT plays an instrumental role in the company's crisis response when the media's clock starts ticking. As we've noted, the RRT is designed to produce fast and accurate public statements within the first moments of a news cycle. When a question regarding a new wrinkle in the crisis is received, the RRT's role is to quickly gather facts (see Chapter 4, "Get the Facts . . . Fast") and formulate a response. The RRT's contacts and relationships gleaned from the earlier question-gathering process will prove to be invaluable resources.

Move Quickly

Just how much time will your spokesperson, supported by the RRT, have to respond to a media inquiry? That depends on several factors. In the experience of the authors, most wire services or other mainstream legacy journalists want to create an accurate story that fairly represents opposing points of view in an impartial manner. As such, media will most often give a spokesperson a reasonable amount time to gather information and formulate a response. Candor with journalists on this point is crucial, letting them know when they might hear from you, which will allow them to work around you while building out their story. But what is a reasonable amount of time? A week? A day? An hour? If, for example, an impatient Associated Press (AP) writer is drumming his fingers, waiting for your statement on a breaking story, and a Reuters story crosses the wire with just a glimmer of information about your issue, the AP reporter will likely issue a teaser story as well, to keep up with the competition.

Bill Koenig has more than 40 years of experience as a journalist, having served as the deputy U.S. autos team leader at *Bloomberg News* from 2011 until 2013, as the lead reporter covering Ford Motor Co. in Detroit, and as a staff reporter for the *Indianapolis Star*. Since the wires often lead the news, they are particularly time conscious. As a former wire service reporter, Koenig says,

> I always got the impression that the PR people were wary of the wire services because they knew we had to get the news out fast. In terms of how much time I would give a company, it depends on the sensitivity of the story but certainly get back to me sooner rather than later. If it's a breaking story such as an announcement has been made, I'd give a little time after the first contact. If it's a scoop or a super sensitive story, I'd give more time, but not much.[10]

Daily publications have the luxury of a little bit more time. Jayne O'Donnell spent 28 years at *USA Today* writing about healthcare policy, consumer affairs, and safety. Her 1996 articles on the dangers that airbags posed to children prompted the introduction of "smart" airbags and the government's requirement that warning labels be placed on every vehicle. In terms of the amount of time she allowed an organization to produce a response to a question she posed, O'Donnell said, "In most cases, the people or organizations I was covering knew that a story was coming. If that's the case, I generally gave them a day to respond to my questions."[11]

Respond in Writing

How should the RRT respond? Most crises involve sensitive matters. A careful choice of words will be essential for an organization under pressure. For the most part, an RRT media response to a new and emerging issue should be in writing and distributed by email. This allows the statement to be delivered quickly, assures absolute accuracy as to what will appear in the news report, and creates a permanent record of what was said. An added benefit is that an emailed statement can be directed only to those journalists who have an expressed interest in the crisis, thus avoiding a more widely broadcast statement on such services as PR Newswire or the Business Wire, which may inadvertently expand awareness of the crisis. For more discussion of effective ways of working with journalists in a crisis, see Chapter 16, "Engaging with Legacy Media."

Prioritize and Streamline

All this speaks to the need for the RRT to act fast and for the approval process to be sleek when a new issue arises. A streamlined approval process should be established that allows RRT statements to receive very little and immediate review.

The fewer reviewers, the faster the statement can ship to the media. Prioritize the approval process based on your assessment of reputational risk:

- **For new matters of no, or very low, risk,** keep the approval process within the RRT itself, which houses your day-to-day spokesperson on the crisis and can expedite your media response.
- **For new matters that may pose some limited risk,** elevate the RRT's proposed response to the Chief Communications Officer and perhaps a line executive responsible for the business area affected by the crisis.
- **For new matters of high risk,** push the statement up through the two levels just described, and on to the crisis response manager for final approval, and perhaps to the CEO.

Once the RRT has responded to the media, any statement should be shared with the larger Crisis Communications Team, monitoring should commence, and the statement should then be added to the Master Q-&-A for future reference.

Other Benefits

The concept of establishing a nimble team of fast writers to speed copy into the hands of decision makers can have value beyond crisis communications. Similar teams can be established in specialized areas for use whenever there is a need for ideas and copy to be generated over a short time period. For instance, Washington, D.C., is constantly sending up public policy trial balloons on which companies are often asked to take a position. Why not establish a standing Government Policy RRT to quickly work the problem and develop a statement? As the social justice movement continues to gather momentum and organizations are asked for their views, an Inclusion and Diversity RRT may be worthwhile to have within your organization. The concept might also work well for other public-facing issues, such as sustainability or labor relations. As with a crisis RRT, you need the right people, all of whom must be exceptional writers with the right expertise and resourcefulness, able to work quickly as a high-performing team.

Crisis Preparation Checklist

The immense benefits of being ready for the communications challenges produced by a crisis will be highly valued by senior leadership once your organization finds itself in trouble. As we conclude our discussion on *crisis preparation*, here is a quick checklist of actions to help get your planning underway or to supplement your existing plans. If you are just getting started, these can be considered in priority order, but all are equally important for comprehensive crisis preparation.

❏ Maintain up-to-date contact information for key personnel.
❏ Train your spokespersons.
❏ Establish a generic Crisis Communications Team template.
❏ Predetermine a clear chain-of-command.
❏ Set up a Rapid Response Team process.
❏ Start a Master Q-&-A.
❏ Establish a social media policy and crisis plan.
❏ Designate and equip a situation room.
❏ Plan for internal communication updates.
❏ Make a crisis scenario playbook.
❏ Create stand-by websites that can be up and running quickly.
❏ Be ready for media who arrive without notice.
❏ Communicate your plan throughout the organization.
❏ Conduct periodic crisis training.

References

1. "Rapid Response Teams. U.S. Food & Drug Administration." YouTube Video. Retrieved online: June 2, 2022. www.fda.gov/federal-state-local-tribal-and-territorial-officials/national-integrated-food-safety-system-ifss-programs-and-initiatives/rapid-response-teams-rrts

2. "Rapid Response Systems." Patient Safety Network, Agency for Healthcare Research and Quality, Department of Health and Human Services. Retrieved online: June 2, 2022. https://psnet.ahrq.gov/primer/rapid-response-systems

3. "Immediate Response Force." Wikipedia. Retrieved online: June 6, 2022. https://en.wikipedia.org/wiki/Immediate_Response_Force

4. Aitken, P. "U.S. Marines Quick Reaction Force Deployed Twice in Last 30 Days to Defend Embassies." Fox News. July 31, 2021. Retrieved online: June 6, 2022. www.foxnews.com/world/us-marine-force-deployed-twice-defend-embassies

5. Dimartino, T. "Rapid Response Team Fights Pandemic at the Deckplates." U.S. Department of Defense. August 21, 2020. Retrieved online: June 6, 2020. www.defense.gov/News/Feature-Stories/Story/Article/2318612/rapid-response-team-fights-pandemic-at-the-deckplates/

6. Balasundaram, A, Begliak, R, and Viswanat, V. *Equifax: Data Protection in the Digital Age*. Notre Dame, IN: Eugene D. Fanning Center for Business Communication, Mendoza College of Business, University of Notre Dame, 2018.

7. Ibid.

8. Federal Trade Commission. "Equifax to Pay $575 Million as Part of Settlement with FTC, CFPB, and States Related to 2017 Data Breach." July 7, 2019. Retrieved online: June 11, 2022. www.ftc.gov/news-events/news/press-releases/2019/07/equifax-pay-575-million-part-settlement-ftc-cfpb-states-related-2017-data-breach

9. Bernstein, L. "Congressman Reacts to Equifax Testimony, 'I can't fix stupid'." ABC Channel 15 News. October 3, 2017. Retrieved online: June 11, 2022. https://wpde.com/news/nation-world/equifax-hearing-i-cant-fix-stupid

10. Interview with Bill Koenig, via Zoom. June 10, 2022.

11. Interview with Jayne O'Donnell, via Zoom. June 10, 2022.

Crisis Management

Chapter 4

Get the Facts . . . Fast

September 11, 2001, began as a routine Tuesday for Morgan Stanley's Managing Director of Corporate Affairs, Raymond O'Rourke, who worked out of the corporate headquarters at 1585 Broadway in New York. Shortly after O'Rourke began conducting the weekly global corporate affairs conference call at 8:30 a.m., though, his secretary burst into the office telling him that he had an urgent call from a *Bloomberg News* reporter.[1]

The reporter told O'Rourke that a jetliner had crashed into the North Tower of the World Trade Center. O'Rourke relayed the message to the Morgan Stanley global affairs team then broke off the call. Stunned by the news, O'Rourke rushed to an office window and watched in horror as a second plane hit the South Tower of the World Trade Center where Morgan Stanley occupied 22 floors, housing 2,500 employees. The firm also had an additional 1,000 employees at Number 5 World Trade Center. As the morning of September 11 progressed, it became obvious that these two events were not accidents but terrorism.[2]

O'Rourke and his CEO, Phil Purcell, knew they had numerous actions to take immediately, almost all of them related to communication. Evacuating Morgan Stanley employees from the South Tower and from Number 5 World Trade Center was the job of Security Director Rick Rescorla. He had written a detailed plan for just such an event, exercised it regularly, and every Morgan Stanley employee knew exactly what to do. Evidence of Rescorla's skill and diligence surfaced several days later when corporate officials announced that all but 6 of Morgan Stanley's 2,700 employees had escaped and survived. Five of those who died in the building were above the entry point of the aircraft and could not escape. The sixth was Rescorla himself, climbing the stairs in search of his colleagues.[3]

Among O'Rourke's more immediate challenges, in addition to notifying clients, business partners, and others about the effects on the business, was locating nearly 3,500 Morgan Stanley employees who, by then, were scattered in the streets of New York. "Some managed to get on the last Path Train beneath the river to Jersey City, some caught the ferry," O'Rourke said. "Others walked over the Brooklyn Bridge and spent the night in Prospect Park. A few just huddled in doorways, uncertain what to do."[4]

DOI: 10.4324/9781003322849-7

Telephone service was completely disrupted in Manhattan's Financial District. Power was out, the internet didn't work. No one knew where anyone was, and fewer still had any idea how to find them. O'Rourke devised an ingenious plan to gather information and focus on finding and helping those who had escaped. "We converted our Discover Card call centers in Chicago and Salt Lake City from a credit application service into a data gathering facility." His next move was to get help moving the message.

O'Rourke hastily wrote a message, put it in a dispatch bag, and gave it to a bicycle messenger. "It was the *only* way to get around lower Manhattan," he said. "I told the messenger to get down to Number 8 Broad Street – the traders' entrance to the NYSE – show his credentials and ask for Bob Zito." He was the New York Stock Exchange's Chief Communication Officer. The note on the envelope's exterior said, "Please give this to Maria Bartiromo." She was CNBC's reporter at the exchange and was still on the air when Zito found her on the trading floor. The message inside the envelope said, "Would all Morgan Stanley employees please call a Discover Card operator." That's it. Just try to find a working phone and call that 800-number. Bartiromo repeated that message a number of times during the day.

Within three days, Discover Card operators had heard from all but a handful of Morgan Stanley employees. In return, they passed valuable information to each of them, providing directions to sleeping accommodations, food, and clean clothing. Employees in the headquarters building at 1585 Broadway in midtown opened a spreadsheet, began organizing the data, and shared it with employee families and loved ones.[5]

Among the more important messages the communication staff were able to pass along was the remarkable news that Morgan Stanley would reopen trading operations at a secure location on the West Side Highway the next Tuesday. The world would know the company had survived and was open for business, welcoming clients, traders, and business partners. Investors would know their assets were safe.

The challenge continued for months afterward, but neither Purcell nor O'Rourke would have been able to communicate with anyone in the absence of current, accurate, reliable information. Converting a retail sales call center to an emergency contact point was just one step in the process of getting the facts as fast as possible.

Deal From an Informed Position

Journalists will tell you that their most important asset is their credibility. If people don't believe them, ranging from editors to readers, they won't be around long. The same is true of corporate representatives and advocates. If you find yourself in that position during an unfolding crisis, your most valuable asset will be accurate, reliable information.

That means two things: first, separating fact from rumor and, second, knowing where you can look and with whom you can speak to find the truth. In a crisis situation, people are often happy to make things up, perhaps to make themselves look important or to disguise ineptitude, incompetence, or inattention to detail.

"I've had people in my own organization lie to my face," said Colonel David Shea, retired Director of Public Affairs for U.S. Air Forces Europe and a career public affairs officer. "That didn't happen often, but, because it did, the lesson for me was to double-check everything I think I know. Update your facts," he said, "find a second source, keep checking."[6]

The key is to document what you know and really don't know for sure, then document the source of your confidence in all that you've gathered. You must be able to explain to your chief executive, your employees, the press, and others how it is you know what you're saying is true.

A colleague who teaches in the Newhouse School at Syracuse University once remarked, "The first thing I do each morning is to ask myself if anything I know is still true." That's a useful question because much of what we've learned in school and in the early days of our careers is no longer true. Keeping up with changes to our store of knowledge and confirming its accuracy are not just helpful, they're essential.

Assess Media Coverage in Real Time

Staying abreast of what newspapers, television, radio, social media and internet news sources are saying about you, your organization, your brand, your products, and your people is equally essential. Just because it's not entirely true doesn't mean it won't make its way into the news cycle and onto a website or Twitter feed.

Appointing staff to assist with this task is fairly easy, but please know that this is a full-time, nonstop job that demands someone's attention 24 hours a day. If your budget will permit, consider hiring a firm that specializes in searching the media landscape and providing real-time alerts regarding your business. Companies such as Cision/Trendkite and Meltwater provide reasonably priced, full-time service so that your own staff won't be burdened with that task.

The vast majority of news outlets will have the same information, thanks to the wire services. Associated Press, Reuters, Bloomberg and others are in the business of gathering and distributing breaking news across the world. Print press as well as broadcasters depend heavily on the wire services, both in the U.S. and abroad, so moving information accurately and rapidly means beginning with the wire services. Once you have determined that your organization must make a public statement, unless you have some compelling reason to speak to local reporters first, it's probably practical and wise to start with a wire service release.

And, since most media outlets will be working with the same set of facts, it's fair to expect just a small bit of variance in the style and accuracy of the coverage. Occasionally, however, you will encounter outliers who gather and report the news entirely on their own. If yours is a story with important local impact, numerous local media outlets will try, at least initially, to cover the events with their own reporters, stringers, and camera crews.

Correcting a media reporting error is particularly important since that error can migrate to the wire services and, from there, to publications all around the world. Very quickly. Dealing with the reporter who wrote a story you think is damaging or erroneous may seem difficult because such people are professionals, accustomed to being told that they "may have gotten it wrong" by any number of people they are sent to interview or report on. The issue here is to explain *why* the story is wrong and how best to correct it.

The advice for correcting an error? It's simple. Contact the reporter or his or her city editor (or news director, in the case of broadcasting) and ask if you can speak for a moment. Thank the reporter for the time and expertise that went into the story. Then, politely say, "I believe the report I've just read on your website concerning our company is inaccurate." Follow that with a complete description of the correct information, facts, or concepts and explain how grateful you are. "I know you don't want your readers to be misinformed," you can say, "so I know you'll do the right thing."

Do not ask for a retraction, an apology, or some admission of bias. That simply will not win you any friends or any better coverage. Reporters deal with angry, upset people every day and try their very best to get to the truth. Show them why you have the correct, factual information. Don't ask how they came by the statement they printed in the paper or posted to their website. Above all, don't pick a fight. That's one you simply cannot win.

Another tussle you cannot win is one that involves opinion. One man's opinion, in a press interview, may well be as good as another's. Do not try to convince a reporter that an opinion from one of their sources is wrong, unflattering, or unfair. Take up only those issues of fact for which you can offer reasonable proof. Senator Daniel Patrick Moynihan (D-NY) famously said in 1983, "Everyone is entitled to his own opinion, but not his own facts."[7]

Among the more important reasons to correct a story that's inaccurate is the morgue file. That's the backlog of all stories reported by a news agency; it serves as a record of what its published and will be the first place another reporter looks if your company's name or brand comes up in the news again. Even if you never see a correction in the paper or on the air, knowing that the permanent record is flagged and corrected is vitally important. In a 1963 speech to overseas correspondents in London, *The Washington Post* publisher Phil Graham said, "Journalism is the first rough draft of history."[8] If you want history to think well of you, historians should at least begin with the truth.

Connect Across Time Zones

In the tragedy Morgan Stanley faced on the morning of September 11, 2001, news of the horrific acts traveled the world instantly. Unfortunately, a casualty of this blizzard of instant information was accuracy. Asian investors received false information that Morgan Stanley was completely "gone." Rumors that Morgan Stanley was "out of business" began traveling quickly throughout the world, primarily via the internet. As realities of the attacks began to sink in, Ray O'Rourke knew he would have to construct an operations plan while simultaneously focusing corporate efforts on the human crisis.[9]

The events of that day were not just a New York story. Nor were they an "American" story exclusively. News outlets in every country published photos, film, and accounts of all that was happening. Unscrupulous financial predators quickly tried to use the confusion, ambiguity, and information vacuum to their own advantage. Countering the reputational damage already done, as well as the very real threat to the business, meant the Morgan Stanley corporate affairs team would have to communicate globally and quickly.

O'Rourke awakened Phil Purcell very early on September 12, explained what was happening overnight in Asia, and then described a plan to deal with that. With a freshly printed newspaper in hand, the two Morgan Stanley executives walked from their hotel back to corporate headquarters on Broadway and headed for a small, undistinguished room the company used as a TV studio. O'Rourke arranged for a satellite uplink and connections to the company's video wire service.

"Hello, I'm Phil Purcell, chief executive of Morgan Stanley. I'm speaking to you live from our headquarters in midtown Manhattan." Purcell's rumpled suit, still covered in the soot floating through the air in New York, held up the Wednesday edition of *The New York Times* with the boldface headline, "U.S. Attacked." He went on to describe how his employees had survived and that the company was safe and ready to resume operations when the NYSE reopened. No one knew when that would be, but Purcell was taking no chances. Every time zone, every locality became important at that moment.[10]

Monitor Social Media

In the presence of breaking news, people no longer seek out a newspaper or news magazine for detail. They may learn about it on drive-time radio or see images on their televisions, but people, regardless of age or demographic, will quickly pull out their phones and turn to the internet. Some will seek out traditional news-gathering organizations such as *The New York Times*, *The Washington Post*, BBC, or NBC News. Others, though, will look for their favorite blog or comment wiki, hoping for insight, opinion, or inside information. Many will look to social media and social networking sites to see what others are saying about the situation.

No organization can afford to ignore what's trending on social media in a crisis. In April 2009, Tim McIntyre, VP of Corporate Communication at Domino's Pizza, experienced a lesson he'll never forget. While wrapping up his workday at the corporate office in Ann Arbor, Michigan, McIntyre received an email from a webmaster he didn't know, alerting him that videos featuring company employees contaminating food in an unidentified store had been posted on the online video sharing site YouTube. What had been a quiet day following Easter weekend suddenly turned into the first day of a full-fledged communications and marketing nightmare.

After just one viewing, McIntyre knew that the five amateur videos could seriously damage the Domino's brand, not to mention put the company at legal risk. He said, "You know what, this is a bad one – they're in uniform, they're in the store. We need to do something about it."[11] McIntyre said that this initial notification came about 15 minutes prior to his corporate social media team discovering the existence of the videos online. Within that same hour, another popular consumer affairs blog site *www.consumerist.com* also posted the videos. Within 24 hours, McIntyre would learn that the most popular video had received 250,000 YouTube views. It had just begun to go viral.[12]

With 122 million active viewers every day, YouTube has a big audience.[13] Facebook has more than 1.9 billion active daily users.[14] And so it goes: TikTok has amassed a billion daily users, and platforms such as Whatsapp, Instagram, SnapChat, Reddit, Pinterest, and Twitter attract even more.[15]

Compounding McIntyre's problem that afternoon at Domino's was the reality that he had no social media monitoring capability in-house. He had no contract monitoring service. He didn't even have a Twitter account. Others came to his rescue, but he'd have been better off with a social media monitoring tool such as Hootsuite, Talkwalker, or Nexalogy. Firms such as Reputology and Radian 6 provide real-time surveillance and notification. Given the anxiety and damage caused to the Domino's brand, their franchisees, and customers, the cost of a monitoring service is both inexpensive and well worth the investment.[16]

Become *the* Source of Reliable Information

Just as the press and the public kept returning each day to hear what Admiral Thad Allen had to say about the Coast Guard's work on the Macondo wellhead, the press and public returned to Ray O'Rourke and his CEO for accurate information about their investment firm. They did so because they knew Allen and O'Rourke could be trusted. What they said each day turned out to be true. It was accurate, reliable, and current.

A public spokesperson who hopes to maintain some form of control over the reporting in a crisis must know that accuracy, reliability, and currency are central to their credibility. American Rubber Products CEO Jeff Bernel discovered that a South Bend, Indiana, television station was running a videotaped interview with an ordinary bystander on the street outside Bernel's LaPorte, Indiana, manufacturing facility. The bystander, with absolutely no knowledge of what had happened, began speculating that the boiler which exploded was old and improperly maintained. On he went, offering baseless comment about things he wasn't witness to.

"Why did they talk to *him*?" Bernel asked. The answer: because Bernel chose not to talk to them. He did not have a designated spokesperson or an advocate to speak up for the company. Having driven that far to cover the story, the WSBT-22 news team was not about to return to the station empty-handed. They began interviewing anyone who agreed to talk. The fellow with no accurate knowledge but plenty of speculation just "wanted to be on the TV."[17]

The best way to counter inaccuracy is to appoint an authoritative, reliable, and knowledgeable spokesperson to interact with the press. You or your designated advocate must become *the* reliable source of information about this story, the company, your brand, your people, and your products. Don't let someone else tell your story for you. Even if it's unpleasant, unflattering, or simply awful, tell it yourself. And make certain that everything you say is actually true.

Keep the Information Flowing

Among the most important things you can do to help control the accuracy, velocity, and direction of a story is to keep communicating. Do that, even though you may not have much to say or any new information. Keep talking, keep listening.

Admiral Thad Allen, on his first day as National Incident Commander for the Deepwater Horizon oil spill, said: "That's about all I have for you. I'll be back tomorrow to take your questions, even if I have no new information. I'll be here until this is resolved."[18] That was a promise he kept, and one which the press and the American public genuinely appreciated.

For more in-depth discussion of news media and social media relations during a crisis, see Chapters 16 and 19, respectively.

References

1. Raymond O'Rourke, whose work at Morgan Stanley is cited here, is no relation to the author of this book.
2. Ulto, S. and Strmiska, D. *Morgan Stanley: The Events of September 11, 2001 (A)*. Notre Dame, IN: Eugene D. Fanning Center for Business Communication, Mendoza College of Business, University of Notre Dame, 2001, p. 1.
3. Grunwald, M. "A Tower of Courage," *The Washington Post*, October 28, 2001. Retrieved online: February 18, 2023: http://www.washingtonpost.com
4. Personal interview. Raymond O'Rourke, Managing Director of Corporate Affairs, Morgan Stanley. Corporate headquarters, New York, NY. February 25, 2004
5. Ibid.
6. Personal interview. Colonel David Shea, USAF, Director of Public Affairs, U. S. Air Forces Europe. Ramstein AFB, Germany. March 4, 1985.
7. Daniel Patrick Moynihan. *Wikipedia*, Retrieved online: February 18, 2023: https://en.wikipedia.org/wiki/Daniel_Patrick_Moynihan
8. Philip L. Graham. *Wikipedia*, Retrieved online: February 18, 2023: https://en.wikipedia.org/wiki/Phil_Graham
9. Personal interview. Raymond O'Rourke. Managing Director of Corporate Affairs, Morgan Stanley. New York, NY: Corporate Headquarters, February 25, 2004.

10. Ulto, S. and Strmiska, D. *Morgan Stanley: The Events of September 11, 2001 (A)*. Notre Dame, IN: Eugene D. Fanning Center for Business Communication, Mendoza College of Business, University of Notre Dame, 2001, p. 4.

11. Jacques, Amy. "Domino's Delivers During Crisis," *The Strategist*, 2009, p. 7.

12. Peeples, A. and Vaughn, C. *Domino's "Special" Delivery: Going Viral Through Social Media (A)*. Notre Dame, IN: Eugene D. Fanning Center for Business Communication, Mendoza College of Business, University of Notre Dame, 2009, pp. 1–2.

13. Global Media Insight. "YouTube Users Statistics." Retrieved online: November 3, 2022: www.globalmediainsight.com/blog/youtube-users-statistics/

14. Hamilton, I. A. "Facebook's User Numbers Shrunk for the First Time in Its History," *Business Insider*, February 3, 2022. Retrieved online: November 3, 2022: www.businessinsider.com/meta-facebook-user-numbers-shrink-first-time-ever-2022-2#

15. Walsh, S. "The Top Ten Social Media Sites and Platforms 2021," *Search Engine Journal*, June 22, 2021. Retrieved online: October 10, 2022: www.searchenginejournal.com/social-media/biggest-social-media-sites/#close

16. Cooper, P. "8 of the Best Social Media Monitoring Tools to Save You Time," *Strategy*, August 6, 2021. Retrieved online: https://blog.hootsuite.com/social-media-monitoring-tools/

17. Personal Interview. American Rubber Products CEO, Jeffrey Bernel, Notre Dame, Indiana. March 12, 1993.

18. Admiral Thad Allen, USCG, national incident commander for Deepwater BP oil spill response, and Dr. Jane Lubchenco, the NOAA administrator, provided an update on ongoing Deepwater BP oil spill response efforts in the BP Training Facility (Unified Incident Command Houma) in Schriever, La. at 8:30 a.m. CDT. Source: The American Presidency Project, UC Santa Barbara. Retrieved online: https://www.presidency.ucsb.edu/documents/press-briefing-national-incident-commander-thad-allen-1

Chapter 5

Determine the Real Problem

"If I were given one hour to save the planet," said physicist Albert Einstein, "I would spend 59 minutes defining the problem and one minute resolving it." Or, at least he is *said* to have said that. The quote may be apocryphal or it may be the thinking of an industrial engineer at Yale.[1]

While the source of the quote is uncertain, it contains considerable wisdom for several reasons. First, without a proper problem definition, no solution is possible. Australian business educator Gary Hadler says a lack of commitment or, perhaps, inadequate information may be a cause for failure in problem-solving, but it's more likely to be a misinterpretation of the problem itself.[2] Second, a methodical analytic approach to a business problem is more likely to lead to root causes than simple symptomatic descriptions.

If a company has put its money, muscle, and mind power behind the wrong solution, failure is inevitable. If that company is small enough or inadequately capitalized, the decision to back the wrong solution – or, perhaps the wrong problem to begin with – may result in bankruptcy and liquidation. The risks are high, and the demand is for managers to get a correct definition of the problem before they commit investor funding to pursue a solution.

Defining a Business Problem

The rigor with which a problem is defined is the most important factor in finding a good solution. Many organizations, however, are not proficient at articulating their problems and identifying which ones are crucial to their strategies. They may even be trying to solve the wrong problems – missing opportunities and wasting resources in the process. The key is to ask the right questions.

Dwayne Spradlin describes a process that his firm, InnoCentive, has used to help clients define and articulate business, technical, social, and policy challenges and then present them to an online community of more than 250,000 solvers. The four-step process consists of asking a series of questions and using

DOI: 10.4324/9781003322849-8

the answers to create a problem statement that will elicit novel ideas from an array of experts.

- **Establish the need for a solution.** What is the basic need? Who will benefit from a solution?
- **Justify the need.** Why should your organization attempt to solve this problem? Is it aligned with your strategy? If a solution is found, who will implement it?
- **Contextualize the problem.** What have you and others already tried? Are there internal and external constraints to implementing a solution?
- **Write the problem statement.** What requirements must a solution meet? What language should you use to describe the problem? How will you evaluate solutions and measure success?[3]

Short-Term vs. Long-Term Problems

During the COVID-19 pandemic lockdown of 2020 and again in 2021, many people in the industrialized world began changing their behavior. Very few trips to restaurants, except for takeout. No evenings in nightclubs or movie theaters. Department stores, retail merchants and local boutiques were closed, so shopping moved online. The family car sat in the garage and long-distance trips, whether for business or vacation, were postponed or cancelled. Zoom meetings, for better or worse, became a regular feature of working from home.

In addition to those behaviors, Americans began spending less and saving more.

- Americans added nearly $4 trillion to their savings during the COVID pandemic, but most of the gains went to upper-income families, according to a new study from Oxford Economics.
- Stimulus checks, rising stock markets, and fewer spending choices led to a massive savings boom over the [2020–2021 period], according to economists Nancy Vanden Houten and Gregory Daco.[4]

By the time a majority of Americans were safely vaccinated against COVID-19 and began to leave the house once more, the retail landscape had dramatically changed: big box retailers and Quick Service Restaurant (QSR) operators experienced serious trouble trying to hire and retain employees. Products and supplies were out of stock and hard to find. A number of small businesses were shuttered for good.

Making matters worse, supplies anticipated from overseas were stuck in ports of entry, such as Long Beach, Los Angeles, and Galveston. Hundreds of container vessels were anchored offshore, waiting for access to those ports, and thousands of long-haul truck drivers simply quit or retired. Warehoused inventory couldn't move from point-to-point because there were too few loaders and drivers to get it there.[5] An important question for business managers is this: will the disruption to our supplies be short-term or permanent?

Problems in the Coffee Industry

What kind of problem are we facing? By mid-2021, Starbucks began experiencing a serious shortage of many products, but most disturbing was hard-to-find coffee. In a statement, a spokeswoman for Starbucks said the company was experiencing "temporary supply shortages" of some of its products. She said the shortages varied by location, with some stores experiencing "outages of various items at the same time." She added that the company was working with its vendors to restock the items as soon as possible, and that the supply chain issues had not affected prices.[6]

Ominously, however, shipments of coffee beans from Mexico, Guatemala, Costa Rica, El Salvador, and a number of other producing regions signaled to coffee shop operators that shortages in coffee supply will continue and prices will increase.[7] While some market forecasters see this as a temporary disruption, others see a long-term decline in the supply of fresh coffee beans.

Starbucks and other coffee shop, restaurant, and beverage industry operators are faced with the challenge of knowing whether the crisis they face will resolve itself in six months or continue indefinitely. In this particular case, company strategists think it's a bit of both. Some issues like the shortage of napkins, lid stoppers, and cups truly are temporary and can be addressed with workarounds, substitutes, and customer patience. Other issues such as global climate change and the depletion of coffee fields in Brazil, Guatemala, Honduras, and elsewhere may, indeed, be permanent. Corporate response, then, would be different in each case. But a short-term solution to a long-term problem will likely result in disaster.

Problems in the Airline Industry

A serious pilot shortage at the legacy domestic airlines was addressed in the near term with adjustment to routes, scheduling, and, in some cases, large bonuses to pilots willing to forego vacation or personal time. That only works for the near term, however. Facing up to what appears to be a chronic, long-term shortage of qualified flight officers, United Airlines has opened its own flight academy, promising entry-level work to graduates at no cost to the students. The steady supply of military pilots and civilian flight school graduates could not keep up with expanding travel demand. The basic model for pilot training in the U.S. has begun to permanently change.[8]

United opened its new Phoenix, Arizona-area flight school in January 2022, branding it as the United Aviate Academy (UAA). At 340,000 square feet and valued at more than $10 million, the venture is clearly a long-term investment.

United officials said they were committed to a tuition-free training experience for 500 pilots a year.[9]

Is This Really Our Problem?

In the 1980s, McDonald's Corporation began to see low customer satisfaction as a problem. The issue, reportedly, was the time span between cooking a hot sandwich and a restaurant customer consuming the product. If the meal were purchased in a drive-through line, the Quarter Pounder or Big Mac might well be cold by the time a customer reaches home. While the company's food and process engineers worked diligently on making the kitchen more efficient, that didn't directly address customer concerns about a hot meal.

The solution seemed almost too good to be true: a device called a "polystyrene clamshell" – made from benzene and refined petroleum – was shown to keep hot things hot and cold things cold. A late-night comedian once said, "That's genius. How does it *know*?" An innovative sandwich called the "McD.L.T." was served in a dual polystyrene container with a hot hamburger on one side and cool lettuce and tomato on the other. That container seemed, on the surface, to be a small bit of retail genius.

Quick Service Restaurant executives and franchisees really did see the clamshell as a form of packaging innovation. As advertised, it did keep hot food hot and cold food cold. It was remarkably inexpensive, easy to ship, and easy to store, and the container simply would not degrade or decompose over time. It could be incinerated but would release carbon black and carbon monoxide to the atmosphere. And it did present a significant challenge to landfill and waste storage managers.[10]

Styrofoam is commonly used in disposable products that are used just once. According to science writer Max Dilthey,

> These products, can persist in the environment for more than a million years, since polystyrene is not biodegradable. Though it is slow to break down chemically, Styrofoam does fragment into small pieces, choking animals that ingest it, clogging their digestive systems. Styrofoam and other plastics currently make up about 30 percent of the landfill volume in the United States.[11]

McDonald's executives and franchisees did not see any of these issues as a business problem until consumer sentiment turned against the company and its packaging. But, by churning out 10 million of these boxes a day – more than 3.5 billion a year in 1990 – McDonald's helped make the packaging a symbol of a throwaway society.[12] Soon everyone from vocal environmentalists to ordinary school children began campaigning against the use of polystyrene clamshells.

The executive team at McDonald's, including Senior Vice President Shelby Yastrow and Ed Rensi, President of McDonald's USA, met in the late 1980s to discuss the problem and explored a collaborative approach with groups such as The

Environmental Defense Fund and Friends of the Earth. The company insisted to the end, however, that its foam packaging was environmentally sound, but "our customers just don't feel good about it," said Rensi. "So we're changing."[13]

The resolution came at a meeting in early 1990 at the company's Oak Brook, Illinois, headquarters. After hearing from franchise operators, supply chain managers, marketers, and more – all of whom continued to defend the polystyrene product – CEO Jack Greenberg quietly said: "Has it occurred to anyone in this room that this isn't our product? We don't make polystyrene clamshells. This isn't our problem." When asked what the company should do, he replied: "Quit using someone else's product. Just wrap the sandwich in paper and hand it to the customer."

Marketing executives howled about the "mouth feel, warmth, customer satisfaction," and much more. Greenberg listened patiently and said, "The market has moved on. This isn't about customer satisfaction, convenience, or anything else we offer. Global sentiment about protecting the environment is telling us we're on the wrong side this issue." In a matter of days, McDonald's issued orders for restaurant operators to return to paper packaging.[14]

Initially, the senior team at McDonald's had thought convenience and customer satisfaction were at the core of the problem and devoted their money, mind power, and public relations muscle to improving all of those. As it happens, that wasn't what people cared about most. Greenberg was right, the market – dominated by a younger generation – had moved on. If it wanted to remain in business, McDonald's would have to move with them. Not long ago, McDonald's Corporation appointed Katie Beirne Fallon as Executive Vice President and Chief Global Impact Officer to build a team and closely monitor such issues. The appointment, according to analysts, environmental advocates, and critics, was strongly positive and well-received.

The lesson Greenberg and others understood is that you must define the problem properly before you try to solve it. And, if it's really not your problem, quit investing in a defense of the product or a solution you cannot implement. If it's not your problem, move on and leave it to others to solve.

Note

1 The earliest relevant evidence of the quote appeared in a 1966 collection of articles about manufacturing. An employee of the Stainless Processing Company named William H. Markle wrote a piece titled "The Manufacturing Manager's Skills," which included a strong match for the saying. Markle, however, credited those words to an unnamed professor at Yale University and not to Einstein at Princeton.

References

1. In *The Manufacturing Man and His Job*. Finley, R. E. and Ziobro, R. "The Manufacturing Manager's Skills" by William H. Markle, Vice President, Stainless Processing Company, Chicago, IL, pp. 15–18. American Management Association, Inc., New York. 1966.

2. Hadler, G. "Why People Fail to Solve Problems Effectively," *ITS Education Asia*. Retrieved online: www.itseducation.asia/article/why-people-fail-to-solve-problems-effectively Accessed 6 February 2022.

3. Spradlin, D. "Are You Solving the Right Problem?" *Harvard Business Review*, September 2012. Retrieved online: https://hbr.org/2012/09/are-you-solving-the-right-problem Accessed 6 February 2022.

4. Frank, R. "Most of America's Extra Savings During the Pandemic Are Going to the Wealthy," *CNBC*, August 3, 2021. Retrieved online: www.cnbc.com/2021/08/03/most-of-americas-extra-pandemic-savings-are-going-to-the-wealthy-.html Accessed 6 February 2022.

5. Sweeney, E. "The Big Challenges for Supply Chains in 2022," *World Economic Forum*, January 19, 2022. Retrieved online: www.weforum.org/agenda/2022/01/challenges-supply-chains-covid19-2022/

6. Creswell, J. "Starbucks, Flush with Customers, Is Running Low on Ingredients," *The New York Times*, June 14, 2021, Section B, p. 1. Retrieved online: https://www.nytimes.com/2021/06/10/business/starbucks-shortages.html?searchResultPosition=1 www.nytimes.com/2021/06/10/business/starbucks-shortages.html

7. Hunt, R. "Why Starbucks Could Emerge from the Coffee Shortage Even Stronger," *The Motley Fool*, July 26, 2021. Retrieved online: www.fool.com/investing/2021/07/26/why-starbucks-could-emerge-from-coffee-shortage/ Accessed 6 February 2022.

8. Wallace, G. and Muntean, P. "United Airlines Has an Answer to the Pilot Shortage: Its Own Flight School," *CNN Business*, January 31, 2022. Retrieved online: www.cnn.com/2022/01/31/business/united-airlines-flight-school/index.html

9. Ewing, R. "Inside United's New $10 Million Arizona Flight School," *AirlineGeeks*, January 27, 2022. Retrieved online: https://airlinegeeks.com/2022/01/27/inside-united-s-new-10-million-arizona-flight-school/#

10. "The Facts on Styrofoam: Reduce and Reuse," *Collier County Public Utilities*. Retrieved online: www.colliercountyfl.gov/government/public-utilities/solid-hazardous-waste/keeping-green-helpful-information-page/the-facts-on-styrofoam-reduce-and-reuse# Accessed 6 February 2022.

11. Dilthey, M. "How Long Does It Take for Styrofoam to Break Down?" *Sciencing*, April 19, 2018. Retrieved online: https://sciencing.com/long-styrofoam-break-down-5407877.html Accessed 6 February 2022.

12. Farhi, P. "McDonald's Trashing Its Foam Containers," *The Washington Post*, November 2, 1990.

13. Holusha, J. "Packaging and Public Image: McDonald's Fills a Big Order," *The New York Times*, November 2, 1990, Section A, p. 1. Retrieved online: www.nytimes.com/1990/11/02/business/packaging-and-public-image-mcdonald-s-fills-a-big-order.html

14. Personal interview. Richard G. Starmann, Senior Vice President for Corporate Communication, McDonald's Corporation. March 21, 1997. McDonald's Corporation Headquarters, Oak Brook, Illinois.

Chapter 6

Put Someone in Charge

A true crisis involves a set of events, resource demands, short-notice requirements, and situational judgments that simply cannot be produced by any organizational staff unit *in addition to* what they're asked to do every day. This is not business as usual. As a result, senior leadership must appoint a response team leader, preferably someone sufficiently senior and experienced to take on the problem.

Four key principles govern the appointment of a Crisis Communications Team leader. The organizational Chief Executive Officer or Chief Operating Officer must give the team leader:

1. **Full responsibility.** This means, simply, that the individual appointed to direct the organizational response to events in the crisis is both responsible for actions taken (or not taken) and fully accountable for the results. Initially, that person will hold accountability for solving the problem, preventing further knock-on effects, and setting the future course of the organization in response to what's happened. Often, this means explaining expenses incurred to deal with ongoing events as well as an explanation about where the money came from to set things right. Obviously, cooperation with other corporate division chiefs, including budget and financial services, will be essential. Marketing, legal, and operations will be quick to follow.

2. **Complete authority to act.** The person appointed to lead the response team should have the authority to act on his or her best judgment and must not be required to receive permission for each action, expenditure, or public statement. Requiring higher-level approval will only serve to slow down the response, limit the effectiveness of the solution, and encourage wrangling among C-suite divisions about "who'll take the blame if this doesn't work." Such moments in a corporate officer's career will not only test what they're made of but also can easily demonstrate who is ready for appointment to a higher grade with much greater responsibility.

3. **All resources required.** The same principle applies to the resources required to solve the problem, deal with those affected, and make things right for all who are involved. If the team leader or section chiefs must formally request

DOI: 10.4324/9781003322849-9

cash, equipment, personnel, external contract assistance, or inventory held by the company, everything will slow down and increase the probability of failure. Full responsibility means the team chief should move quickly to take action, employ corporate resources, and use his or her best judgment in the moment, then brief the senior team in a timely fashion.

One additional principle applies here: the CEO or COO must tell people who is in charge of the corporate response. This serves two purposes. First, all within the organization, including contractors and consultants, will know to contact the response team chief and not an operating agency within the company. Second, those external to the company – including the news media, regulatory agencies, elected officials, and others with a direct interest in events – will see a consistent face for the company's response and will adjust their expectations accordingly.

An important distinction here exists between the Crisis Communications Team leader and the day-to-day media spokesperson, who is likely to be quoted in news media articles and stories. The response team leader would be known to government officials, for example, because that individual would likely be the one to appear before hearings or lead press conferences. Daily updates and media statements, by contrast, would likely come from the chief of corporate communications (CCO). As long as external agencies know who is responsible for each activity, it should be easy for them to find the right person to speak with.

A Crisis in the Pharmaceutical Industry

On the afternoon of Friday, September 24, 2004, Joan Wainwright, Vice President of Public Affairs at Merck & Company, sat in the jury waiting room in a Baltimore, Maryland, courthouse. "One last time," she thought, as she checked her phone for email, just to see if there were any last-minute issues to address before the weekend. It was 3:00 p.m.

An urgent message asked her to call Merck's general counsel about news from the FDA's Data and Safety Monitoring Board. Wainwright asked the court bailiff for permission to use the phone and quickly returned the call. What she learned wasn't good: the latest clinical study on Merck's blockbuster arthritis drug, Vioxx, had produced strongly unfavorable results. The Data and Safety Monitoring Board recommended stopping the Vioxx study with eight weeks remaining, citing an increased risk of heart attack and stroke in patients taking the drug.[1]

Following the court's adjournment for the day, Wainwright rushed home to participate in a 5:00 p.m. conference call with other Merck executives, including the general counsel and chief of the U.S. marketing group. The conference call discussed scenario planning, leaving Merck with two viable options: leave Vioxx on the market with a "black box" warning or pull the drug.

While Wainwright spent the weekend contemplating the logistics of communicating the company's decision to many different audiences, Merck's Chief

Executive Officer, Raymond Gilmartin, assigned Dr. Peter Kim, the company's Research and Development Chief, full authority to make a decision on Vioxx based on patient safety.[2] Regardless of the decision Kim would soon make, Wainwright knew that life in the near term would change dramatically for her communications and public affairs team at Merck.

The Recall

With overwhelming results showing Vioxx's cardiovascular risks, Kim made the final decision to pull the drug from the market on Monday, September 27, citing patient safety as motivation for the decision. For the next three days, Joan Wainwright and a team of Merck officials assembled in a "war room" to discuss communication of the recall.

On September 30, Ray Gilmartin, Merck CEO, made an announcement that would change the face of the enterprise and the entire pharmaceutical industry. Gilmartin announced that Merck was in the process of withdrawing its popular arthritis painkiller Vioxx from the worldwide market. At the time of the recall, about two million people were taking Vioxx. Since the drug's approval in 1999, more than 100 million prescriptions had been written.[3]

The Merck Team

"We began thinking about who we would have to notify, how we might go about that, and what resources would be available to us," Wainwright said, "so we prepared grids with the audiences and channels. But because we didn't yet have a decision, we couldn't begin preparing any of the message content."[4] Beginning Monday morning, Wainwright assembled a team of 25 people, all experienced professionals from Merck public affairs, investor relations, U.S. and worldwide marketing, Merck research labs, and Merck's corporate counsel. All would be responsible for helping to communicate the message as soon as a decision regarding Vioxx was available to them. She made certain to include a chemist, a pharmacologist, a medical doctor, and a corporate liability attorney.

The team's work on Monday, September 27, was aided by their experience just a year earlier, when the company stopped the development of two very promising drugs that were in Stage III clinical trials. "We went back and reviewed the plans we used to announce the cessation of those two drugs," said Wainwright, "but because neither was on the market yet, we knew we would have additional audiences to reach with Vioxx."[5]

Complications in the Withdrawal

As Wainwright knew, it would not be difficult to stop the flow of her company's drug to retailers and patients. Of roughly 60,000 retail pharmacies in the U.S., one-third are independent and two-thirds are retail chains, supermarkets, or mass retailers.[6] Merck's marketing and distribution divisions could make those contacts. Wholesalers would quit shipping Vioxx to the pharmacies. The company's "detailers" or sales representatives would be asked to call on doctors and prescribers to explain the withdrawal of the drug. Those calls would be easy.

The more difficult issue would be the patients who'd been prescribed the drug for post-surgical recovery or an injury of some sort and would likely still have some in their bathroom medicine cabinets. Unwilling to throw away an expensive painkiller like Vioxx, they would reach for the container if they felt a twinge or some unrelated pain. The real danger would come for millions of people who continued to take the drug and had no idea of the risk involved.

Multiple audiences would have a direct interest in this action by Merck, including investors, stock analysts, retail partners, channels of distribution, and patients and physicians worldwide, among others.

The Announcement

At 8:00 a.m. on Thursday, September 30, Merck & Co. issued a press release announcing the worldwide recall of the company's $2.5 billion drug. At 9:00 a.m., Wainwright held a press conference in New York at which CEO Ray Gilmartin repeated the announcement and took questions from news media representatives. The company also conducted an investor relations teleconference at 10:00 a.m. that morning to explain the news to Wall Street and the financial community.[7] And, at the moment the press release was moving, Wainwright sent an email to all Merck & Co. employees worldwide explaining what had happened. A second email sent each employee a link to view the webcast of the press conference in New York.

For the balance of the day, Kim and Gilmartin spent most of their time responding to press queries, physician concerns, and questions from regulatory agencies. Wainwright said later,

> I was in the fortunate position that when I asked Dr. Kim and Mr. Gilmartin to make these announcements personally and to make themselves available for press statements and interviews, I received complete cooperation from them and their staffs. They were more than willing to do whatever we asked of them.[8]

On October 2, the Sunday following the announcement, Merck & Co. ran full-page display advertisements in 25 major newspapers throughout the country explaining the Data and Safety Monitoring Board's findings and the company's decision to withdraw Vioxx from the market. The advertisement was in the form of a letter to patients letting them know where they could find more information about the drug and the reason for the withdrawal.

Using This Case as an Example

We'll have more to say in Chapter 7 about activating the crisis team and much more in Chapter 9 on goals and measurement of success. For now, it's important to think about what we've learned from Joan Wainwright's experience in helping her company to withdraw a potentially dangerous pharmaceutical compound from the marketplace.

1. If you're confronted with a crisis, learn everything you can about the issue and make sure you can stand behind the story. Don't accept anything at face value. Ask questions, talk to people who are knowledgeable, do your own research. You have to understand the story and you have to believe in the story.
2. Think about the worst-case scenario, plan for it, and recognize that you'll be involved in the issue for a very long time.
3. Don't underestimate the power of your critics or overestimate the power of the press. The media will often give airtime or print space to people who aren't really experts. They'll be uncovered before long but can do serious damage in the near term. Similarly, the press isn't your enemy, but obsessing over one reporter or one publication can derail your efforts to tell the entire story fairly and completely.
4. Understand that every day offers a new opportunity. If the media is paying attention to you, don't ignore the opportunity to explain issues or aspects of the story it hasn't asked about or covered either thoroughly or accurately.
5. Have faith in your decisions. Once you've made a decision, don't spend time endlessly second-guessing yourself. Everyone outside the organization, particularly those who've only come to the issue recently, will consider themselves an expert. Rely on your staff and have confidence in their work.
6. Measure, measure, measure. It's the only way to show your staff and senior management what you've done.
7. Understand that employees are your greatest asset. This includes not only those in your own department but also others throughout the entire organization. They can carry your message to friends, family, neighbors, and others.
8. Keep an eye on your team. Look for stress, disappointment, and burnout. Respond quickly to address the needs of those who are most affected.
9. Develop a team to handle the issues full time in the days and months ahead. Let employees return to their previous day jobs, get special expertise if you need it, and don't leave anyone on the team too long.
10. Finally, realize that life goes on outside the office. It's important that you have a life as well as a job.

References

1. Wainwright, Joan, Vice President for Public Affairs, Merck & Company, in a teleconference interview from her offices at Merck corporate headquarters, Whitehouse Station, NJ, 11:00 a.m. (EST), December 9, 2004.

2. Ibid.
3. Gust, A. M. and G. D. Bartucci, *Merck & Company, Inc.: The Recall of Vioxx© (A)*. Notre Dame, IN: Eugene D. Fanning Center for Business Communication, Mendoza College of Business, University of Notre Dame, 2005, p. 1.
4. Wainwright, Joan. op. cit.
5. Ibid.
6. Dabora, M. C., N. Turaga and K. A. Schulman, "Financing and Distribution of Pharmaceuticals in the United States," *JAMA* 318, no. 1 (2017): 21–22.
7. Freudenheim, M. "A Blow to Efforts to Close In on Rivals," *The New York Times,* October 1, 2004. Retrieved online: https://www.nytimes.com/2004/10/01/business/health/merck-and-vioxx-the-company-a-blow-to-efforts-to-close-in.html?searchResultPosition=1
8. Wainwright, Joan. op. cit.

Chapter 7

Activate the Crisis Communications Team

Communications professionals who have experienced a crisis agree on the value of establishing a Crisis Communications Team to help an organization manage any situation that threatens its reputation. A keystone of crisis preparation, which we examined in the first part of this book, was the need to develop a generic Crisis Communications Team template and populate it in advance with seasoned leaders from cross-functional areas. After all your preparation, once a sudden, unwanted event strikes from any quarter, it is time to convene the situation room, put the right team members' names in the right boxes, and quickly activate the team.

Writing in the *Harvard Business Review*, Ben W. Heineman, former GE General Counsel and a senior fellow at Harvard University's schools of law and government, says of corporate leaders' response to a crisis, "The mantra for all leaders in crisis management must be: 'It is our problem the moment we hear about it. We will be judged from that instant forward for everything we do – and don't do.'"[1]

As soon as a crisis becomes evident, says Heineman, "The CEO or top business leaders should then form appropriate multifunctional teams relating to: design problems and solutions; internal personnel and processes; duties to regulators; management of litigation; a communications strategy with various constituencies; and any other relevant functions."[2]

The Team's Mission

In broad strokes, organizations form crisis communication teams to collectively develop and execute tactics and strategies that will help them weather the storm, emerge from difficult circumstances as soon as possible, and then prepare for an optimistic future. The team's main job is to lead and coordinate all activity related to the threat at hand and contain its growth. The members will be confronted with incomplete information on which to make quick decisions. They will define and communicate the organization's top priorities. They will decide what to do and, just as importantly, decide what *not* to do.

The means of achieving success will include identifying potential short-term and long-term problem areas that may arise, devising effective solutions, and allocating

DOI: 10.4324/9781003322849-10

resources to fix the problem. We will have more to say on the usefulness of centralizing all communication activities and functions into one team in one location and reporting to one senior official in Chapter 10, "The Value of Centralization."

On a more granular level, the Crisis Communications Team must consist of senior leaders who can work well together when the going gets tough. Collaborative, creative, open-minded, thick-skinned leaders must coalesce to form a high-functioning unit to solve the crisis. While senior decision makers are absolutely required on the team, title should be a secondary consideration to knowledge and proficiency. Who has the expertise? Who has the proper interpersonal relations skills? Who has right communication skills? Who has the patience and focus?

At the onset of a crisis, the team should ideally be isolated from other day-to-day concerns and allowed to concentrate entirely on the immediate challenge. While difficult to keep high-level leadership away from their daily responsibilities over a sustained period, deputizing subordinates to keep the lights on over the short term will allow the team to get organized and give the crisis the full attention it requires.

Composition

The makeup and size of the team will scale up or down based on the size of the organization and the magnitude of the crisis. The Crisis Communications Team should include all the company stakeholders that may be affected by a crisis as well as all areas responsible for developing and deploying the organization's crisis response. Make it large enough to be effective across the entire organization but not so large that it becomes unwieldy. Avoid unnecessary horse-holders, note-takers, and hangers-on, but, by all means, be sure that each team member has a trained and high-level replacement. What if a key member suddenly disappears? Who is the backup? At the same time, keep it small enough to be nimble, able to make quick decisions, and instantly shift direction as a single coordinated unit, much like a school of fish.

Cadence

How often will the team meet? Whether in a virtual situation room or a well-equipped, bricks-and-mortar conference room, the crisis leader must establish a regular meeting cadence, most likely at the same time each day, to fit the intensity of the situation. Based on the experience of the authors, in the early days of a breaking crises, the team should meet several times a day to identify and prioritize problems, divide up tasks into subgroups, and then reconvene to discuss potential resolutions well into the night, including weekends. No business as usual.

Some crises last much longer than anyone ever hopes or imagines. On December 12, 2019, a cluster of patients in Wuhan, Hubei Province, China began to experience shortness of breath and fever. Within less than two months, CDC's

Dr. Nancy Messonnier, Incident Manager for the COVID-19 Response, held a briefing where she braced the U.S. for the spread of the virus stating that the "disruption to everyday life may be severe." After two chaotic, disruptive and tragic years for billions of people, for society, and certainly for businesses everywhere, the global COVID pandemic is just showing signs of abatement.[3]

The Volkswagen emissions crisis, known in the media as Dieselgate, began in September 2015. The United States Environmental Protection Agency (EPA) accused German automaker Volkswagen Group of intentionally tweaking certain diesel engines to turn on their emissions controls only during laboratory emissions testing, thereby falsely appearing to meet U.S. regulatory standards. Volkswagen used this deceptive software in about 11 million cars worldwide, including 500,000 in the United States.[4]

After seven months of intense global media and governmental scrutiny – following the resignation of Volkswagen Group CEO Martin Winterkorn – a subsequent police raid on Volkswagen's headquarters in Wolfsburg, Germany, several arrests, and a $2.8 billion criminal fine in the U.S., Volkswagen agreed to pay $15.3 billion to resolve several public and private civil actions, the largest automotive-related consumer class action settlement in history.[5]

Not all crises are as persistent and world-gripping as COVID-19 or as protracted and expensive as the Volkswagen debacle. Often, in life and in business, no correlation exists between the size of a problem and the time it takes to solve it. On the one hand, an apparently minor matter involving executive indiscretion may drag on for months as a parade of new and intriguing stakeholders appears in front of the cameras to stimulate continued media interest. On the other hand, what at first may appear to an organization to be a potentially thorny and sizeable problem may be quickly resolved by a decisive stroke on the part of company leadership, such as a sincere and well-received apology from the top. Or, a crisis may be averted and removed entirely from public view by an unrelated and dramatic event that diverts the public's attention elsewhere.

Some crises last for years, months, or weeks. Others for just a day or two. Generally, once the facts are all gathered by the Crisis Communications Team, the stakeholders are identified, and the organization's position is clearly communicated, the turmoil and immediacy that gripped the early days of the crisis will begin to subside, and the meeting cadence can adjust accordingly. After a concentrated period of daily or twice-daily huddles in the situation room, the team may switch to meeting three times a week, and then gradually two, and eventually once a week. One good indicator that things are getting better is when the Crisis Communications Team is reduced in size and renamed the "Project Team."

Follow the Sun

The Volkswagen crisis was a global communications nightmare. One of the largest automakers in the world, the Volkswagen Group operates in 153 countries, with 120 production plants in Europe, the Americas, Asia, and Africa.[6] As such, the emissions crisis attracted sustained worldwide media attention for years as numerous governments took civil and criminal actions against Volkswagen and imposed fines and prison sentences in several countries. Due to the company's mismanagement of the truth from the start and a constant flow of new revelations, the challenge facing Volkswagen – trying to keep its global communications consistent and appropriately timed – was nearly impossible to overcome. Volkswagen's predicament serves as an important lesson for any international organization facing a crisis.

An adage in corporate communications states that the best time to announce bad news is on a Friday night. The theory is that reporters are heading out, hoping for an early start to the weekend. Even if a negative story does appear on a Saturday, fewer people are paying attention to the news. And there is still an entire Sunday acting as a buffer until the Monday morning news. Further, a lot of bad things can happen to *someone else* between Friday and Monday that could take your story off the front pages. At least, that is the conventional wisdom. Don't count on it.

Global companies must regularly follow the sun as they make announcements, taking careful account of time differences in all the regions where they operate. Imagine that an organization hopes to bury some bad news by announcing it at 6:00 p.m. in New York, too late for any evening news broadcasts. Across the world, the U.S. news bureaus in Tokyo are coming alive at 7:00 a.m. and can flash a story back to the States in seconds.

The wire services are all globally matrixed, 24 hours a day, so corporate communications teams must make international time zone integration an operational standard. The tools for global connectedness exist, from videoconferencing, to email, to texting, to mobile phone calls. Every spokesperson around the world should be armed with the updated Master Q-&-A and kept in the loop about what will be announced, or said, and when, in every time zone where the organization operates. Where such systems often fail, even in the best of companies, is when a spokesperson in a faraway time zone answers a reporter's question, goes home, and fails to tell anyone about it. The resulting story can be an unwelcome surprise that undermines the organization's efforts to control the timing and content of its messaging.

A Tale of Two Races

On Father's Day in June 2005, the French tiremaker Michelin experienced a major embarrassment at the United States Formula 1 (F1) Grand Prix at the legendary Indianapolis Motor Speedway (IMS) when all seven racing teams using Michelin tires, a total of 14 race cars, withdrew from the race due to concerns over the safety of the tires. Only three teams, totaling six cars, all riding on Bridgestone tires, completed the lackluster race.

In contrast to F1 venues outside the United States, Michelin did not have the opportunity to test the tires on the IMS prior to the race and, by race day, decided that the tires were potentially unsafe.

Michael Fanning, Vice President of Corporate Affairs for Michelin North America at the time, now retired, explained the unprecedented decision to withdraw: "Out of an abundance of caution for the safety of the drivers and spectators and people working the race, we felt we could not in good conscience complete the race on the tires we constructed for that particular track."[7]

With the sudden and dramatic race day exit by the seven race teams on Michelin tires, a perfect storm consisting of live worldwide weekend media coverage for the event, 100,000[8] fans with expensive tickets in the IMS grandstands, and political feuding within the sport of Formula 1, produced an enormous communication challenge and major risks to Michelin's image and reputation.

Racing was in Michelin's DNA from its founding, when brothers Édouard and André Michelin of Clermont-Ferrand, France, established their pneumatic bicycle tire company in 1889. Two years later the brothers patented the tire used to win the first long-distance bicycle race in history. Today, Michelin is the largest tire manufacturer in the world and is also known for its travel guides, road maps, and coveted stars in the *Michelin Guide* to restaurants.[9]

In addition to competing in Formula 1, Michelin tires have achieved substantial motorsports success, contending in both the European and American Le Mans Series, in the World Rally Championship Series, and in MotoGP motorcycle racing.[10]

Early during the ill-fated 2005 Grand Prix, as the remaining six race cars circled the IMS track, many of the frustrated spectators left the grandstands. Thousands of fans descended on the IMS ticket office to demand refunds, and police were called to maintain order. Booing could be heard throughout the race, and some infuriated fans raised their middle fingers and tossed beer cans and water bottles on the track.[11]

"Race fan reaction at IMS was intense. Team personnel were physically threatened on site, and we received hundreds of calls to our customer relations numbers and faxes," Fanning said. One fax read, "Screw Michelin. I spent $3,200 this weekend."[12]

Another customer wrote, "Hopefully, the fallout will extend beyond Formula 1 Racing, well into lowered tire sales. I will do everything possible to see that it does." Still another wrote, "We will NEVER again purchase a Michelin product."[13]

Unrelenting and fiercely negative media coverage followed. Of the nearly 7,000 news stories, 38 percent were decidedly negative and the rest were simply factual; the simple facts in this case were not good.

On the legal front, the threat of protracted litigation loomed against Michelin, against the IMS, against Formula 1 and against Federation Internationale de l'Automobile (FIA), the sport's governing body. Immediately following the race, three class action lawsuits were filed on behalf of disgruntled fans seeking punitive damages and compensation, charging that Michelin, Formula 1, and FIA did not hold the race as advertised.[14]

The controversy and its aftermath threatened the Michelin brand and its proud racing tradition. "The hallmark of the company from its very earliest days was racing, and racing has been instrumental to Michelin as a strategic communications platform since its founding, affecting dealers, consumers, original equipment manufacturers, and many others," explained Fanning. "So when this happened on a worldwide stage in 2005, everyone in the company sat up and took notice. From a communications point of view, we determined it was going to be a very strategic response."[15]

Michelin's Response

Michelin had previously announced in December 2005 that it would depart F1 after the 2006 season because the series was moving to a single tire supplier, and Michelin felt that change would eliminate a significant element of competitiveness and technical development from the sport. Despite having no long-term commitment to F1 in the U.S. beyond the coming 2006 Grand Prix at IMS, Michelin mounted a major strategic communications campaign to protect its brand and demonstrate sincerity and loyalty to its race fans, customers, dealers, and the racing teams and automotive companies whose vehicles ran on Michelin tires.

Activating the Team

Fanning, who reported to Michelin North America's top executive, was put in charge of the crisis response. He quickly flew to France with Michelin's lead U.S. lawyer to meet with the heads of communications, public affairs, and senior company management to decide how they were going to address the problem. The legal team was important because the first lawsuits were filed the day after the race and because more were probably in the works.

Fortunately, good crisis communication was always an imperative at Michelin. Embedded within the company communications philosophy was the idea that effective crisis communication would always be a high priority. Michelin held regular crisis simulations. The company even had one individual dedicated to help implement a worldwide crisis communication approach.

"The infrastructure for our team was already in place, and the actual implementation plan for our crisis team was pretty well set beforehand," Fanning said.

> We used a team approach. Because this was a global crisis, our main task was to parse out exactly who would handle what. Since we had such a strong crisis communications philosophy, we were able to quickly map out responsibilities and our means of communicating with one another.[16]

The team divided the work. Even though the 2005 Grand Prix happened on U.S. soil, it was a global issue, and there were global stakeholders to be reckoned with, including Formula 1 and FIA. France would handle those factions. North American operations would focus on the IMS, Michelin dealers, and its consumers and on handling the U.S. media, including the business, consumer, enthusiast, and trade press. Media monitoring was constant, and the team would "follow the sun," with daily comparisons of the French and U.S. media reports in real time.

"In terms of strategic communications, this is an example of a company that had to really double down and make sure that all the piece parts were aligned before we went ahead and started addressing tactical issues," Fanning said.[17]

Michelin faced significant risks relating to both the 2005 Grand Prix debacle and to the race the following year in June 2006. If thousands of disappointed fans from 2005 did not return for the 2006 race, Michelin would be blamed for a poorly attended event and the negative story from 2005 would be kept alive indefinitely. Local Michelin dealers could be harmed by a potential downward spiral in passenger tire sales, especially in the Indianapolis area. Worse yet, automotive and motorcycle companies who use Michelin tires as original equipment on their vehicles might lose confidence in their tire supplier.

Michelin's Sincere Gesture

Company leadership moved quickly and decisively to limit damage and shorten the duration of the crisis. The biggest and most important step was the announcement of Michelin's "sincere gesture of goodwill toward the people present at the [Grand Prix]."[18] The gesture guaranteed the unprecedented refund of the cost of tickets for all 2005 spectators and declared that Michelin would purchase an additional 20,000 tickets for the 2006 race, to be given away to fans who attended the 2005 Grand Prix. In addition, Michelin would provide a companion ticket for anyone who purchased one for 2006, above and beyond the 20,000.

"Michelin exercised real moral authority. This was an expensive proposition, but it was the brand at stake," Fanning said.[19]

These three steps aimed to satisfy disgruntled fans and help set the stage to assure a successful and well-attended 2006 contest. Such a burst of good news sought to change the tone of media coverage to at least neutral and to move the story from national headlines to the enthusiast press.

"Our goal was to appeal to what we called the 'middle group' of racing fans who were disappointed in 2005 but who were willing to move on, by giving them the opportunity to show their support," Fanning said. "If they were willing to 'forgive and forget,' then the negative story would die out."[20]

The 2006 Grand Prix

Things were looking considerably better a year later. In an extraordinary stroke of timing, three weeks before the race, Federal Judge Sarah Evans Barker dismissed the consolidated class action lawsuits against Michelin and others, saying that sports fans ought to expect that participants in a sporting event could suddenly be sidelined because of injury, or suspended, or benched. Judge Barker wrote that such expectations are a "risk that sports fans assume when they buy a ticket of admission to a sporting event."[21]

Regardless of having announced its departure from Formula 1 following the 2006 season, Michelin made a strong commitment to the 2006 Grand Prix and to its fans in several ways. As race week 2006 approached, the ticket refund was more than 97 percent complete and the 20,000 tickets were distributed. In the community, a new local dealer activation was underway as was a philanthropic program with the Boys & Girls Clubs. An aggressive plan to put Michelin Formula 1 drivers in front of fans and a new fan appreciation program were announced.

"We were also pleased to see that the event prestige was being retained. Ticket sales and hotel bookings were running at 2005 levels, and that meant the fans were coming back," Fanning said.[22]

Michelin assets were intentionally everywhere leading up to the race. Several thousand Michelin-branded T-shirts, caps, and flags were handed out and the famous Michelin Man (Bibendum) circulated through the crowds. Following a media breakfast, Fernando Alonso, 2005 Formula 1 World Champion, held a news conference attended by several national news outlets and then participated in media interviews, in all-day fan activities, and in autograph signings with several other Michelin F1 drivers – all hosted by Michelin.

On race day, attendance rivaled the prior year's race, with one ESPN columnist comparing the number of spectators at the two years' races noting, "Fans were furious, many of whom said they never would return. But most of them did return."[23] The contest got off to a bad start with two major accidents that took out seven cars but with no injuries. Michael Schumacher and his Ferrari teammate took first and second on Bridgestone tires, while Giancarlo Fisichella's Renault took third on Michelin tires.[24]

Fanning said of race day media coverage that Michelin's media tracking showed a drop in the total number of stories from nearly 7,000 stories in 2005, to just over 1,000 stories in 2006. The story tone went from 38 percent negative, to over 99 percent neutral. Although there were many positive stories, Michelin took a conservative approach and counted any reference to the problems of 2005 as a "neutral" measure of tone.[25]

"One of my favorite stories was this one, right at Ground Zero," Fanning said. The headline and lede in the *Indianapolis Star* on the morning after the 2006 race read:[26] " 'Fans Forgive and Forget Debacle at Last Year's Race.' This time last year, fans waved their middle fingers at Michelin. Before Sunday's race, many instead hoisted the French tire maker's flag in the air."[27]

The Crisis Communications Team

A crisis large enough to attract the attention of the news media and stakeholders in a company of about 30,000 employees might consider having the following key functions and roles on its Crisis Communications Team. For smaller organizations, consolidate some of these roles:

Leadership. As discussed in Chapter 6, "Put Someone in Charge," a senior leader must take the helm and hold the final decision-making authority to order and approve strategy, greenlight consequential tactics, and break any logjams that may slow down the response process. That senior leader is in place to:

- Prioritize the issues into those that must be handled immediately and those that can be deferred to a slightly later date.
- Encourage all the members to operate as a single unit, and inspire the confidence, enthusiasm, determination, courage, and optimism that are critically important to success in a crisis.
- Manage the often-considerable resources to resolve the problem and allocate them to the right areas.
- Report to the CEO, establishing a direct and confidential link to the organizational chief executive, moving information from the team to this person and back again.

Corporate Communications. The organization's communications team serves as the nerve center and overall coordinator of all crisis communications activity. The team:

- Usually provides the main day-to-day spokesperson for the crisis.
- Collaborates constantly with all internal business functions involved in the crisis.
- Assures international connectedness and coordination for all announcements.
- Serves as the millwork from which the crisis response is built by writing most of the copy for both internal and external communications.
- Works closely with the Rapid Response Team to develop public statements and answers to media questions.
- Leads interaction with the news media to answer inquiries, issue approved statements, and negotiate interviews.
- Monitors news coverage in real time and quickly corrects errors-in-fact.
- Develops and regularly updates the crisis-specific website and media-specific website, working with marketing to make sure all commercial websites are clearly linked to the crisis site.
- Oversees any crisis communications consultants and commissions any requested research to gauge the perception of external stakeholders.
- Coordinates communication to key internal and external stakeholders.

- Aligns both strategic and tactical crisis communications initiatives with marketing, social media, legal, government relations, investor relations, product PR, overseas markets, customer relations, human resources, and others.
- Works most weekends!

Rapid Response Team. The RRT is a small, agile subset of the entire Crisis Communications Team, drawn primarily from corporate communications staff, but also includes social media, legal, a content expert on the topic, the day-to-day spokesperson, and government relations if the crisis has the interest of public officials. The team:

- Is staffed with the organization's very best writers.
- Produces fast and accurate public statements within the first moments of a news cycle in order to be immediately reactive to news media inquiries.
- Develops the initial Master Q-&-A and updates it daily with new, officially approved language for future use.
- Operates as part of a larger process. For further detail, see Chapter 3, "Set Up a Rapid Response Team Process."

Social Media. This leading-edge function is a complex and essential player in the organization's crisis communications strategy. This relatively small team:

- Guides and manages both the company's proactive and reactive social media engagement on platforms such as Facebook, Twitter, and Instagram.
- Chooses the appropriate channels based on the desire to either pinpoint information or widely disseminate it.
- Monitors, analyzes, and reports to the Crisis Communications Team on social media activity, with a focus on useful quality data versus huge quantities of dense information, typically employing a monitoring service such as Cision, Digimind, Agility, or Newsexposure.
- Coordinates with marketing on social media geo-targeting to reach stakeholders with messages on social media in specific markets.
- Serves on the Rapid Response Team.
- For further detail, see Chapter 19, "Social Media Has Changed the Crisis Communications Landscape."

Marketing. Maintains the capability to develop and deploy local and, if needed, national print, digital, and broadcast advertising consistent with the overall crisis communications strategy.

- Interacts closely with corporate communications and social media to align any public efforts on commercial websites or other marketing platforms.
- Monitors audience sentiment to avoid alienating customers and others by appearing to be tone-deaf or insensitive.

- Establishes a fast process with agency partners to remove, modify, or replace advertising and marketing communication of all types, including mass mailing or product-related emails to the customer base.
- Scrutinizes all current contracts during a crisis to identify those that automatically renew and might unintentionally post content that may offend audiences.
- Determines the impact of a crisis on current advertising campaigns and recommends changes if necessary. Evaluates and reports to the Crisis Communications Team on the brand impact of any proactive crisis-related marketing efforts.

Customer Relations. Sometimes called customer or client service, this group serves as the vanguard for communicating directly with customers in a crisis.

- Provides call center employees with regularly updated call scripts and a Q-&-A of approved responses as the crisis evolves.
- May establish a customer service call center team with dedicated management to work exclusively with customers impacted by the crisis, particularly for product quality or safety concerns, such as a recall.
- Engages customers in an empathetic manner and informs them of specific steps to resolve their issue.
- Transparently refers customers to the crisis website for detailed information.
- Monitors customer complaints and reports their volume and nature to the Crisis Communications Team.
- May have a distinct and specialized customer relations crisis social media function for direct engagement with customers and coordinates this activity with the larger social media team.

Legal. Plays a central role in the organization's crisis-related activity.

- Reviews and approves all crisis-related internal and external communication, including the Master Q-&-A, prior to top-level approval.
- Coordinates with corporate communication to balance communication goals with legal risk. If possible, a single attorney should be on point for these approvals to allow for the lightning quick reactions required for effective news media relations.
- Advises leadership on the legal implications of the organization's actions to solve the crisis.
- Supervises any internal investigations.
- Coordinates any crisis-related civil or criminal enforcement actions, such as the organization's legal strategies and theories of defense against class action lawsuits, personal injury lawsuits, criminal procedures, or other litigation-related matters.
- Interacts directly with law enforcement.
- Manages outside counsel and technical experts.

- Interacts with state and federal regulatory bodies and issues any required notices to them.
- Serves on the Rapid Response Team.

Government Relations. Interacts with state and federal legislative, regulatory, and administration officials who oversee and regulate an organization's activities.

- On a federal level, this group works closely with the two U.S. Senators and U.S. House member who represent geographic locations where the organization operates and keeps these influential stakeholders apprised of the organization's activities and positions on the crisis.
- Manages state or federal legislative hearings and testimony.
- Oversees consultants who gather intelligence.
- Maintains contact with trade associations to help control messaging and demonstrate industry consensus.
- Serves on the Rapid Response Team if public officials are involved in the crisis.

Within the Capital Beltway in Washington, D.C., is a microcosm of America, and what happens there resonates throughout the country. However, to quote Representative Thomas "Tip" O'Neill (D-MA), the renowned former Speaker of the House, "All politics is local."[28] Federal, state, and local officials pay very close attention to what happens in their home districts, so companies located there must keep their government leaders up-to-date. No politician likes to be surprised by the actions of the corporate constituents in his or her district. In addition, a well-briefed member of Congress can be helpful in protecting his or her constituent from a harsh response.

Three members of the Crisis Communications Team must work particularly hand in glove in any crisis: (1) government relations, (2) legal, and (3) corporate communications. An unexpected comment made by the company spokesperson to a local newspaper could draw fire from a U.S. Senator in Washington and spark congressional hearings. A surprised local city council member may decide to make a name for himself by calling a news conference to skewer your organization. Intensive intelligence gathering and collaboration by these three key members of the Crisis Communications Team, enhanced by robust information sharing to public officials by the government relations team, may be able to head off unwelcome political problems of this nature.

Human Resources. HR is a crucial partner in crisis communication because of its focus on employee welfare and morale. This corporate staff division:

- Serves on the frontline for employee relations in a crisis.
- Should be aware of and consulted on any communications, particularly content posted on internal sites and publications related to a crisis.[29]

- Must be promptly involved if a crisis is related to behavior of an employee or to concerns regarding hostility, harassment, ethnicity, gender, hiring, or other human capital matters, as well as company policies.
- Serves as a welcoming haven for employees to share concerns about the crisis, and HR can then anonymously share the voice and sentiment of the employees with the Crisis Communications Team.
- Coordinates employee activity if employees are engaged by the organization to support resolution of the crisis.

Content Experts. Flexible members of the crisis team, depending on the issues involved. For example, a cyberattack or customer data breach may bring in the IT head and team to provide reasons for the problem, along with proposed solutions and a timeline.

- A product defect or recall requires the presence of a senior product manager knowledgeable about the safety and technical issues related to the product and to provide analysis on the root cause of the problem.
- A financial crisis calls in the investor relations team to help shareholders understand its monetary repercussions.
- A manufacturing stoppage brings in plant managers and lead production engineers.
- Disruption in the supply chain calls for involvement by senior purchasing and logistics experts.

If an operational crisis primarily affects a single location, that location's leadership must be in constant touch with the Crisis Communications Team. We know of no substitute for local, ground-level knowledge, and reporting on the actual situation firsthand.

References

1. Heineman, B. "The Crisis Management Lesson from Toyota and GM: 'It's Our Problem the Moment We Hear About It,'" *Harvard Business Review*, March 20, 2014. Retrieved online: June 21, 2022: https://hbr.org/2014/03/the-crisis-management-lesson-from-toyota-and-gm-its-our-problem-the-moment-we-hear-about-it
2. Ibid.
3. "CDC Museum COVID-19 Timeline." United States Center for Disease Control and Prevention. Retrieved online: June 21, 2022: www.cdc.gov/museum/timeline/covid19.html#
4. "Volkswagen Emissions Scandal." *Wikipedia*. Retrieved online: June 21, 2022: https://en.wikipedia.org/wiki/Volkswagen_emissions_scandal
5. Ibid.
6. The Volkswagen Group. "Portrait & Locations." Retrieved online: June 22, 2022: www.volkswagenag.com/en/group/portrait-and-production-plants.html#
7. Interview with Michael I. Fanning, Vice President of Corporate Affairs for Michelin North America, via Zoom. June 30, 2022.

8. "Controversy at U.S. Grand Prix." *History.com*. Retrieved online: July 5, 2022. www.history.com/this-day-in-history/controversy-at-u-s-grand-prix

9. "Michelin." *Wikipedia*. Retrieved online: July 6, 2022. https://en.wikipedia.org/wiki/Michelin

10. Ibid.

11. "2005 United States Grand Prix." *Wikipedia*. Retrieved online: July 5, 2022. https://en.wikipedia.org/wiki/2005_United_States_Grand_Prix

12. Fanning. op. cit.

13. Ibid.

14. "Three Lawsuits Filled Over US GP." *Autosport*. June 22, 2005. Retrieved online: July 5, 2022. www.autosport.com/f1/news/three-lawsuits-filed-over-us-gp-5328939/5328939/?nrt=54

15. Fanning. op cit.

16. Ibid.

17. Ibid.

18. Michelin News Release. *WTHR.com*. June 28, 2005. Retrieved online: July 6, 2022. www.wthr.com/article/news/michelin-news-release/531-357073ec-7171-4e75-944c-21fdc2a45e16

19. Fanning. op. cit.

20. Ibid.

21. "US GP Class Action Lawsuit Dismissed." *Autosport.com*. June 16, 2006. Retrieved online: July 7, 2022. www.autosport.com/f1/news/us-gp-class-action-lawsuit-dismissed-4403480/4403480/

22. Fanning. op. cit.

23. Blount, T. "F1's U.S. Grand Prix on Shaky Ground at Indy." *ESPN.com*. June 16, 2007. Retrieved online: July 8, 2022. www.espn.com/racing/columns/story?columnist=blount_terry&id=2906439&seriesId=6

24. "2006 United States Grand Prix." *Wikipedia*. Retrieved online: July 8, 2022. https://en.wikipedia.org/wiki/2006_United_States_Grand_Prix

25. Fanning. op. cit.

26. Ibid.

27. "Fans Forgive and Forget Debacle at Last Year's Race." *Indianapolis Star*, July 3, 2006.

28. "All Politics is Local." *Wikipedia*. Retrieved online: February 7, 2022. https://en.wikipedia.org/wiki/All_politics_is_local

29. *Author's note*: HR should be consulted on any outgoing communication, but experience indicates that the written word may not be HR's strongest suit. One senior corporate communications executive who asked not to be identified because he was not authorized to speak for the company, paraphrasing the great Jim Croce, put it this way: "Don't tread on Superman's cape, don't spit into the wind, and don't let HR write *anything*".

Chapter 8

Develop a Strategy

Every enterprise needs a strategic plan, but there is no one-size-fits-all template to accommodate every situation. Business strategy often entails developing a strong set of plans, steps, and objectives that detail how a business will compete in a defined market with services or products. Military strategy consists of planning and conducting campaigns; deploying air, land, and sea forces; and deceiving the enemy. Crisis communication strategy shares some of those traits. But all crisis strategy, no matter the enterprise, is distinctive in that it shares a common ultimate objective: end this thing.

More than 60 years ago, Alfred Chandler, a professor of business history at Harvard Business School and Johns Hopkins, devised a clear and simple definition of strategy that is still relevant today. Chandler wrote, "Strategy is the determination of the basic long-term goals of an enterprise, and the adoption of courses of action and the allocation of resources necessary for carrying out these goals."[1]

Although Chandler was not writing specifically about crisis communications strategy, his classic definition applies directly. A company facing a crisis should develop a strategy rooted in its fundamental principles to determine its "long-term goals," by looking past the day-to-day tactical concerns of managing and focusing on the desired result. At the onset of a crisis, that view of the future means establishing an overarching plan and set of goals that guide the organization through its crisis response over the long term. A benefit of such long-view thinking is that easily understood, clearly communicated goals reinforce an organization's sense of purpose and knit it together around a common intention and hope for the future. What do we stand for? Where do we want to be when this is over? How do we want our many stakeholders to view us? How will the outcome affect our employees? How do we want the government to regard us?[2]

Once the ideal image of the future destination is fixed, the process shifts to how we get there. Chandler refers to this part of strategy as "the adoption of courses of action," consisting of the means of achieving its stated objectives. Those strategic courses of action make up much of the purpose and content of this book. Who should be in charge in a crisis? How should we collect the

DOI: 10.4324/9781003322849-11

facts, define the problem, and assemble the crisis team? How will we handle employee communication? How and where do we deploy advertising? Whom do we engage with on social media? What's the most effective way to navigate a sea of hostile reporters?[3]

The third pillar of Chandler's definition refers to "the allocation of resources" required to help the organization reach its established goals. Fighting to overcome a crisis is often expensive, requiring resources for advertising, web development, special PR agency support, social media monitoring, outside legal counsel, and customer goodwill, such as replacing a product or extending a warranty. These expenditures are an investment in the future, and, while there are no guarantees that an enterprise will ultimately prevail, the consequences of short-sighted underfunding of a crisis response can be serious indeed.[4]

When Michelin's business and brand were threatened – due to tire safety concerns – all seven race teams using Michelin tires withdrew from the 2005 Grand Prix at Indianapolis Motor Speedway. In response, the company took a strategic approach to solving the crisis that might well have come directly from the pages of Chandler's book. Michelin recognized the foundational importance of its racing heritage and knew that preserving and maintaining it was fundamental to the "basic long-term goals," of the enterprise. By mounting a year-long major strategic communications campaign aimed directly to win back the hearts and minds of its race fans, customers, dealers, racing teams, and automotive companies, it "adopted impactful courses of action" to limit damage and reduce the extent and duration of the crisis. Michelin's "sincere gesture of goodwill"[5] to provide refunds for all 2005 spectators, to purchase an additional 20,000 tickets for the 2006 race, and to provide companion tickets to anyone else who bought a ticket was an expensive and effective action, and a literal example of "the allocation of resources necessary" to achieve its goals.[6]

Campbell Soup and GMO – Just Label It!

Enlisting celebrities to join a cause raises its visibility. When young celebrity mothers Jennifer Garner and Gisele Bundchen attended the *Conceal or Reveal* launch event for Campbell Soup Company's "Just Label It" campaign in Los Angeles in the spring of 2015, they added to the growing list of notables who were "fed up with being kept in the dark about GMO and non-GMO labeling." Opposition to GMOs, or genetically modified organisms, had been spreading quickly across the country. Growing tensions between the food production industry and those in support of GMO labeling set the stage for the Campbell Soup Company to make a highly strategic, forward-looking, and industry-changing decision.[7]

In 1895, the Campbell Soup Company introduced its first can of "ready-to-eat" soup and, nearly 100 years later, produced its 20 billionth can of condensed tomato soup. In addition to soup, Campbell produces foods such as Pepperidge

Farm baked goods, V8 beverages, and Prego pasta sauces. Today, Campbell generates approximately $8.5 billion in annual sales revenue, sells its products in 100 countries worldwide, and employs more than 19,000 people.

What exactly did the celebrities want to "conceal or reveal"? GMOs are living organisms whose genetic material has been modified in a laboratory through genetic engineering (GE) and modern biotechnology. GMOs were first commercialized in the United States in the early 1990s to enhance particular traits within organisms. Genetic engineering isolates specific genes to alter the genetic makeup of a plant for specific purposes, such as better flavor, higher crop yield, and greater resistance to drought, insects, and other plant diseases. However, there was no requirement that food producers disclose the presence of GMOs in their products. Battle lines were drawn, and the celebrities, and millions of Americans, wanted the food industry to disclose whether or not products contained these genetically altered organic substances.[8]

The widespread impact of GMO technology on human food sources is substantial. In the United States today, GMOs are present in as much as 80 percent of conventional processed food. The plants most associated with GMOs include soy, cotton, canola, corn, sugar beets, alfalfa, and squash. GMO are also common in a large percentage of processed food ingredients, such as amino acids, high fructose corn syrup, and aspartame. About three-quarters of Campbell Soup's products include ingredients from the largest genetically engineered crops.[9]

Consumers across the globe questioned the safety of GMOs, asking whether they are carcinogenic or are harmful to the human brain, and some studies have pointed to potential health problems. In one study, mice fed with genetically engineered corn developed fertility problems and hamsters fed with GMO soy were unable to produce offspring.

Growing numbers of younger millennials demanding transparency and healthier foods and a mounting distrust in larger established food companies among consumers were reflected in studies showing that shoppers wanted mandatory GMO labeling. According to research published by *Consumer Reports* in 2015, nearly 90 percent of Americans wanted mandatory labeling of GMOs.[10]

Opponents of GMO technology had a clever strategy. Requiring companies to label their products "with" and "without" GMOs would, in turn, lead consumers to question the safety of products and potentially cease purchasing GMO products, driving consumers to look for the "non-GMO" label on all products. This frightened the farming and food processing community, which feared mandatory GMO labeling would lead to product boycotts or completely drive cost-saving GMO technology out of the marketplace.

The food industry closed ranks, fighting against GMO labeling on either the state or federal level. Campbell spent approximately $1 million to oppose GMO labeling requirements in California and Oregon in 2012 and 2013.[11] The Grocery Manufacturers Association (GMA), representing more than 300 food, beverage, and consumer product companies including Campbell, was spending millions of dollars on anti-labeling efforts to defeat pending state and federal requirements that food companies identify products containing GMO ingredients. It was an industry battle line entrenched in the statehouses and on Capitol Hill, shouting "Hell no!"

Enter Denise Morrison, who became the CEO of Campbell Soup Company in August 2011, at a time when the company was facing declining sales, a rising cost structure, turmoil in the industry, and rapidly changing consumer preferences. Morrison determined that Campbell Soup lacked two key ingredients for success: effective decision-making and courage. Under Morrison's leadership, Campbell took a deep, introspective look into its corporate purpose, what it does, and what it stands for as a company: "Our purpose begins with these simple words: Real food that matters for life's moments. We make real food for real people. They trust us to provide food and drink that is good, honest, authentic, and flavorfultr."[12]

With the company purpose clearly defined, Campbell started shifting its product lineup to the outer shelves of the grocery store. It began moving away from processed food items and toward the more-visited produce and deli sections of the store in order to appeal to consumers' increasing desire for fresher, less processed products.

In a sudden and industry-changing reversal of position on January 7, 2016, Campbell Soup Company announced its support of mandatory national labeling of products that may contain GMOs. In doing so, Campbell Soup strategically differentiated itself from industry rivals as the first major food company to begin disclosing GMO ingredients in its products. Morrison also stated in her announcement that Campbell would withdraw from any efforts led by groups opposing mandatory GMO labeling legislation, including GMA.

Morrison said Campbell Soup's decision to change direction and support mandatory labeling of GMO ingredients "was guided by our purpose, rooted in our consumer-first mindset, and driven by our commitment to transparency – to be open and honest about our food." Following the announcement, Campbell's stock price rose steadily, from $50.82 on January 7, 2016, to $52.62 per share on February 25, 2016.[13]

Campbell's against-the-grain move was accompanied by a solid communication strategy to cover several audiences. To evolve and adapt to the changing food preferences of millennials, the food conglomerate had a strong presence on several social media platforms. To reach baby boomers, it courted major legacy media as ongoing sources of unpaid exposure through coverage of Campbell's movement in the marketplace.

In response to consumer concern about GMOs, Campbell also operated a website, *www.whatsinmyfood.com*. The landing page states, "We Believe People Should Know What's in Our Food," and the site encouraged online discussion of GMO ingredients in its products. For each product, the website listed key ingredients and the purpose of each (i.e., flavor, texture, color), including any GMOs.[14]

For more ideas on how such websites can be helpful in a crisis, see Chapter 18, "Deploy Your Websites."

By switching sides, Campbell Soup Company established a precedent as the first in the processed foods industry to call for mandatory federal GMO labeling standards. Leading up to this decision, the company conducted a deep analysis of its purpose, which helped it determine its long-term goals. Company executives evaluated a changing marketplace with major consideration to the impact of millennials on its business. At the same time, they saw the political writing on the wall. Societal momentum and, thus, political energy were moving toward some form of GMO labeling requirement, and Campbell recognized that if each state imposed its own set of regulations, an unworkable crazy quilt of state-by-state requirements would ensue. Embracing a single set of federal regulations was the strategic choice, and Campbell Soup was the first to make it.

The Campbell Soup Company's foresight became a reality for everyone in the food industry as of January 1, 2022, when food manufacturers, importers, and retailers in the U.S. began to comply with a new federal labeling standard for food that has been genetically modified. While the term GMO is no longer widely used, labels on some foods now say "bioengineered food" or "contains a bioengineered food product." The U.S. Department of Agriculture has approved two new disclosure labels for companies to use on their food packaging or they can include a QR code to scan or a phone number to text that will provide more information about the ingredients in the food.[15]

Don't Confuse Strategy With Tactics

As we briefly noted in Chapter 2, "Be Strategic in Your Planning," the terms "strategy" and "tactics" are often used interchangeably, sometimes to a reckless extent. Given the frequent use and significance of these two words in most organizations, especially in business, anyone who mixes up the meaning of the two terms is practicing uninformed business communication. Similarity in the definition of these terms does exist in that they both concern what an organization is prepared to do in the future, but that's about it.

Simply put, while strategy means determining the long-term goals of an organization and creating an action plan with sufficient funds to support it, tactics are the individual specific steps and actions that will execute the initiatives charted in the strategy.

Tactics are the tangible actions an enterprise will take to achieve its objectives, but they must be supported by an underlying strategy. The two terms should not be seen as opposites but rather as complementary to each other, working in tandem to achieve success. Strategy without tactics can result in endless planning without taking action. Tactics without strategy can result in work without purpose. If strategy is understood to be the long-term plan, tactics should be viewed as the short-term steps that help you achieve more limited goals. Strategic planning is the creation of an enduring and ideal image. Tactical planning consists of deconstructing your strategic plan into short-term activities.

Thinking about the differences between strategy and tactics another way, consider that strategies are *transformational*, whereas tactics are *transactional*. Strategies are transformational because they involve long-term endeavors, embedded as a core principle of any crisis response, designed to eventually reverse the entire crisis narrative from bad to good. Thus, transformational strategy requires significant investment of resources, such as commissioning a high-dollar market research study on which to base a long-running and expensive corporate advertising campaign across print, television, online, and social media channels.

Conversely, tactics are transactional because they involve short-term actions, such as editorial board meetings, executive speeches, op-eds, YouTube videos, targeted social media posts or a simple corporate apology in a news release. As such, these shorter-term activities usually require fewer resources than the bigger, strategic initiatives.

Know Yourself

In the wake of the 2005 Grand Prix crisis, Michelin acknowledged the importance of its long-standing racing heritage to the long-term goals of its brand, and then moved decisively to restore and reinforce its reputation with its key stakeholders. Once the Campbell Soup Company had defined its corporate purpose as producing "food and drink that is good, honest, authentic, and flavorful" to maintain the trust of its customers, its path to transparency became clear: they would embrace a federal standard to require labeling of genetically engineered ingredients in products.[16]

Zenia Mucha is the recently retired Senior Executive Vice President and Chief Communications Officer of The Walt Disney Company. During her 19-year career at the helm of a 500-person global media relations team, Mucha advised Disney on both communications and business strategy. She says a number of important considerations inform corporate thinking about what kind of strategy to develop.

Foremost is the need to understand the nature and purpose of the enterprise.

"How you define a company, its brand as well as its values, should serve as the basis for developing a strategic communications plan," said Mucha. "How many diverse stakeholders is it important to? What is its public perception? Communications plans for a business-to-business company are very different from those for direct-to-consumer businesses."[17] An organization's scale, purpose and history all come into play when developing a strategy, Mucha said:

> If it's a start up, you obviously have a different strategy than you do for a well-established brand like Disney. You have to ask if the strategy is to continue to simply grow the business or to redefine and/or reinvent it. In the case of an almost 100-year-old company like Disney, obviously historical perspective is critical to developing any kind of a long-term strategy, whether it's a business strategy or communication strategy.[18]

We'll hear more from Zenia Mucha about The Walt Disney Company in the chapters that follow.

References

1. Chandler, Alfred. *Strategy and Structure: Chapters in the History of Industrial Enterprise.* New York: Doubleday, 1962. Retrieved online: June 25, 2022. https://en.wikipedia. org/wiki/Strategy#cite_ref-21
2. Ibid.
3. Ibid.
4. Ibid.
5. Michelin News Release. *WTHR.com*, June 28, 2005. Retrieved online: July 6, 2022. www.wthr.com/article/news/michelin-news-release/531-357073ec7171-4e75-944c-21fdc2a45e16
6. Chandler, op. cit.
7. Buffington, G. and Fasano, S. *Campbell Soup Company: Support for Mandatory GMO Labeling.* Notre Dame, IN: Eugene D. Fanning Center for Business Communication, Mendoza College of Business, University of Notre Dame, 2016.
8. Ibid.
9. Ibid.
10. Ibid. and Kopicki, Allison. Strong Support for Labeling Modified Foods. *The New York Times*, July 27, 2013. Retrieved online: www.nytimes.com/2013/07/28/science/strong-support-for-labeling-modified-foods.html?_r=0 and Jalonik, Mary Claire, "AP-GfK Poll: An Appetite for Labeling Genetically Modified Foods." *Associated Press and Gesellschaft fur Konsumforschung (Society for Consumer Research)*, January 13, 2016. Retrieved online: http:// ap-gfkpoll.com/featured/ap-gfk-poll-an-appetite-for-labeling-genetically-modified-foods
11. Paul, K. Campbell's Decision to Label GMOs Destroys Monsanto's Main Argument Against Labeling, 2016, January 15. Retrieved online: February 25, 2016. http:// www.alternet.org/food/campbells-decision-label-gmos-destroys-monsantos-main-argument-against-labeling
12. Campbell Team. "Real Food That Matters for Life's Moments." *Campbell Soup Company*, June 9, 2014. Retrieved online: February 25, 2016. www.campbellsoupcompany.com/newsroom/news/2014/06/09/real-food-that-matters-for-lifes-moments/
13. Campbell Team. "Why We Support Mandatory National GMO Labeling." *Campbell Soup Company*, January 7, 2016. Retrieved online: www.campbellsoupcompany.com/newsroom/news/2016/01/07/labeling/
14. Hernandez, J. "GMO Is Out, 'Bioengineered' Is in, as New U.S. Food Labeling Rules Take Effect." *National Public Radio*, January 5, 2022. Retrieved online: July 9, 2022. www.npr.org/2022/01/05/1070212871/usda-bioengineered-food-label-gmo
15. Buffington, G. and Fasano, S. op. cit.
16. Ibid.
17. Interview with Zenia Mucha, Executive Vice President and Chief Global Communications Officer, the Walt Disney Company, January 7, 2022. Via Zoom.
18. Ibid.

Chapter 9

Establish Goals

In retrospect, 2011 was not the best of years for the General Electric Company (GE). Several crises followed one after another: the continuing fallout of the global financial crisis, a damning story in *The New York Times* about the company paying little or no federal tax for a number of years, then the Fukushima nuclear disaster. Just one of these would have been bad enough to tarnish the company's reputation. Taken together, the situation called for immediate action.

General Electric's communication and marketing teams, led by Gary Sheffer and Beth Comstock, met to discuss what the company might do to improve everything from reputation scores to perceptions of the brand among investors and the general public. Building on the highly successful "Imagination at Work" campaign launched in 2001, Sheffer and Comstock argued for a bigger investment and more powerful approach to influencing reputation called "GE Works."[1]

"The goal," according to Sheffer, "was to remind people of the positive influences of GE in their daily lives and to re-emphasize GE's manufacturing chops. He added, "'Imagination at Work' remained the company's tagline during this campaign, and the company still uses GE Works ('A World that Works') to describe the outcomes it produces."[2]

The reinvigorated campaign, fostered jointly by GE's communication and marketing departments, was not an attempt to distract investors, the media, customers, or the public from the sizable problems the company was experiencing, but – as Sheffer said – to remind us of all the good the company was doing. Their previous tagline for many years had been, "We bring good things to life." The goals were clear, and success would show up in numbers tracking sales, share price, reputation indices, net promoter scores, and more.

Why Set Goals?

As Joan Wainwright explained following Merck & Co.'s removal of a profitable pain reliever from the worldwide pharmaceutical market, "The mantra is 'Measure, Measure, Measure.' It's the only way to show your staff and senior

DOI: 10.4324/9781003322849-12

management what you've done." The process is not simple, though. Wainwright said,

> I knew we had to begin with goals that would be easy to understand and relatively easy to achieve. If you set impossible metrics for your team early in the process, you'll fall short, people will lose confidence in themselves and in you, and it could all spiral out of control.[3]

Wainwright said she would periodically encounter her CEO, Ray Gilmartin, in the hallways at corporate headquarters, and he would call her name and ask about the withdrawal. "He was eager to know how we were doing, even though I would brief him at least once a week." Simple, easy-to-understand metrics were helpful. "I reminded him that we set as a goal an 80 percent adult public awareness within 30 days," she said. "We made the announcement on September 30, and I was determined that our externally conducted surveys would show that figure by Halloween."[4]

As it happened, her optimism was rewarded, and the company's recall campaign hit 89 percent within 30 days. "Once you get into the 90s," she added, "it gets really tough. This country is about 8 percent communication-resistant and 2 percent communication-immune." Wainwright, of course, was an optimist. She moved on to other metrics and other objectives, quickly listing pharmacies contacted, wholesalers in compliance, and physicians who had been briefed. Other, more ominous measures dealt with reports of cardiovascular events and adverse outcomes for patients. Her team even tracked negative press reports and editorials, just to see if the trend in public outrage had a downward track.[5]

According to Wainwright, she and her public spokespersons should be ready to speak about at least three of the most current measures available on a moment's notice, along with the more serious remaining challenges and next steps the company would take.

Defining Crisis Communication Goals

Goals set by communication teams in response to a genuine crisis seem to fall in three broad categories: (1) problem-solution goals, (2) financial goals, and (3) nonfinancial goals.

Problem-Solution Goals

These are specific measures, dates, accomplishments, or actions related to solving the problem that created the crisis. For Coast Guard Admiral Thad Allen, number one on his list was stopping the leak. If his team and the phalanx of contractors hired to work the issue were unable to stop the flow of crude oil into the Gulf of Mexico, none of the rest would matter. Vessels and people on scene, progress in drilling a shaft to intercept the pipe below the wellhead, and gallons of oil removed from the water's surface would all be irrelevant. Everyone from the president to the fishermen whose livelihood depended on the Gulf wanted the leak stopped.

The Macondo wellhead blew out and the Deepwater Horizon caught fire on Tuesday, April 20, 2010. In the face of continuing inaction on BP's part, on April 30, President Obama declared a national emergency and named Adm. Allen as National Incident Commander.[6] Among the admiral's first statements was the acknowledgment that he didn't know how to stop an oil leak, had no specialized equipment, and no budget. He promised, however, that he and his team were already working the problem and would have regular updates. Within a few weeks, Adm. Allen offered a realistic assessment, saying that they should have the intercept shaft completed and the oil leak shut off by the second or third week of August. That announcement came in early May.

In the time-honored tradition of under-promising and over-delivering, Adm. Allen returned to the press room podium on July 15, 2010, to announce that the leak had been stopped, just 87 days after the disaster began. With the oil shut off, staff members on the Incident Response Team said – off the record – they were confident they could cap the leak well before mid-August, but were leery of promising a date they couldn't deliver. "After the story is all over, that's all they would talk about . . . how we couldn't meet our goals and deliver what we promised." Others on the team, however, added that the drilling process moved rapidly and without complication. "I think even we were surprised at our luck," they said.[7]

If it's a recall, get the contaminated product off the shelves and away from consumers. If it's a defective product, devise a solution, prove that it works, then repair the equipment or product you've already sold to customers. If it's a threat you've discovered in your software package, work diligently around the clock to produce a patch or an intervention that will remove the risk to those who depend on your technology. Solve the problem first. You can talk about the process, the cost, and the way forward later on.

Financial Goals

No business can operate without adequate financing. Numerous business writers, in fact, list inadequate financing or capitalization as the number one reason for small business failures. Virtually all business writers list this as a prominent cause of failure in businesses of all sizes.[8]

Many stakeholders worry about the financial condition of a company in crisis, including the company's chief executive and C-suite officers, shareholders, investment bank analysts who follow the stock, auditors, regulators, vendors, customers, employees, and the communities in which they operate. Often, managers and executives are directly compensated in stock with the financial performance of the company as a base measure.

Among the many problems here, of course, is that shareprice is not the only measure of a company's health or success, nor is it necessarily the most important.

Other financial measures include quarterly and annual earnings, the market capitalization of the business, the firm's price-to-earnings ratio, and annual statements of retained earnings. Add to that the liabilities a company may incur as a result of a crisis. Did the funding to respond to a crisis situation come from current income or was it borrowed? What's the payback schedule and rate of interest attached to the debt the company just acquired?

Many small to midsize firms take out lines of credit that include adequacy-of-capitalization clauses. If a company suddenly experiences a sharp decline in revenues, or an unexpected increase in its cost structure, the bank or lending institution may decide to call the loan. Under the terms of such agreements, the capital lent to an enterprise may be due in full, on demand. Where can you go to borrow more money to cover that? A crisis can set off a cascading series of financial problems if financial managers have not properly anticipated an emergency requirement for funding or a change in cost structure.

Nonfinancial Goals

Almost every business manager has seen a company balance sheet or been part of an annual review that gives updates on the organization's financial health. But not as many people are familiar with how success is determined without focusing on finances.

The easiest way to define nonfinancial performance measures, according to consultant Amanda Atrash, is to explain what they aren't. "Nonfinancial [key performance indicators] are not expressed as monetary values – in other words, they aren't directly associated with dollar signs," she says. "They focus on other aspects of the business and are often leading (forward-looking) measures, whereas financial KPIs are lagging measures."

She adds,

> While it's true that nonfinancial KPIs aren't associated with finances, that doesn't mean they can't be numeric. These types of measures can be either quantitative or qualitative. Many organizations view employees' "soft skills" as the biggest contributors to nonfinancial performance, which can be measured in various ways.[9]

Consultants at VisionEdge Marketing in Austin, Texas, list four primary nonfinancial metric categories that can serve as leading indicators of future financial performance and provide insight on an organization's impact on stakeholders and society. These include:

- Company reputation.
- Customer influence and value.
- Competitiveness.
- Innovation.[10]

The arrival of a genuine crisis in a company can directly affect brand preference, take rate, and customer retention. It can also influence customer experience, innovation, and market share. A company in the midst of an unresolved crisis may lose customers who no longer trust the brand. It may find that long-time, loyal clients no longer see the company as innovative. A loss of market share may result. While each of these issues is unlikely to happen quickly, given the measure of forgiveness afforded strong brands, the insidious loss of trust with those who matter most – investors, suppliers, customers, and others – can cripple a business and, perhaps, lead to bankruptcy or liquidation.[11]

Social Media Goals

When a company opens a Twitter account, a Facebook page, or a YouTube channel, most people assume, first, that whatever appears on those pages is what the company wants you to know about it. And, second, that the marketing and reputation management effort comes at very little cost. Neither, of course, is true.

Many companies have discovered that outsourcing the design, construction, and daily management of everything from their websites to their social media pages is expensive but worthwhile, given the number and levels of skill involved in the process, as well as the astounding rate of change in the social media landscape. Given the number of regular viewers on such platforms, though, social media is a phenomenon no manager can afford to ignore.

Service firms such as Radian 6 will (for a fee) measure the number of daily mentions of your company's name, brand, products, and services. It's one way of telling whether a new marketing or advertising campaign is getting any traction. It's also a relatively easy way to determine whether anyone is paying attention to your brand if a full-blown crisis has broken out.

During the Domino's Pizza food contamination crisis of 2009 (discussed in Chapter 4), Radian 6 tracked all blogs, microblogs (Twitter), news sites, forums, replies, comments, and videos for the company. On average, the Domino's brand would appear on one of those platforms about 570 times a day. During April of that year, the company had little to worry about until Sunday, April 12, when recorded images of the contamination prank were posted to YouTube. Within 24 hours, the most popular video had received 250,000 views, and by the following Wednesday, when YouTube finally removed them, those videos had been viewed nearly a million times. That sounds bad (and it was), but the daily buzz rate and online comment numbers only reached 8,000 by that time. The monitoring service documented that the daily online buzz rate returned to normal by the April 19, just four days later. That's just over a week of online chaos, but relative normality quickly resumed. The real damage was measured in sales, which dropped 50 percent in the Charlotte, North Carolina, area and to a lesser extent elsewhere in the country. The stock price took a hit, lawsuits were filed, and the Domino's brand was damaged as a result of two thoughtless employees.[12]

While online platforms can be risky, they can prove useful as well. During a mini-crisis involving an online advertisement for the pain relief product Motrin, Johnson & Johnson (J&J) communicators looked at a Twitter account owned by the airline JetBlue for inspiration. J&J Social Media Director, Marc Monseau, viewed the JetBlue Twitter account as a perfect example of a customer service account but one with real potential in a crisis. JetBlue uses Twitter to keep customers up-to-date on flight delays and cancellations and allows passengers to file complaints about lost luggage. Twitter has other advantages, as well:

- **Expert source:** Twitter can provide information and key insights by a corporate official who is both knowledgeable and publicly recognized.
- **News gatherer:** The account can gather information about the business and the industry the company is a part of and provide it to customers as a news source.
- **Suggestion box:** The account can solicit input and experiences from Twitter followers that can be redistributed to all interested parties.
- **Special offer source:** The account can be a tool to reach out to customers when a crisis is resolved to offer coupons and provide special offers.[13]

Platforms such as this that are used primarily for marketing can easily be repurposed to either push information or gather valuable intelligence in a crisis situation. We'll have more to say about how social media has changed the communication landscape in Chapter 19, but for now, please know it's just one of many ways in which business executives can measure and manage their social standing and the flow of information in a crisis.

The Value of Reputation for an Organization

"Corporate reputation," according to New York University professor Charles Fombrum, "is the outcome of a competitive process in which management signals its firm's key characteristics to constituents to manage its social standing."[14] *Reputation*, at its heart, is a measure of how outsiders see an organization, while *identity* is an organization as seen by insiders, and *image* is the tangible appearance of an organization to all. So, if brown trucks are an example of the *image* of UPS or golden arches the image of McDonald's, the question of "who we are" is part of the *identity* of those who work for a business. *Reputation*, though, is far broader and more encompassing than either of those, sometimes confused, synonyms.

Let's begin with what reputation is:

- Composed of numerous attributes.
- Relative to the reputation of others.
- Usually quite enduring.
- Based on public perceptions.

Thus, in measuring and managing reputation, corporate executives are not looking for just one number, as we'll see in the next examples. It's also relative to those with whom they compete and the industry they occupy. Just as not everyone in a given industry (healthcare, consumer packaged goods, apparel, overnight delivery services, and so on) is perceived in precisely the same way, not every industry is held in equal regard (tobacco, petroleum, airlines, cable and internet providers, among others). The important thing to remember about reputation is that it is based largely on public perception, which can change on a moment's notice.

Further, reputation is *not:*

- Objective.
- Easily measurable.
- Uniform across all constituents.

What people think of you and your business is entirely subjective and dependent on their experience with your products and services and your employees as well as with others in your industry. It's tough to accurately measure such perceptions not only because they can change quickly but also because such changes often come at no cost. A customer with no switching barriers can change his mind about your product and begin doing business with another provider at very little personal cost in money, time, quality, or convenience.

Reputations, once established, are usually quite durable, but the market can (and will) move on if you do not change in ways that continue to meet stakeholder expectations. Just ask Sears, Montgomery Ward, GameStop, Toys "R" Us, J. Crew, or Pier 1 Imports. Protecting the reputation of a business or brand, particularly in a crisis situation, is of paramount importance.

Factors affecting reputation include financial performance, the reputation of the CEO and management team, the industry, situational events (i.e., crisis reaction), demands by various stakeholder groups, and government regulation. A number of organizations, consulting firms, and publishers have taken up the task of measuring what people think of various businesses and publish survey lists of the results. Here are a few that most communication executives pay at least some attention to:

Fortune 500: Based solely on financial performance and market capitalization.
World's Most Admired Companies: Rated by executives, directors, and securities analysts.
Best Companies to Work for: Based in part on the responses of randomly selected employees. Measures the quality of workplace culture.
100 Best Companies for Working Mothers: Companies complete an application, submit benefits handbooks, and provide other information.
Most Socially Responsible Companies: Several publishers and NGOs consider characteristics such as diversity, employee satisfaction, greenhouse gas emissions, waste products, and efficiency in energy use.

Larger, more complex organizations have the resources, time, and expertise to complete the surveys and position themselves in the best possible light. Landing a spot on a most admired or best-in-category list is generally an occasion for a press release and celebratory gathering, but it's not a guarantee of continued success or widespread admiration across all constituencies. Different groups of people, clearly, are looking for different things from the businesses they frequent.

Good corporate reputation can lead to:

- Enhanced financial performance.
- Enhanced shareholder value.
- Improved business partner relations.
- Happier, better employees.

These, in turn, can lead to greater client or consumer loyalty, increased public support, credibility in times of crisis, and achievement of key business objectives. Here's the bottom line: corporate reputation is difficult, though not impossible to manage. Successful companies usually have strong identities and high product quality. And, good reputations, because of their inertial qualities, allow organizations maneuvering room during mediocre performance periods as well as genuine crises.

Setting goals as you begin to understand and manage a crisis is essential. Be sure to include nonfinancial outcomes and social media comment as well as financial metrics you hope to achieve.

References

1. "GE's 'Imagination at Work' and 'Ecomagination' Rack Up *Advertising Week* Honors." *Press Release: General Electric Company*, October 14, 2005. Retrieved online: www.ge.com/news/press-releases/ges-imagination-work-and-ecomagination-rack-advertising-week-honors-0
2. Sheffer, Gary. in an e-mail exchange with the authors, February 20, 2022.
3. Wainwright, Joan, Vice President for Public Affairs, Merck & Company, in a teleconference interview from her offices at Merck corporate headquarters, Whitehouse Station, NJ, 11:00 a.m. (EST), December 9, 2004.
4. Wainwright, Joan. Teleconference interview, December 9, 2004.
5. Ibid.
6. Schleifstein, Mark. "Disaster Response Should Mimic Human Immune Response, Thad Allen Says," *NOLA.com*, June 3, 2015. Updated July 18, 2019. Retrieved online: www.nola.com/news/environment/article_fe0412b4-8e07-53fb-8a13-d7513586d769.html
7. "Deepwater Horizon – BP Gulf of Mexico Oil Spill," *Press Release: EPA United States Environmental Protection Agency*, Retrieved online: www.epa.gov/enforcement/deepwater-horizon-bp-gulf-mexico-oil-spill
8. Olsen, Erica. "Ten Common Causes of Business Failure," *On Strategy*. March 16, 2021. Retrieved online: https://onstrategyhq.com/resources/ten-common-causes-of-business-failure/ See also: Horton, Melissa. "The 4 Most Common Reasons a Small

Business Fails," *Investopedia*. March 31, 2021. Retrieved online: www.investopedia.com/articles/personal-finance/120815/4-most-common-reasons-small-business-fails.asp

9. Atrash, Amanda. "15 Examples of Non-Financial Performance Measures to Track," *ClearPoint Strategy*, nd. Retrieved online: www.clearpointstrategy.com/nonfinancial-performance-measures/

10. "Six Non-Financial Metrics Every Marketer Should Measure," *VisionEdge Marketing*. February 20, 2022. Retrieved online: https://visionedgemarketing.com/non-financial-metrics/

11. Keller, Kevin L. "Brand Synthesis: The Multidimensionality of Brand Knowledge," *Journal of Consumer Research*, Vol. 29, No. 4 (March 2003), pp. 595–600. Oxford University Press. See also: Keller, Kevin L. "The Brand Report Card," *Harvard Business Review*, January-February 2000. Retrieved online: https://hbr.org/2000/01/the-brand-report-card

12. Peeples, A. and Vaughn, C. *Domino's "Special" Delivery: Going Viral Through Social Media (A)*, Notre Dame, IN: Eugene D. Fanning Center for Business Communication, Mendoza College of Business, University of Notre Dame. 2009, pp. 1–2.

13. Eisele, Kathryn and Patrick Fishburne. *Johnson & Johnson's Strategy with Motrin: The Growing Pains of Social Media*, Notre Dame, IN: Eugene D. Fanning Center for Business Communication, Mendoza College of Business, University of Notre Dame. 2010, p. 5.

14. Fombrun, Charles. *Reputation: Realizing Value from the Corporate Image*, Cambridge: Harvard Business Review Press. 1996.

Chapter 10

Centralize Communication

Properly managing a situation that has unexpectedly turned critical will require a number of assets, most of them tangible. As we've discussed, you'll need adequate, knowledgeable staffing, leadership, and financial support. You'll also require access to both data within the company and those who control it.

Beyond that, no one will be able to successfully see a crisis through to its conclusion without the visible and audible backing of the organization's senior leadership. That means access to the Chief Executive Officer and others within the C-suite, as well as regular statements and acts of support for those managing the crisis. Few in the organization will be willing to help you if they do not believe you represent the senior-most decision makers in the company. And no one in the enterprise will jeopardize his or her own career if support for your actions are either unclear or indifferent.

One tool essential to managing C-suite support and facilitating control of events during a crisis is centralized communication. Most large and complex organizations delegate communication authority, quite properly, to the level of management most responsible and best able to produce the needed results. In most cases, that means working downward through layers of management to identify and engage those who'll do the work of writing, speaking, and creating images, along with those who'll reach out to the media and corporate stakeholders.

In other instances, delegation or distribution of the task will mean giving responsibility and accountability for communication goals to regional or national offices where culture, language, and customs play a large role in the messaging process. Corporate headquarters, on a day-to-day basis, is often not the proper point of origin for the substantial flow of communication in a truly global enterprise. The same is true to a large extent in organizations whose boundaries and ambitions are more limited.

That all works, of course, when nothing's gone wrong. Once an issue goes critical and shareholders, creditors, vendors, franchisees, the media, and dozens of others are demanding answers, a decentralized system just doesn't work. It's ponderous, slow, and prone to avoiding risk, and – surprisingly – the information it produces is frequently inaccurate, dated, incomplete, and unhelpful. The

DOI: 10.4324/9781003322849-13

only answer is to centralize all communication related to the crisis. Let others go on about their business in the organization, but make certain those responsible for managing the crisis have fully centralized their operations, technology, work schedules, daily goals, and communication flow.

We'll say more, later in this chapter, about what that might look like and how it might work, but first we'll visit the communications team in one of America's most recognized retail brands and examine how they managed an entirely unanticipated critical situation.

Sears, Roebuck and Co. and the United Colors of Benetton

Since day one, Arthur C. Martinez's career as CEO at Sears, Roebuck and Co. was – to say the least – challenging. The hyper-competitive retail industry had been flooded with new businesses that positioned themselves in specific segments where Sears had been the market leader for decades. Throughout his tenure, Martinez was constantly faced with the challenge of making strategic decisions quickly. Issues concerning growth and expansion, alliances, earnings, corporate reputation, employee welfare, and marketing came across his desk daily, and each action contributed to the massive financial turnaround of Sears that occurred in the late 1990s – a recovery widely credited to Martinez's management expertise.

The morning of February 16, 2000, brought with it an opportunity for yet another strategic decision. What had been hailed as a brilliant alliance for both Sears and Benetton, a cutting-edge Italian fashion label, had turned into a situation in need of immediate attention. The sensitive nature of the most recent Benetton advertising campaign, "We on Death Row," had prompted protests from Sears employees who demanded that Benetton merchandise be immediately removed from Sears stores.

Should Martinez heed the demands of his employees, widely believed to reflect the overall attitudes of Sears's consumers, or remain true to the alliance recently established with the stylish and sophisticated Italian retailer? Would continued protests and publicity negatively affect the successful turnaround efforts? Was it necessary to stop selling Benetton merchandise in order to quell the controversy? Additionally, would Ron Culp, Senior Vice President for Public Relations and Government Affairs, and Tom Nicholson, Director of Public Relations, be able to handle this issue well enough to satisfy the many different parties affected by and interested in this issue? Martinez realized the critical need to answer these questions quickly and that swift, careful action would be essential.

Sears and Benetton Split Over Advertising Strategies

When Sears entered into an agreement with Benetton in October 1998 to sell the Benetton USA line of clothing in more than 800 Sears outlets, the company

knew that Benetton had a history of producing controversial print advertisements. Sears, however, was assured that the Benetton USA line (exclusive to
Sears stores) would carry advertising and signage distinct from that of other
Benetton stores and product lines and that this separate advertising campaign
would shield Sears against any controversy that might arise from other Benetton
ad campaigns.

Apparel sales at Sears stores had fallen dramatically over the previous few years
and a new look and feel to product offerings was the only way to salvage this segment of operations. An alliance with Benetton seemed a logical way to proceed
as that company sought to increase U.S. sales in order to supplement its primarily
European base. Tom Nicholson, Sears's Director of Public Relations, expressed
the situation clearly:

> We always knew there was some risk in any type of joint marketing venture
> with Benetton. They were hip, edgy and were known for a chic urban style.
> However, everything about this venture was separate from United Colors
> of Benetton, styles were more mainstream, the merchandise was made by a
> third-party manufacturer, and the marketing message was to be completely
> different. Quite simply, we knew that at some point Benetton's overall image
> and advertising would no longer be compatible with that of Sears but we cer-
> tainly did not expect this to occur so soon, just months after our agreement
> was signed.[1]

What Sears did not realize was just how far Benetton would continue to "push
the envelope" in terms of advertising designed to stimulate brand awareness and
encourage consumers to buy more of its apparel – all under the guise of promoting social and political awareness. Sears found out when Benetton launched its
campaign "We on Death Row."

The ad campaign featured 26 men and women who were either facing the
death penalty or who had been executed by the time the ads went to press. The
advertisements only mentioned the charges of which the individuals were convicted and provided no detail of their crimes. The ads did not display any Benetton clothing in the pictures.

Sears corporate communication staff knew that the company's primary customer base consisted of middle-American people with traditional, conservative
values. As demonstrations were held outside Sears Houston offices to protest
Benetton's "We on Death Row" ad campaign, and employees who had lost
loved ones to those profiled in the Benetton ads contacted Sears headquarters,
Ron Culp knew the company had to take action. Not only were employees and
customers hurt by the painful memories dredged up by seeing convicted felons
on billboards and in telephone kiosks in New York City, Sears found itself in
the especially precarious situation of appearing to take a position on the death
penalty.[2]

The Franchising Contract

In the fall of 1999, Sears and Benetton executed a contract through which Sears agreed to carry Benetton USA merchandise in approximately 400 Sears stores. In part, this deal was an attempt by Benetton to re-establish itself in the U.S., after years of decline had led to the U.S. market accounting for only 5 percent of Benetton's total business. Likewise, the agreement was an attempt by Sears to reposition itself in the youth clothing market and attract younger consumers to its stores. The deal was lauded as an excellent move for both companies.[3]

Benetton's Advertising History

Although Benetton's early advertisements were entirely conventional, focusing on the product and stressing the quality of the wool the company used, Benetton grew accustomed to controversy surrounding its advertising campaigns. The first U.S. advertising campaigns were handled by a small agency and emphasized the European origins and international success of Benetton. In 1982, however, Luciano Benetton, Chairman of Benetton Group, met Oliviero Toscani, a well-known fashion and advertising photographer who lived in Tuscany and had studios in Paris and New York. Toscani convinced Benetton that the company had to promote its brand as a lifestyle, not as a clothing business.[4]

Benetton's initial campaigns with Toscani were conventional in style. They underscored social status and conformism and featured groups of young people wearing Benetton clothes. The first real departure from the original styling arrived in 1984 with the concept of "All the Colors in the World." Advertisements in that campaign portrayed groups of teenagers from different countries and ethnic groups dressed in colorful knitwear. While some negative reactions to these advertisements emerged, overall the public greeted the campaign with enthusiasm. During the late 1980s, Benetton continued to use multiracial messages to promote its apparel, a "united" Benetton. The company also believed that it was promoting a message of racial equality. But over the years, the advertisements grew more controversial and began to offend various groups around the world with their shocking nature.

By the 1990s, Benetton campaigns took on issues beyond racism. Also designed by Toscani, the ads featured images of a man dying of AIDS, a priest kissing a nun, a newborn child covered in blood, and two horses, one black, one white, copulating. According to Benetton, all the campaigns presumed to offer some social message, and the company was merely trying to promote debate on serious social issues.[5]

In order to increase sales at the United Colors of Benetton retail stores, Benetton introduced the advertising campaign conceived by Toscani called "We on Death Row." In the U.S., Benetton opened the campaign with a 96-page supplement that was attached to the February issue of *Talk* magazine. The campaign included interviews with convicted killers and featured photographs of 26 convicts in different U.S. states. Only the charges of which they were convicted were mentioned. No details of their crimes were provided, and no photographs or images of Benetton clothing were shown.

The written profiles were mostly sympathetic, focusing on the men's regrets about their plight and offering few details about the crimes they were convicted of committing. The photographs were shot in the photojournalist style of Toscani, who had developed Benetton's branding for two decades. He claimed that his campaigns were all based on the same premise: "We are all equal. There is no reason to slaughter each other, to fight, not even to hate each other. We can wear whatever we want, whatever colours, we want just to live."[6] Toscani also insisted that his advertisements do not exploit sensitive social issues in order to sell knitwear. He asserted:

It's the other way 'round. I exploit clothing to raise social issues. Traditional advertising says if you buy a certain product, you will be beautiful, sexually powerful, successful. All that [stuff] doesn't really exist. I'm not doing that.[7]

Benetton also claimed that the portraits, with accompanying interviews, would "give the prisoners back their human face and highlight the present of those without a future."[8]

To create the campaign, Toscani joined forces with the National Association of Criminal Defense Lawyers, which strongly opposes the death penalty. Benetton and the Association told prison officials they were making an "international photo documentary" project sponsored by Benetton. There was no mention of the advertisements, and Toscani was described only as a "photojournalist."[9] Ken Shulman, who conducted the interviews for Benetton's magazine was described as a "*Newsweek* magazine contributor."[10] Prison officials, however, felt they were misled and claim that they did not know the prisoners were being used for advertising.

Benetton has said the following about its communications campaigns:

The choice of new communication channels has prompted advertising campaigns on issues of social and current interest worldwide, such as racism and AIDS, conservation, life and death. Oliviero Toscani's photos for Benetton picture reality but, perhaps because they do, the images themselves become a focus for debate and discussion, transcending the bounds of advertising to enter the realm of artistic expression and depict our era.

Exhibitions of Benetton ads have been mounted by museums and cultural institutions throughout the world, including the Old England Museum in Brussels, the Corporate Art Museum in Tokyo, the Bienal in Sao Paulo, Brazil, and the Cable Factory in Helsinki. Communication is complemented by initiatives in support of international humanitarian associations, like SOS Racisme, for whom Benetton organized the first world conference in Treviso in 1996, and FAO (Food and Agricultural Organisation of the United Nations), who invited Benetton to devise a communications campaign for the first World Food Summit held in Rome in 1996.[11]

Negotiations Begin

Fortunately, Arthur Martinez received advance warning of the "We on Death Row" campaign several weeks prior to launch. After previewing the campaign in a marketing trade publication, Martinez immediately realized the delicate implications of such a message reaching the community. He sent an urgent message through Ron Culp to Tom Nicholson and the public relations staff saying, "Begin talks with Benetton and review all options from A) how to better differentiate United Colors of Benetton to Z) actually removing merchandise from our stores." Martinez hoped that a compromise could be reached and either production of the Benetton USA merchandise could be stopped or the ad campaign halted.[12]

The Sears Communication Team Organizes

Ron Culp, who oversaw all of corporate communication and public relations at Sears, later said in an interview that the events involved in the Benetton deal were both surprising and very fast moving. "When the deal was signed in autumn of 1999, there was a lot of excitement around the company. This was a major effort aimed at improving the 'softer side' of Sears."[13] He noted, in particular, that the Benetton merchandise was "very high quality, unlike anything we'd seen in Sears," and everyone in merchandising and marketing was highly enthusiastic about the relationship. "The curious thing," Culp noted, "was that Benetton insisted on complete control over marketing and merchandising." Sears would have nothing to say about that.

Culp knew, for perhaps the first time, that the relationship would be fraught at the launch party for the Benetton USA brand in New York. "It was late autumn and we were in a very hip loft in SoHo. All the major apparel magazines and trade publications were there – all of them." As soon as he and Tom Nicholson walked into the party, they both knew Sears was in some trouble. "It was a prison-themed event," Culp recalled, "so all of the catering people and servers were in prison garb. Tom looked at me and said, 'Uh-oh.'"[14]

Sears managers asked if they could see any of the advertising, store displays, or other copy prior to the arrival of merchandise and were told flatly, "That's none of your business." Culp added, "So, when the advertising dropped, so did our jaws."[15]

Culp pulled together a small team that same day, "just so we would be ready." He explained why it would be easy to centralize communication for this issue with a surprising story from four years earlier.

I asked for a meeting of everyone in Sears who had anything to do with communications and, to my surprise, we wouldn't fit in any space other than the enormous Merchandise Review Center. I had invited Arthur Martinez to join us and, when he walked in the room, he asked, "Who are all these people?" I told him, "Therein lies the problem."

That meeting gathered more than 400 people, all of whom worked for Sears.

These folks were scattered throughout the organization in the divisions, the business units, various entities. I asked for an audit of how many people fit that description and, in fact, it was more than 400. We promptly began either separating people or offering them jobs in other units. Our corporate communication team shrank to about 60.

The move not only centralized communication but saved Sears money. "That was material to the balance sheet," Culp said. "We went from eight PR agencies to two, and from 400 people to about five dozen. The final savings figure was greater than $20 million."[16]

The Crisis Management Team

Pulling together a team of seven or so senior managers to address the Benetton case was, as a result, relatively easy:

Our team included stores operations, community relations, legal, marketing, merchandising, logistics, and myself. We met about twice a day in a designated conference room which belonged to us for as long as we needed it, and then reported up and back to the business units.

Culp briefed Martinez twice daily and the team's specialists briefed their counterparts elsewhere in the business late each morning.[17]

Once Benetton national advertising hit the market, Sears heard from multiple sectors of their business, and none of them was happy. Culp said, "We heard from the Fraternal Order of Police, from store managers who were getting grief from customers, and from our loyal, long-time customers themselves." He related a phone call from a woman in St. Louis who described herself as a lifelong Sears customer. "Can you imagine picking up a magazine," she said, "and seeing the name and image of the man who brutally raped and murdered my daughter – all to sell clothing to young people?" Culp said, "I was speechless. That conversation just gave me chills." When asked about the potential for boycotts and demonstrations, he replied, "We got those all the time, maybe one a week. But this was different. People were angry and the anger was widespread. We had to act."[18]

The time span from the launch press event to the arrival of merchandise in the stores was just two months. Advertising quickly followed. "Less than a month later," Culp recalled, "I ran into Arthur on the sixth floor. 'Tell me the latest,' he said." Culp briefed him and Martinez simply asked, "What do you think we should do?" Culp replied, "We've seen a lot of threats over the years, but this one is different. I think we should pull the merchandise." "All of it?" Martinez asked? "Yes," said Culp, "all of it and now."

The CEO conferred with a few C-suite officers, including legal, and gave the order. Part of the evidence that convinced him to act quickly was news that fewer than 300 of Sears 800 retail stores had received Benetton merchandise. The loss at that point would be about $15 million. If they waited, the figure could be two or three times that large.[19]

It helped as well that Culp had a couple of figures ready following a confidential conversation with a friend. It happens that Benetton was less than 1 percent of Sears revenue ("No better than a rounding error," he said), while Sears was poised to become between 20 and 25 percent of Benetton's annual revenue. As a $44 billion company, Sears could afford to absorb the loss and move on.

Culp recalled,

> I knew the crisis was over when I opened a letter from that woman in St. Louis who had called me a month earlier. She thanked me and the company for the decision to remove the merchandise from our stores. Included in the envelope was a sales receipt for school supplies she had purchased the day before for her younger children. That was so sweet. She was a customer again and I knew this was over.[20]

The Value of Centralization

Centralizing all communication activities, functions, responsibilities, and products into one team, in one location, reporting to one senior official has two important values:

- **Incoming communication provides intelligence.** Anything learned by anyone in the organization that may be relevant to management of the crisis must be directed immediately to the team's operations center. That information can then be verified or corroborated with other sources and shared with all. This becomes particularly important if the CEO and other corporate officers have requested daily briefings on the matter. You can confidently report what you know, how you've learned it, and why you believe it to be true.
- **Outgoing communication provides (some measure) of control.** The organization will be able to confidently limit official statements to one source who has cleared the content with the crisis team and other senior corporate officials. This will preclude others in the organization from claiming inside knowledge, though unnamed sources are often a staple of investigative reporting. If you centralize communication, gather the facts, determine which actions to take, and move quickly, you will be able to set the *direction, velocity,* and *vocabulary* of the conversation around this crisis. Others will follow with your

language and repeat your assumptions and statements. That alone will confer an early advantage to firms operating in a highly speculative environment.

Appointing a public spokesperson is a crucial task that the team leader must take early in the process. The best crisis managers recommend against allowing the company's regular media relations team to take on this task in addition to their daily duties. How many spokespersons will you need? Clearly, more than one if overseas operations, language issues, and time zone complications will prevent one person from addressing all media queries. For long-term, complex crisis management situations, you may need as many as three to allow others to take days off or, perhaps, go on vacation. Certainly, three would be sufficient. Each of them must be:

- **Knowledgeable**: Spokespersons who are consistently misinformed or uninformed are not only of no help to the company or its stakeholders, they're really counterproductive. These people must work each day with the crisis management team and its leader to document what they know for sure, what they don't know, and what they may never know. Explaining how you know something is true will be particularly helpful. Updates, corrections, and revisions to previous statements are essential if you hope to remain respected as *the* go-to source for information.
- **Authoritative**: People speaking on behalf of the organization must be sufficiently senior in rank and experience to command the respect of those whom they're briefing. They cannot simply appear in public and read from a press release, but they must be available to answer questions confidently. Authority comes from the top of the organization, so to speak authoritatively, you must be near them regularly.
- **Responsive**: It's helpful if at least one of the three designated spokespersons is awake. Crises cross time zones and news-gathering deadlines are no longer daily, but on a constant, rolling cycle. Someone must be ready to respond to legitimate queries at any hour of the day. You needn't speak with everyone who calls; that's a professional judgment. But you cannot ignore the most important of the media, government regulators, creditors, business partners, and others.
- **Collaborative**: The best public spokespersons are willing and eager to collaborate with others in the enterprise. Gathering information, vetting the leads you've received, and composing potential questions and answers are indispensable parts of the job. It's far easier if the person representing the company can collaborate with others who are dedicated to managing and resolving the crisis.
- **Patient**: The legendary communicator Arthur W. Page once said that the best public relations results are produced by people who are "calm, patient, and good humored."[21] A capable spokesperson never picks a fight, never takes the bait for a mal-intentioned question, and never takes the process personally.

Good spokespersons know their job is to remain professional and to help the world understand what's happened and what the company is doing about it.

Centralization provides one-stop-shopping for anyone with an interest in the issue and its management. One location, one source, one telephone number and website. All of it under the watchful eye of a crisis manager appointed for specifically that job.

References

1. Hellwig, A. and Loughney, E. *Sears, Roebuck and Company and The United Colors of Benetton (A),* Notre Dame, IN: Eugene D. Fanning Center for Business Communication, Mendoza College of Business, University of Notre Dame. 2000, p. 2.
2. Personal Interview. E. Ronald Culp, Senior Vice President, Public Relations and Government Affairs, Sears Roebuck and Company. March 22, 2022, 3:15 p.m. to 4:13 p.m. (EST), via telephone.
3. Hellwig and Loughney, p. 3.
4. Ibid.
5. Hellwig and Loughney, p. 4.
6. Ibid.
7. Ibid.
8. Kerrigan, Michael, *The Scotsman,* The Scotsman Publications Ltd., January 28, 2000, p. 22.
9. Ibid.
10. Ibid.
11. Benetton. "Who We Are, Our Communications." March 2000. Retrieved online: www.benetton.com/wws/aboutus/ourcomms/index.html
12. Personal Interview, E. Ronald Culp, March 22, 2022.
13. Ibid.
14. Ibid.
15. Ibid.
16. Ibid.
17. Ibid.
18. Ibid.
19. Ibid.
20. Ibid.
21. The Arthur W. Page Society. "The Page Principles." March 3, 2023. Retrieved online: https://page.org/site/the-page-principles

Chapter 11

Consider All Stakeholders, All Markets You Serve

In drafting a plan to deal with a situation that has or may become critical, virtually every communication executive will look at a similar range of responses. To quote former AT&T executive Arthur W. Page, first tell the truth, then prove it with action. Above all, though, Page wrote, "Listen to the stakeholders." Good advice, though it is just a bit thin on specifics. Those will be left to the managers and executives directing the organization under siege.

In response to the 2010 explosion aboard the Deepwater Horizon and subsequent spill of 4.9 million barrels of oil, Coast Guard Admiral Thad Allen saw his obligation as twofold: be honest and accurate, but first . . . stop the leak.[1] Solving the immediate problem that is creating grief, suffering, and loss for others must always come first, whether it's an oil leak, a contaminated food product, or defective consumer goods on store shelves. Communication begins with those media most capable of passing accurate information to consumers and others who may be in danger, followed by conversations with those who may be of some immediate help.

Beyond that first press release or statement to the wire services, we begin to realize that no two crisis situations are exactly the same, in scope and scale, in immediate jeopardy, or in duration. And certainly, the people who have an interest in management's actions will vary widely, depending on the circumstances. The advice here, prior to reviewing the checklists and action items, is simple: please consider all stakeholders and all markets you serve.

The Death of an Intern at Bank of America

After Moritz Erhardt did not come early to work as usual and skipped a very important 2:00 p.m. meeting, his flatmates, colleagues, and work friends began to worry. This was not like Erhardt. They contacted Claredale House, the East London student housing where he had been living for the last six weeks, to get someone to check on him. He had pulled "all-nighters" with "magic-roundabouts" for the last three days consecutively, and they feared something may have happened.

DOI: 10.4324/9781003322849-14

Erhardt was an undergraduate student at a prominent business school in Germany. He had participated in an international exchange program with a top American university and was considered hardworking by nature. He had also completed placements at KPMG Consulting, Morgan Stanley, and Deutsche Bank before starting his summer internship at Bank of America's Merrill Lynch London office.

It was 8:30 p.m. on August 15, 2013, when the body of Moritz Erhardt was found unconscious on the shower floor of his flat in Claredale House student housing. Following unsuccessful attempts at resuscitation, he was pronounced dead at the scene by responding paramedics. Erhardt had suffered from an epileptic fit, just a week from completion of his seven-week summer internship. He was just 21 years old.

John McIvor, Bank of America's head of communication for Europe, Middle East, and Africa, said in a statement referring to Erhardt, "He was popular amongst his peers and was a highly diligent intern at our company with a promising future." He also stated that Erhardt was in line to receive a job offer from Bank of America of about £45,000 a year by the end of his internship.[2]

The Investment Banking Culture

Investment bankers work very long and often unpredictable hours, typically between 90 and 100 hours a week.[3] On a usual day, in fact, an analyst can expect to work about 15 hours. Additionally, most work both days of the weekend. Some days, an investment banker will be incredibly busy and work late into the night.[4] The driving factor behind the long hours is an expectation within the investment banking community.

That culture often pressures employees to work such long hours, often through the night, in order to meet tight deadlines imposed by their directors.[5] Occasionally, they will work overnight through consecutive nights. These are sometimes referred to as "magic-roundabouts," which occur when a banker takes a taxi early in the morning home from the office after remaining there all night and has the taxi wait outside his or her apartment while he or she showers and changes clothes and then returns to work.[6] The culture drives young bankers to outwork and outstay the others.

Investment Banking Internships

Business students in all major money centers of the world anxiously seek summer internships at the best investment banks. Such internships are intense since they are regarded as a summer-long interview. They are said to be designed to identify and help select the brightest and most hardworking applicants.

British finance author Polly Courtney lived through this world herself for two years, including a summer internship with Merrill Lynch in London, and described in an article some aspects of her "so-called life" as an intern at Merrill Lynch.[7]

> We thought we knew what we were letting ourselves in for. The long hours and hard work were no secret among university undergraduates. Even before I joined the firm, I'd heard tales of junior bankers collapsing from exhaustion and analysts who slept under their desks.
>
> During our internship, all-nighters were a rite of passage. You weren't deemed a "proper" banker until you'd worked through the night. Hundred-hour weeks were standard.[8]

Bank of America Merrill Lynch's Initial Response

The bank had a very limited response to this tragedy. John McIvor made statements to several news groups, including CNBC. He repeatedly told reporters that "he could not confirm the circumstances surrounding Erhardt's death."[9] McIvor also said that "all the rumors and comments are just that" and that Bank of America would "wait and see what the post-mortem examination [revealed]."[10] He reiterated multiple times that "nobody knows what happened and until that is established, . . . any conclusion is premature. As such, Bank of America is waiting until the coroner's report is released."[11]

McIvor added that there would be an investigation into Erhardt's death and anything else "is speculation."[12] Additionally, the Bank stated they had "convened a formal senior working group to consider the facts as they become known, . . . to review all aspects of this tragedy, to listen to employees at all levels, and to help us learn from them."[13] The company said it planned to look especially into the working conditions faced by junior employees and interns.

Furthermore, Bank of America said it would offer support to the family, the other interns, and the employees affected by this tragedy. McIvor remarked, "Our first thoughts are with his family, and we send our condolences to them at this difficult time."[14] The bank also offered to allow the other interns to "end placements early" but all interns declined.[15]

Public Reaction

In addition to a flurry of Google and Twitter reactions and other social media responses, many newspapers, wire services, broadcasters, and blogs covered the events. *The Independent*, a British national morning newspaper, headlined an article about the event as:

> "Slavery in the City: Death of 21-year-old intern Moritz Erhardt at Merrill Lynch sparks furor over long hours and macho culture at banks."[16]

This headline, in turn, created the impression that Merrill Lynch was employing what amounted to slave labor. News accounts additionally raised the issue of long hours and a "macho" culture at London's banks. The article was one among several covering the story that led to a large public outcry for improved labor conditions for interns.

The Challenge for Corporate Communication

Employees often die while still employed, but that's not what is most disturbing about this case. What's most distressing is that the circumstances of this young man's death appear to have been the product of a work environment his employer not only knew about but also encouraged. On the surface, this appears to have been entirely preventable.

Should the bank wait for a coroner's report before commenting in the hope to avoid speculation and assuming full responsibility for what may have been an underlying condition? John McIvor appears to offer a "let's wait and see" approach favored by C-suite executives, lest they be held responsible for all that's happened. Others on the Bank of America communication team, including those in the United States, favored a more forward, sympathetic response, knowing that this story would not go away quickly, nor would the conditions that created it. While this case was genuinely tragic, other crises can still threaten a brand's reputation and future.

A Product Contamination Crisis in Europe

Doug Ivester, CEO of Coca-Cola, thanked former Johnson & Johnson exec James Burke for his time and returned the phone to the handset. On June 18, 1999, four weeks after the first report was filed in Europe citing adverse health effects suffered following the consumption of Coca-Cola products, Ivester sought to reformulate his communication strategy. Ivester called Burke, the former J&J CEO who successfully managed the Tylenol scare in the 1980s, to discuss how Coke could regain its reputation and credibility. He hoped it was not too late to mend Coke's relationship with European consumers.

A Timeline of Events

During May and June 1999, hundreds of consumers in Europe became ill after consuming Coca-Cola products. In the biggest recall in Coca-Cola history, products, including Coke, Coke Light, Fanta, and Sprite, were pulled off the shelves in Belgium, France, Luxembourg, the Netherlands, and Germany. Here is a timeline of the specific events that took place from mid-May through the end of June 1999:

May 12: A bar in Belgium reports to the Belgian Health Ministry and to Coca-Cola that four people who drank Coke products had become ill.

Samples of Coke from the same batch are sent for analysis at a government-licensed laboratory in Belgium. Results prove inconclusive and no poison is found. The incident is not widely reported and no public safety warnings are issued.17

June 8: School children in Bornem, Belgium, reportedly experience dizziness, nausea, and other symptoms after drinking Coke. Forty-two people are hospitalized during the next 24 hours.18

June 10: Eight children are hospitalized in Bruges, Belgium, after drinking Coke and Fanta.19

June 11: The German Health Ministry summons Coca-Cola officials for a meeting regarding the reported illnesses. Thirteen children are hospitalized in Harelbeke, Belgium.20

June 12–14: The Belgian government establishes a telephone hotline for health complaints about Coca-Cola products and receives more than 200 calls.21

June 14: Forty-two children are taken to a hospital in Lochristi. The Belgian government orders all Coca-Cola products off the market and halts production at bottling plants in Antwerp and Ghent.22

June 15: Eight children are reported sick in Kortrijk, Belgium. Luxembourg bans Coca-Cola products. Health authorities in France close a bottling plant in Dunkirk. The Netherlands bans all Coca-Cola products shipped through Belgium. At the same time, Coca-Cola Enterprises (CCE) holds a press conference in Brussels to provide an explanation for the cause of the illnesses.23

June 16: Germany bans Coca-Cola products produced at the Dunkirk plant. Coca-Cola issues its first apology to European consumers in the form of a written release under CEO Doug Ivester's name. German officials empty store shelves of Coke products.24

June 17: The ban on products is eased in Belgium with the exception of thousands of Coca-Cola vending machines.25

June 18: Ivester arrives in Belgium to oversee management of the crisis.26,27

Coca-Cola's sales and reputation suffered throughout Europe. Following product bans issued by the French and Belgian governments, the Netherlands, and Luxembourg also restricted sales of certain Coca-Cola products until possible health risks could be fully identified.[28] Reports emerged that Saudi Arabia and Germany had banned imports of all Coca-Cola beverages produced in Belgium and that the Spanish government had stopped a shipment of Belgian-bottled Coca-Cola and other brands for fear of contamination.[29]

Even the health minister of the Central African Republic took a stand on the issue, saying citizens of that country shouldn't drink Coke "until further notice" because of the health questions. Sweden's *Svenska Dagbladet* ran a headline on June 16 claiming, "200 Poisoned by Coca-Cola." An Italian newspaper's front-page headline reported, "Alarm Across Europe for Coca-Cola Products."[30] *The*

Wall Street Journal reporters James Hagerty and Amy Barrett describe the rapid movement of news about the crisis across international borders:

> It amounted to a harsh lesson for Coke in the perils of global marketing in the electronic age. No one has been better than Coke at creating an enticing image and sending it flashing around the world. Now Coke is learning that an image can come unraveled in an instant.[31]

The Source of the Problem

The outbreaks were apparently caused by two sources: fungicide sprayed on wooden pallets used to transport the product and contaminated carbon dioxide that found its way into the product at a bottler in Belgium. The company was unable to determine whether the carbon dioxide was already contaminated when the bottler received it or whether contamination occurred later, at the bottling facility. In an interview with *The Wall Street Journal*, Anton Amon, Coca-Cola's chief scientist, said that "contrary to Coke procedure, the plant wasn't receiving certificates of analysis from the supplier of the gas, Aga Gas AB of Sweden. This certificate vouches for the purity of the CO_2." A Coca-Cola Enterprises spokesman confirmed this statement and acknowledged that the company did not test the CO_2 batch at the Antwerp plant.[32] In either case, key quality control procedures were not followed.

At the Coca-Cola bottling facility in Dunkirk, France, the plant received wooden pallets that had been sprayed with a fungicide that left a medicinal odor on a number of cans. Jennifer McCollum, a spokeswoman for Coca-Cola, described the substance as "a chemical commonly found in wood preservatives and cleaning fluids." The substance, she said, can be absorbed through the skin and cause redness, burning sensation, pain, and skin burns. If inhaled, the chemical can cause symptoms such as cough, sore throat, shortness of breath, headache, dizziness, nausea, vomiting, and unconsciousness and may cause effects on the central nervous system, liver, and kidneys. These more severe conditions are said to require large doses or chronic exposure to the chemical.[33]

Coca-Cola said that the substance was sprayed on approximately 800 pallets used to transport cans produced in Dunkirk to Belgium. The supplier of the pallets was said to be Dutch. The company, however, declined to name the supplier, stating only that it was not one of their regular ones. The foul odor is believed to have caused numerous symptoms, including upset stomachs, headaches, and nausea after drinking the product.[34]

Dr. Hugo Botinck, Medical Director at St. Joseph's Clinic in Belgium and one of the first physicians to see these patients, stated in an interview that affected persons were treated for, "headaches, dizziness, nausea, and muscular vibration." He added that "some of them were vomiting, but there was no fever."[35]

Bottling and International Distribution

One of Coke's greatest strengths lies in its ability to conduct business on a global scale while maintaining a "multilocal" approach. At the heart of this approach is the bottler system. Bottling companies are, with only a few exceptions, locally owned and operated by independent business people, native to the nations in which they are located, who are contractually authorized to sell products of The Coca-Cola Company. These facilities package and sell the company's soft drinks within certain territorial boundaries and under conditions that ensure the highest standards of product quality and uniformity. Coca-Cola Enterprises (CCE) manages most of the European bottlers. The Coca-Cola Company now controls about a 40 percent interest in CCE.[36]

External Factors Involved

In May and June 1999, it is fair to say that Coca-Cola executives vastly underestimated the sensitivity of European consumers to food contamination issues in light of the existing social and political environment. Contributing to the anxiety was the "mad cow" crisis involving contaminated beef that had taken place three years earlier. Additionally, the Coke incident coincided with a recent governmental ban on the slaughter of pork and poultry in Belgium. Earlier in June, cancer-causing dioxin was found in a large shipment of meat, which was believed to have originated through contaminated animal feed. In the end, this scandal forced the resignation of Belgian Prime Minister Jean-Luc Dahaene as well as the country's health minister. With the Belgian government facing elections on June 13, all political platforms were under scrutiny.

In the wake of the Coke crisis, European government agencies were scrambling to protect their reputations as watchdogs, taking a high-profile role in contamination issues. Consumers had previously considered Coke invulnerable to contamination concerns due to the artificial, manufactured nature of the product.

In addition to its proximity to other food scares in Europe, the crisis also occurred at a time when Coke was looked upon unfavorably by the European Commission. Earlier that year, Coke had made plans to acquire Cadbury Schweppes brands around the world. The European Commission was opposed to this acquisition, viewing Coca-Cola as excessively dominant. The company was forced to scale back its acquisition plans.

Coca-Cola's Response

By the time the recall was completed, 249 cases of Coke-related sicknesses were reported throughout Europe, concentrated primarily in Belgium. A total of 15 million cases of product were recalled, costing the bottler, Coca-Cola Enterprises, an estimated $103 million dollars.[37] When the outbreak began, Coca-Cola executives waited several days to take action. Viewing the issue as low priority, an apology to consumers was not issued until more than a week after the first public reports of illness. Top company officials did not arrive in Belgium until June 18, ten days after the first incident was reported.

The company's casual and muted approach to the crisis was first made evident in its neglect to mention the May 12 incident – in which affected consumers suffered similar symptoms – once the other cases were reported, beginning in June. Ivester remained largely silent, at least publicly, throughout the crisis. He admitted that he happened to be in Coca-Cola's Paris office on June 11, shortly after the first wave of illness reports surfaced, and was briefed in person on the Belgian situation. At the time, Ivester and Belgian Coke executives attributed the problem to a bad batch of carbon dioxide and "hardly a health hazard."[38] The next day, Ivester boarded a plane back to Atlanta, as planned.

On June 14, the Belgium government ordered all Coca-Cola products off the market and halted production at bottling plants in Antwerp and Ghent. The government took the lead to protect consumers from the health scare, rather than Coca-Cola management. Coca-Cola issued a statement on June 15 from Atlanta refuting the contamination claims. The next day, Ivester released a statement under his name expressing regret for the problems, but he mostly left the public side of the damage-control campaign to company spokesmen and CCE.

On June 18, Ivester realized the magnitude and impact of the crisis and arrived in Belgium for the first time to manage it. Ivester's mission to Europe was his most visible step during the crisis and came only after the number of reported cases had ballooned to more than 200.

Coca-Cola officials avoided the media, however, stating afterward that this decision was in response to a request from the Belgian Minister of Health, Luc van den Brossche, asking that the crisis be handled out of the public eye.

Key investors in the Coca-Cola Company, including Warren Buffet, Don Keough, and Herbert Allen, following a face-to-face conversation with Doug Ivester, decided it was time for him to go. He was removed by a vote of the board and the president of Coca-Cola Australia, Doug Daft, was named CEO. Ivester was officially retired by December.[39]

Considering All Stakeholders

As we've already said, a true stakeholder is someone with something to win or lose, depending on the actions of management. Others are simply interested observers. That doesn't mean observers can't influence the outcome of a crisis or react in a way that will be adverse to the interests of the company. It simply means they have different kinds of interests in such circumstances. True stakeholders would commonly include:

Customers. Any business's first concern would be for those immediately affected, beginning in the Coca-Cola case with customers who had consumed drinks containing contaminated carbonation. Preventing further illness or discomfort would be high on the list of actions for responding managers. Coca-Cola was warned, however, by the European Union competitiveness minister not to use coupons or rebates to lure customers back to the brand.40 In every instance, trust is at the center of the relationship between a business and its customers. Responding to their immediate needs and working to reinforce or restore trust will be essential.

Employees. If corporate image is an organization as seen by insiders, it's clear that this will occupy a considerable amount of time and attention as a crisis unfolds. Bank of America would have been well advised at the time of its tragedy in London to think about Moritz Erhardt's coworkers and fellow interns. Their ability to attract, hire and retain top-level business students for such positions will be jeopardized if those students sincerely feel the bank just doesn't care about them. Senior investment bankers have noted that such positions are very hard to come by, so most students will just compete for an opening and suffer the consequences regardless. Regulators and others, including the parents of those young people, may not feel the same.

Investors. Often, shareholders, bondholders, and investors will be top-of-mind for an executive facing a brand crisis. Indeed, Coca-Cola's sales fell sharply in Europe during the spring and summer of 1999, but rebounded by autumn and seemed to suffer little in the way of long-term consequences. The Coke brand, of course, is among the most recognized globally, and the Coca-Cola Company is large and well capitalized. Coca-Cola's brand value by 2022 was about $87.6 billion.41 And, for the record, brand value is the monetary worth of a brand if you were to sell it.42

Vendors and suppliers. Very few businesses are vertically integrated to the point at which they need no suppliers or vendors. Just about everyone needs to purchase raw materials, semifinished goods, supplies, and more from outside vendors. If another business no longer trusts you or is unwilling to be seen as cooperating with or assisting your business, you will find it difficult to continue in business. Sears experienced this sort of problem when hedge fund investor Eddie Lampert bought the company in 2013. Suppliers of dry goods, appliances, tires, and more began asking Sears for "collect on delivery" payments when the Chicago retailer experienced severe cash shortages. Keeping the shelves stocked proved more and more difficult, and the company resorted to selling wholly owned brands, such as Kenmore and Craftsman, just to stay afloat, clearly, an unsustainable strategy. What your suppliers think of you can matter a great deal.

Business partners. The same is true of business partners. BP found it difficult to contract with petroleum extraction firms following their ecological disaster in the Gulf of Mexico. Having blamed its partner Transocean for the wellhead blowout and the death of 11 men working on the Deepwater Horizon, neither Transocean nor any other extractors were willing to collaborate with BP in recovering assets beneath the crust of the earth. Such partners may well say, "It's better for us to lose the revenue than to remain in business with these folks."

On the other hand, when Yum! Brands and their Taco Bell subsidiary encountered trouble with the taco shells manufactured by Kraft Foods for grocery store sale, Greg Creed, Taco Bell's Chief Brand Officer, told the world that Kraft was a valued Taco Bell partner and they would continue to work with each other. That cooperation has been a profitable partnership for more than 25 years.

Communities. Even though many of the people in the communities in which you operate may not own shares in your company, may not work for you, and may not buy your products, they still have an interest in your operations and, perhaps, your survival. They need to know that the air they breathe, the water they drink, and the land they live on are safe from contamination. They need to know that you and your company are good neighbors. They want to trust you. They may even be able to help.

Jeff Bernel was able to save American Rubber Products in LaPorte, Indiana, because the community cared about him and his company. His banker wanted him to succeed, as did a local construction firm and the dozens of people who worked for him. They saw him and his enterprise as a valuable part of the LaPorte community and went to work immediately to help save his business. Jeff's never forgotten that and neither has the community.

Considering Interested Observers

Interested observers will closely follow events and company responses, as well. These are people who may have little or nothing to gain (or lose) when the organization in crisis reacts, but they will have a role to play in what influential others think of the company in question.

The News Media

The principal reason for cooperating with the news media is because so many people are paying attention to them. What those people think of your business and how you've behaved during a crisis may depend largely or entirely on what the news media write and say about you. Another reason to respond to the media is that you may need their help in moving valuable, life-saving information to thousands or, perhaps, millions of people in a very short time.

Joan Wainwright had no other alternatives when pharmaceutical giant Merck decided to withdraw its analgesic prescription drug Vioxx from the market. Millions of prescriptions had been written and hundreds of thousands of Americans still had Vioxx tablets in their medicine cabinets. Without the assistance of radio, television, newspapers, and news aggregators on the internet, she and her company would never have been able to reach those who needed that information.

Industry Analysts

If you operate a publicly traded firm, you already know the role and value of those who follow your company for investment portfolio managers and traders. Their buy-sell-or-hold recommendations will have a huge impact on the market value of a share of your stock. Calm, rational explanations of what's happened, actions you've already taken, and plans for the days ahead will help to reduce volatility and uncertainty in the market for your stock. It's especially helpful if the things you say to them turn out to be true. Further, analysts are often sought out by the news media for comment, so it's particularly important that those who follow your company be well-informed.

Regulators and Government Officials

Direct contact with state or federal regulators may not be high on the list of immediate actions for managers responding to a crisis, but that will eventually come to pass. Your CFO or COO should be thinking about a U.S. Securities and Exchange Commission (SEC) Form 8-K, though. That form, known as a "current report," must be filed with the SEC to announce previously undisclosed material, market-moving information that shareholders should know about. Companies generally have four business days to file a Form 8-K for an event that triggers the filing requirement.[43]

Other elected officials may prove helpful, as well. Your local mayor, congressional representative, senator, or county commissioners may have ideas on who can assist or how they may be of use to you. They, quite honestly, do not want you to fail and will do what they can to see that doesn't happen. You pay taxes, you employ the people who vote for them, and you're an asset to every community in which you operate. Keep them informed and, when necessary, lean on them for help.

Non-Governmental Organizations

No matter what business you're in, it's likely that some non-governmental organization (NGO) has an interest in what you do. Environmental organizations are keen to know how you treat the air, water, and land around your facilities. Consumer protection groups want to know more about the ingredients in your products and the safety record of what you make and sell. Animal protection advocates may be concerned that you're involved in animal-based testing or that your products may somehow affect the welfare of animals. This is a long list of single-issue advocates, but you must become familiar with them and work to understand their values and beliefs long before they show up on your doorstep. Or, perhaps, at a press conference they've staged with your brand prominently on display.

Outside Experts

If you've been wrongly accused, if you've been attacked by opportunists, or if you're simply looking for some expertise in your business category, you might consider the assistance of an outside expert. For one thing, they bring high credibility to the conversation. The press and the public already know your own employees will say – more or less – what they're asked to say, but a laboratory scientist, university professor, or think tank analyst will bring extra gravitas, credibility, and third-party insight to your situation. A small honorarium may be in order, but in many cases, they'll offer insight or opinion pro bono.

Emergency Services

If some disaster has befallen your organization, first responders are among the very first people you want to speak with. They'll quite literally risk their lives to save you and your employees or endanger themselves to save your business. Cooperate with them, thank them personally and publicly, and support them when they ask for it. Without men and women dedicated to this sort of work, none of us could continue in business.

Law Enforcement

The same is, of course, true for law enforcement. While you do not want to put yourself in the position of speaking on their behalf (Question: "What's the FBI doing on your plant property?" Response: "That would be a good question for the FBI, sir."), you should devote as many people and resources, and as much time as necessary, to cooperate fully and answer their questions. We all benefit from a stable, orderly society, and business cooperation is often essential to their investigating and solving crimes and misdemeanors.

Considering All Markets

The markets your organization serves will strike close to home for a business enterprise because they are – for the most part – the reason you are in business. Your purpose in life is to serve them: to provide high-quality, reliable goods and services. The reason they reward you with their business and their loyalty is because you help them in clearly definable ways, whether they are also a business or, perhaps, an end consumer. You have to think of them all.

Local

Just because your business is considered national or, perhaps, larger is no reason to ignore local reporters, civic officials, or others. A thoughtful, well-edited statement to the Associated Press, UPI, or Reuters will move the story quickly, but when an authoritative member of your staff takes the time to offer comment to a local reporter, you have a much better chance of having your story told accurately, fairly, and completely.

Regional

Issues related to a business calamity or product failure frequently do not respect state lines. What people in a neighboring state or another nearby city think of you will have a direct effect on your ability to resume activity and continue in business. This is true of your relationship with civic officials in those communities, just as much as the news media there. Showing them and the people of the region that you're a good neighbor can go a long way toward building goodwill.

National

Things get complicated when a crisis is no longer just a local issue. Moving your message to millions of people is challenging, and sampling what they think of your brand can be difficult. A national agency-of-record may be helpful as you think about media contacts, community relations, and legislative liaison. While communication consultants are never cheap, your investment can, and often will, pay huge dividends once you've righted the ship and solved your immediate problems. It's especially helpful to have the phone number of a knowledgeable professional who understands your business, your industry, and the challenges you face. It's also helpful to have another set of eyes and ears on the problem. Manage the contact carefully, pay only for what you need, but do not reject the idea that professional outside advice may help. It may just save the day.

International

The problem is immensely more complex when you begin doing business in other nations and regions of the world. Not only can the languages be different, so are the cultures, customs, laws, and an understanding of who you are. Play by local rules. Look, listen, and think carefully before speaking. And realize that, even though we may not always fully understand one another, we're more alike than we are different.

References

1. Weber, H. R. "Blown-Out BP Well Finally Killed at Bottom of Gulf," *Boston Globe*, September 19, 2010. Retrieved online: http://archive.boston.com/news/nation/articles/2010/09/19/blown_out_bp_well_finally_killed_at_bottom_of_gulf/
2. Ibid.
3. Joulle, Anabelle. "Investment Banking Lifestyle." *Ibanking FAQ.* October 8, 2013. Retrieved online: www.ibankingfaq.com/category/banking-lifestyle
4. "Life of an Investment Banker." *Street of Walls. Reuters.* October 8, 2013. Retrieved online: www.ibankingfaq.com/category/banking-lifestyle/

5. Joulle, Anabelle. "Investment Banking Lifestyle." *Ibanking FAQ*. October 8, 2013. Retrieved online: www.ibankingfaq.com/category/banking-lifestyle/.

6. Asa, Bennett. "Moritz Erhardt's Death Sparks City Internship Culture Concern." *Huffington Post* [United Kingdom]. August 21, 2013. Retrieved online: October 8, 2013. www.huffingtonpost.co.uk/2013/08/21/moritz-erhardt-bank_n_3789124.html

7. Courtney, Polly. "My So-Called Life as an Intern at Merrill Lynch." *The Independent*, August 23, 2013. Retrieved online: October 8, 2013. www.independent.co.uk/news/uk/home-news/my-socalled-life-asan-internat-merrill-lynch-8782735.html

8. Ibid.

9. Cox, Jeff. "BofA Intern Dies After Reportedly Working 3 Days Straight." *NetNet*. *CNBC*, August 20, 2013. Retrieved online: October 8, 2013. www.cnbc.com/id/100974434

10. Gallagher, Paul. "Slavery in the City: Death of 21-year-old intern Moritz Erhardt at Merrill Lynch sparks furor over long hours and macho culture at banks." *The Independent*, August 20, 2013. Retrieved online: October 8, 2013. www.independent.co.uk/news/uk/home-news/slavery-in-the-city-death-of-21yearold-intern-moritz-erhardt-at-merrill-lynch-sparks-furore-over-long-hours-and-macho-culture-at-banks-8775917.html

11. Mohney, Gillian. "Bank of America to Revise Working Conditions after Intern Death." Good Morning America. *ABC News*, August 24, 2013. Retrieved online: http://abcnews.go.com/Business/bank-america-review-working-conditions-intern-death/story?id=20055735

12. Melendez, Eleazer. "Moritz Erhardt, Investment Banking Intern, Dies in London." *The Huffington Post*, August 19, 2013. Retrieved online: October 8, 2013. www.huffingtonpost.com/2013/08/19/moritz-erhardt-investment-banking-dies_n_3781016.html

13. Ibid.

14. Mohney, Gillian. "Bank of America To Revise Working Conditions After Intern Death." Good Morning America. *ABC News*, August 24, 2013. Retrieved online: October 8, 2013. http://abcnews.go.com/Business/bank-america-review-working-conditions-intern-death/story?id=20055735

15. O'Connor, Sarah; Emma Jacobs; et al. "Interns Keep Working at BofA after Colleague." Business. *The Financial Times*, August 21, 2013. Retrieved online: October 8, 2013. www.ft.com/intl/cms/s/0/d709c2bc-0a8d-11e3-9cec-00144feabdc0.html

16. Gallagher, Paul. "Slavery in the City: Death of 21-year-old intern Moritz Erhardt at Merrill Lynch Sparks Furor Over Long Hours and Macho Culture at Banks." *The Independent*, August 20, 2013. Retrieved online: October 8, 2013. www.independent.co.uk/news/uk/home-news/slavery-in-the-city-death-of-21yearold-intern-moritz-erhardt-at-merrill-lynch-sparks-furore-over-long-hours-and-macho-culture-at-banks-8775917.html

17. "U. S., European Coke Analyses Find No Health Threat," *Reuters News Service*, June 22, 1999. Retrieved online: http://famulus.msnbc.com

18. Hagerty, J. R. and Carreyrou, J., "Coke Drinks' Safety Arises Again as Children in Belgium Feel Ill," *The Wall Street Journal*, October 25, 2999, p. A-4.

19. Ibid.

20. Hayes, C. L., "Concern About Coke Products Spreads to Spain and Germany," *The New York Times*, June 19, 1999, pp. B-1, B-2.

21. Sellers, P., "Crunch Time for Coke," *Fortune*, July 19, 1999, pp. 72–78.

22. Cowell, A., "The Coke Stomach Ache Heard Round the World," *The New York Times*, June 25, 1999, pp. C-1, C-2.

23. "Coke Says Found 800 Tainted Pallets from Dunkirk," *Reuters News Service*, June 24, 1999. Retrieved online: http://famulus.msnbc.com

24. Hayes, C. L., "Concern About Coke Products Spreads to Spain and Germany," *The New York Times*, June 19, 1999, pp. B-1, B-2.

25. "Belgium Re-Opens Coca-Cola Vending Machines," *Reuters News Service*, July 8, 1999. Retrieved online: http://famulus.msnbc.com

26. Andrews, E. L., "Coke's Chief Apologizes for Response on Contamination," *The New York Times*, June 17, 1999, p. C-4.

27. "Coke Chief Ivester in Belgium to Head Crisis Control," *Reuters News Service*, June 20, 1999. Retrieved online: http://famulus.msnbc.com

28. Hagerty, J. R.; Deogun, N., "Coke Scrambles to Contain a Scare in Europe," *The Wall Street Journal*, June 17, 1999, pp. B-1, B-4.

29. Hayes, C. L., "Coke Products Are Ordered Off the Shelves in Four Countries," *The New York Times*, June 16, 1999, pp. C-1, C-2.

30. Deogun, N.; Hagerty, J. R.; Stecklow, S.; and Johannes, L., "Anatomy of a Recall: How Coke's Controls Fizzed Out in Europe," *The Wall Street Journal*, June 29, 1999, pp. A-1, A-6.

31. Hagerty, J. R. and Barrett, A., "France, Belgium Reject Pleas to Lift Ban," *The Wall Street Journal*, June 18, 1999, p. B-1.

32. "Coca-Cola Tests Find No Problem," *The New York Times*, October 26, 1999, p. C-1.

33. Hagerty, J. R. and Carreyrou, J., "Coke Drinks' Safety Arises Again as Children in Belgium Feel Ill," *The Wall Street Journal*, October 25, 1999, p. A-4.

34. "European Report Doubts Explanation by Coke," *The New York Times*, August 18, 1999, p. C-4.

35. Li, L.H., "Origin of Coke Crisis in Europe Is Termed Psychosomatic," *The Wall Street Journal*, April 2, 2000, p. A-21.

36. Press Release. The Coca-Cola Company, "The Coca-Cola Company Finalizes Transaction with Coca-Cola Enterprises," October 3, 2010. Retrieved online: February 19, 2023. https://investors.coca-colacompany.com/news-events/press-releases/detail/281/the-coca-cola-company-finalizes-transaction-with-coca-cola#:~:text=The%20acquisition%20of%20CCE's%20North,of%20%248.88%20billion%20in%20debt.

37. Smith, H. and Feighan, A., "Coca-Cola and the European Contamination Crisis," pp. 6–7, August 2001. Fanning Center for Business Communication, University of Notre Dame. Retrieved online: https://ndcasestudies.kendallhunt.com/search-products-keyword?combine_filter2=Coca-Cola

38. Ibid.

39. McKay, B. and Deogun, N., "After Short, Stormy Tenure, Coke's Ivester to Retire," *The Wall Street Journal*, December 7, 1999, pp. B-1, B-4.

40. Mitchener, B. and McKay, P. A., "EU Warns Coke Not to Use Rebates to Give Sales a Pop," *The Wall Street Journal*, July 23, 1999, p. A-5.

41. "Coca-Cola's Brand Value, 2006–2021," *Statista Research Department*, July 13, 2021. Retrieved online: www.statista.com/statistics/326065/coca-cola-brand-value/

42. "What Is Brand Value and How Can You Measure and Improve It?" *Qualtrics*. March 13, 2022. Retrieved online: www.qualtrics.com/experience-management/brand/value/

43. U. S. Securities and Exchange Commission form 8-K. Retrieved online: www.sec.gov/files/form8-k.pdf

Chapter 12

Expect the Best, Plan for the Worst

When someone advises for you to always "expect the best, but plan for the worst," that does seem as if it's counsel from your mother. It's both encouraging and cautionary at the same moment, but it doesn't seem particularly helpful. As anyone anticipating or managing a crisis will tell you, though, it *is* good advice. The questions for any manager are: "How do I go about that? What should I think about? How do we make our plans come to life?"

The keys here are to draft an actual plan, rather than merely think about it. Exercise it regularly. Then, spend some time defining what real success looks like. We've talked about these three actions in earlier chapters. Let's take a moment now to see what that meant to two companies deeply involved in memorable crisis situations, some of it of their own making.

A Crisis at Alaska Airlines

January 31, 2000, was not a normal day for Lou Cancelmi, Vice President of Corporate Communications for Alaska Airlines. Cancelmi rarely left the corporate offices in SeaTac, Washington, before 7:00 p.m., but that day he had a pressing obligation – a rare chance to see his son at an Italian language lesson in Seattle. As he settled in to enjoy the occasion, he turned off his cell phone and started to relax. He closed his eyes, listened to the lesson, and thought about his son's progress.

After the lesson, Cancelmi walked outside and turned on his phone. Much to his surprise, there were several messages left during the brief time he had it turned off, and he wondered what they could be about. He dialed his voicemail, started listening, and had trouble believing what he was hearing. "Lou, we need you back at the office. We've lost an airplane." That was just the beginning of what would be many sleepless nights for Cancelmi and his team at Alaska Airlines.[1]

Flight 261

Shortly before Cancelmi left work to attend his son's Italian lesson, Flight 261 was departing from Puerto Vallarta, Mexico, piloted by Captain Ted Thompson and

DOI: 10.4324/9781003322849-15

First Officer Bill Tansky. During the flight, they experienced a warning about an inoperative horizontal stabilizer, not normally considered an emergency to well-trained pilots. Thompson and Tansky took measures to compensate for the problem and flew uneventfully for two hours.[2]

At 4:03 p.m., however, the situation had worsened, and the pilots contacted the dispatch control to request landing at Los Angeles International Airport, which was closer than their scheduled destination in San Francisco. The pilots were trying to control the aircraft, which had just taken a sudden nosedive – dropping 6,500 feet in 60 seconds. After regaining control, the two men had a brief discussion about what course of action to take. Captain Thompson got on the public address system and calmly announced:

> Folks, we've had a flight control problem up front here. We're workin' it . . . uh, that's Los Angeles off to the right there . . . that's where we're intending to go. We're pretty busy up here working this situation. I don't anticipate any big problems once we get a couple of sub-systems back online, but we will be going into LAX, and I'd anticipate us parking there in about 20 to 30 minutes.[3]

Conscious of the severity of the situation, the two pilots headed the plane out over the bay to avoid populated areas. First Flight Attendant Allison Shanks entered the cabin and reported that loud bumps were heard from the rear of the plane and then returned to calm the passengers and prepare for landing. Just minutes later, one of the aircraft's flight control jackscrews failed, causing the plane to roll upside down and pitch downward into the sea below. Tragically, all 88 passengers and crew members perished in the crash.[4]

Aeroshell 33

Later that month, five Federal Aviation Administration (FAA) officials conducted a four-day hearing, investigating the accident and Alaska Airlines's conduct. Two senior auditors involved in the post-accident audit confirmed that the company had taken all necessary precautions and followed all FAA-mandated safety procedures, while a third auditor discovered incomplete safety documentation but concluded that it played no part in the accident and that the airline did have skilled employees.[5] Following the release of the audit, William Ayer, CEO and President of Alaska Airlines, said: "We all want to find out what happened to Flight 261 so we can take necessary steps to prevent it from happening again."[6]

The hearing, however, was not without controversy. Much of the discussion focused on the specific grease used to lubricate the MD-80 jackscrews. Alaska Airlines had been using Aeroshell 33, a multipurpose grease invented and endorsed by Boeing. During the course of the accident investigation, technicians discovered that a copper alloy in the grease is corrosive to the jackscrew assembly found in the plane's gears and flight controls. Subsequently, Alaska Airlines switched back to Mobil 28, which they had used until three years earlier.

The audit also uncovered proof that the maintenance engineering order for the initial switch in lubricants lacked all the required signatures, causing some to question Alaska Airlines's procedural effectiveness. The lack of proper documentation would have prohibited the switch but, despite the mistake, witnesses in the hearing remained convinced that the error was ultimately unrelated to the accident. The investigation findings also reported that the airline was lubricating the jackscrews every 2,500 flight hours, well under the FAA guideline lubrication interval of 3,600 flight hours. After the crash, the FAA mandated all airlines lubricate every 650 flight hours and Alaska Airlines complied. Public blame shifted between Alaska Airlines and Boeing following the investigation though, ultimately, both companies assumed legal liability following the investigation in 2003 and agreed to compensate survivors of the victims.[7]

Media Coverage

As in all commercial airline accidents, the media coverage of Flight 261 was relentless. Alaska Airlines was put under a microscope for months and was openly questioned in the local and national media about maintenance practices at its Oakland base. At first, the coverage focused on identifying the cause of the crash. Discussion and conjecture regarding the flight deck recording and subsequent investigation transcripts became a nightly television ritual. Later, the exposure revealed that the company had been involved in a federal grand jury probe into its Oakland, California, maintenance base operations since late 1998. The controversy stemmed from a former Alaska Airlines employee who prompted the FAA to investigate after relaying information regarding company maintenance records on the MD-80 fleet. His allegations, coupled with the emotional response to the accident, painted a public picture of a negligent airline.

Media coverage was especially sensitive in Seattle. The accident made the front page of the local newspapers and was the top story on the evening news for months. Balancing the media's duty to serve as a "watch dog" and Alaska Airlines's efforts to preserve its integrity made for an uneasy relationship between the company and local media outlets. Many stories blamed company culture for what appeared to be sloppy maintenance practices, and one newspaper printed a headline proclaiming the downed MD-80 had experienced mechanical problems on its way to Mexico – which was untrue.[8]

Another newspaper even contended that Alaska Airlines had knowingly and intentionally slacked on safety protocol and then pressured the FAA to overlook the infractions. The article, headlined "U.S. Looks Into FAA's Alaska Air Oversight," ran in the *Seattle Post-Intelligencer* in April 2000 and offered the opinion that:

> Such an investigation would focus on whether Alaska encouraged criminally improper maintenance practices that were either sanctioned by or ignored by the FAA . . . several FAA inspectors in the agency's Flight Standards Division office in Renton [Washington] say they have been pressured by superiors to take it easy on Alaska, and were punished when they tried to strictly enforce FAA regulations.[9]

Confounding the situation were reports that were easily misinterpreted by the public. For example, a *USA Today* article reported on December 11, 2000, that the FAA found "exemplary programs at every airline except Alaska." The inference was that Alaska Airlines was not airworthy. The truth, however, was that Alaska Airlines was excluded from the audit since the FAA had conducted such an extensive investigation that spring, following the crash.

Similarly, an article in the *Tacoma News Tribune* said the FAA fined Alaska Airlines for putting an unairworthy aircraft back into service. The reality was that the FAA did fine the airline, but the infraction resulted from an April test flight carrying no passengers that took off without proper documentation. The media did not reveal that distinction, and the public was led to believe the fine was the result of an unsafe passenger flight.[10]

In June 2000, the FAA threatened to shut down Alaska Airlines's major repair centers in Seattle and Oakland unless the carrier showed it could quickly improve maintenance practices. While these threats never played out, the company feared its image was tarnished in the minds of its customers due to the unrelenting negative publicity following the accident. In order to find out what effect the negative media coverage was having on its brand, the company contracted with an outside party to conduct research on customer perceptions. Remarkably, the survey showed no negligible effect on customers' perceptions of Alaska Airlines.[11]

Although most media coverage during the months following the crash was not flattering to the company, a number of stories hailed the flight crew as heroes. The crew was praised for their professionalism and conduct during the emergency. In the year following the crash, the Air Line Pilots Association International awarded Ted Thompson and Bill Tansky the Gold Medal for Heroism because of their courage in responding to the emergency aboard their airliner.[12]

Nonetheless, the negative publicity took a toll on employee morale. In response, Cancelmi offered the following statement to employees:

> Given the negative publicity . . . I'd like our employees to keep several things in mind. First is the outstanding way they all responded to the tragedy of Flight 261. Then there's the fact we have cooperated fully with every investigating

agency that has made a request of us, not to mention the tremendous effort and progress we've made to improve our operation. The bottom line is, as a company, we have committed ourselves to becoming the model for safety and regulatory compliance in the commercial aviation industry.[13]

Activating the Crisis Management Plan

Lou Cancelmi and the senior team at Alaska Airlines had drafted a solid crisis communications plan and, to their credit, exercised the plan regularly. Even though no one gets up in the morning anticipating a major crisis, each of them knew that, on any given day, landings may not equal takeoffs. They had to be ready.

The crisis response team organized at the company headquarters in SeaTac, a city in southern King County, Washington. Following an immediate statement detailing what the company knew about the accident, the team began responding to numerous stakeholders and key observers.

Local and national media were unrelenting with requests for information, much of which was not even known to the company itself. At the same time, Alaska Airlines was cooperating with government agencies and crash investigators. Timely and clear communication would be critical because of the sheer number and concern of stakeholder groups.

Victims' Families

The most important priority was addressing the needs of victims' families. Immediately following the tragedy, John Kelly, Alaska Air Group CEO at the time, made the trip to Southern California to meet personally with the families and to convey his condolences. He also pledged publicly that the company would do "everything possible to find answers" to the questions about their loss. The company also activated the Family and Friends Care Team to assist in helping people cope with such a difficult situation. Airline executives felt that these actions constituted the "right thing to do," as opposed to tools that would help mitigate possible litigation or create good press.[14]

Customers

Although the management team's world stopped spinning moments after the crash, there was still a company to run. With more than 1,000 daily departures, they realized that it would be crucial to continue filling the seats in their airplanes, especially in light of the challenges they faced. The airline enjoyed fiercely loyal customers and had been recognized on numerous occasions as a leader in customer service by publications such as *Condé Nast Traveler* and *Travel+Leisure* magazine.[15] The company hoped the goodwill and strong feelings they had worked to build over their 68-year history would serve as an insurance policy of sorts and keep customers flying the airline.

Employees

The Flight 261 tragedy shook the foundation of the organization. The integrity of the company was based on core values, which included safety and performance, both of which were under scrutiny following the crash. In addition, 12 passengers on board Flight 261 were employees, and many people at the company were affected in a very personal way.

Together, Alaska and subsidiary Horizon Airlines, employed more than 16,000 people; making information available and accessible to staff was both a challenge and a priority. Among the company's principal means of communication with employees was the internal website, *www.alaskaworld.com*. This platform was mainly used to pass along information published and broadcast in the news media as well as to keep everyone up-to-date on breaking news. The company also went on the road with a team of key managers to talk to employees in outstations about the accident and what they were doing to prevent future tragedies. Some supervisors at Alaska Airlines took it upon themselves to recommit their teams to the organizational values and held impromptu sessions with their direct reports to talk and listen to concerns.[16]

Community

Aviation has long been a cornerstone industry in the Puget Sound region, starting with William Boeing and the Boeing Company in the early 1900s and later with Alaska Airlines and Horizon Airlines in the 1930s. The company was proud of its Northwest heritage and being actively involved in the communities it served. It was important to the company that the tragedy not negatively affect its relationship with the community. Rather, it hoped its response to events would actually bring it even closer to the people and places it served.

Interested Observers

In addition to those with a stake in these events – people or organizations who stand to gain or lose something, depending on the actions taken by management – others are keenly interested in the company, its products and services, and how those might be regulated. In addition to the news media, the Federal Aviation Administration (FAA), the National Transportation Safety Board (NTSB), and the Air Line Pilots Association (ALPA) are all key players in this incident. These organizations and agencies are integral parts of the daily operations of every airline and play a more active role following accidents, as in the case of Flight 261.

Federal Aviation Administration

The FAA's mission is to provide a safe, secure, and efficient global aerospace system that contributes to national security and the promotion of U.S. aerospace safety. They are the leading authority in the aerospace community and are mandated by law to promote aviation safety in the interest of the American public by regulating and overseeing the civil aviation industry. The FAA investigates airline policies and practices but is not directly involved in investigating airline accidents.[17] The policies and practices of Alaska Airlines at its Oakland maintenance base were part of an FAA probe prior to the crash of Flight 261. Some people within the FAA argued that the agency had a track record of treating Alaska Airlines with "kid gloves,"[18] which led to speculation following the accident that the FAA should be forced to take some responsibility.

National Transportation Safety Board

The NTSB is an independent federal agency charged by Congress with investigating every civil aviation accident in the United States and significant accidents in the other modes of transportation – railroad, highway, marine, and pipeline – and issuing safety recommendations aimed at preventing future accidents. The agency works with many different constituencies and is responsible for the final report and causal analysis following its investigation.[19] The NTSB worked closely with Alaska Airlines in its investigation of Flight 261 and coordinated with the FAA to use the information it had obtained from its look into the airline's Oakland maintenance facility.

Air Line Pilots Association

ALPA is a union representing 64,000 airline pilots at 42 U.S. and Canadian airlines. ALPA provides all of the traditional union representation services for its members, including lobbying airline pilot views to Congress and government agencies. The organization is also a proponent of aviation safety and is usually granted "interested party" status in most major airline accidents, which means that ALPA accident investigators assist NTSB staff at the on-site investigations and participate in the ensuing public hearings.[20] Following the crash of Flight 261, the union (which does not normally criticize specific airlines for safety issues,) said that both Alaska Airlines and the FAA were to blame for the circumstances leading up to the accident. The group essentially claimed Alaska Airlines fostered a culture that sacrificed safety for profits and said the FAA officials in Renton (near Alaska's company headquarters) had relationships with management at the airline that were "too close."[21]

Protecting the Brand

In May of 2003, when Bill Ayer became CEO of Alaska Airlines, among the first steps he took was to create a position for a vice president of safety, who would report directly to him. Further, the company employed another 300 maintenance technicians and increased the quality assurance staff fivefold. The company also conducted an internal self-audit of its safety and operational processes, and commissioned an outside review of its safety precautions. The external review recommended 175 specific changes, all of which were completed.

Cancelmi and others on the Alaska Airlines senior team knew that customer service, safety, and value were principles core to the company's foundation. The concept of "Alaska Spirit" is the essence of the airline's brand. The actions Cancelmi and his team took immediately following the accident off the California coast essentially saved the Alaska Airlines brand. Today, the company is profitable and flourishing, despite the loss of revenue during the 2020–2022 COVID pandemic. Today, the company maintains operations at 5 hubs and serves 115 cities with nearly 1,200 daily flights in the United States, Mexico, Canada, and Costa Rica.[22]

A Crisis at Carnival Cruise Lines

> "The boat started shaking. The noise – there was panic, like in a film, dishes crashing to the floor, people running, people falling down the stairs."
>
> ~ survivor Fulvio Rocci.[23]

The Crisis

At 4:00 p.m. on the evening of January 13, 2012, *Costa Concordia* set sail from Rome, Italy, for a seven-day cruise, as it did every week. The ship was due to arrive in Savona, Italy, the next day. Around 9:15 p.m., the ship took a five-mile detour to pass closer to the picturesque Tuscan island of Giglio. Captain Francesco Schettino appears to have misjudged the maneuver, and at 9:30 p.m., the ship collided with a well-mapped reef known as Le Scole. The collision ripped a 160-foot gash in the hull of the ship, and *Concordia* lost power.[24]

The captain is said to have performed the sail-by as a spectacle for head waiter Antonello Tievoli, who was a native of Giglio, and as a salute to former Costa captain Mario Palombo, who retired in 2006. Tievoli had been invited to join the captain in the bridge as the vessel was steered by the island. Captain Palombo was reported to have not even been on the island to see the spectacle on the night of the incident.[25]

Within 15 minutes of the collision, the ship started to take on water and began to list. At that point, Captain Schettino likely realized his ship was in trouble and turned the vessel back toward shore in what appeared to be an effort to make it easier to evacuate.[26] Shortly following the collision, at 10:30 p.m., according to one of the ship's cooks, Captain Schettino ordered dinner for himself and a woman.[27] At 10:35 p.m., the crew directed the passengers to report to their muster stations, saying that the issue was an electrical problem and technicians were working on it. At 10:58 p.m., Captain Schettino ordered "abandon ship."

What followed can only be described as pure chaos. Most passengers did not know the emergency procedure or where their muster station was, as there had been no lifeboat drill yet for the 600 passengers who boarded the ship that afternoon.[28]

The Company

Costa Cruises is based in Genoa, Italy, and, at the time of the accident, operated 15 ships. The company was established in 1854 as a fleet of trading vessels, but it wasn't until 1948 that Costa Cruises began passenger voyages. In 1997, Carnival Cruise Lines – a British-American cruise operator with more than 100 vessels – and another firm, Airtours, jointly acquired Costa Cruises. Carnival became the sole shareholder of Costa after purchasing all Airtours shares in 2000, which was also the year Costa saw the Italian flag return to its ships. In 2004, Costa Cruises became the first company to receive BEST 4 recognition, acknowledging its effort in quality, safety, environmental protection, and social responsibility.[29]

The Ship

Costa Cruises commissioned *Costa Concordia* in 2004, and, at the time of its launch, *Concordia* was the largest Italian cruise ship in history. The vessel was 952 feet in length with a beam of 116 feet. At full capacity, she could carry up to 1,013 crew members with 3,780 passengers occupying the 1,502 staterooms.[30]

The Aftermath

In the chaos that followed Captain Schettino's order to abandon ship, passengers looked for leadership that simply was not available. Under maritime safety regulations, the captain of a ship is obligated to assist passengers and crew members in times of distress. However, Captain Schettino is reported to have left his command and was sailing to safety in a lifeboat before the evacuation of his ship was complete. In the course of the ship sinking, Captain Schettino had a heated exchange with the Coast Guard who ordered him to get back on board the ship and oversee the evacuation. He refused.[31]

Following his arrest, Captain Schettino was recorded telling a friend that management put pressure on him to pass by Giglio in order to provide a spectacle for passengers and a salute to Captain Palombo, a veteran Costa Captain. Schettino was recorded saying:

> Management was always saying "pass by there, pass by there." Someone else in my position might not have been so amenable to pass so close but they busted my balls: "pass by there, pass by there," and now I'm paying for it.[32]

Captain Schettino was held under house arrest at his home in Meta di Sorrento, facing charges of causing a shipwreck, abandoning ship, and multiple counts of manslaughter.[33]

The Italian Civil Protection Agency led the frantic search efforts for survivors. Five days after the incident, on Wednesday, January 18, with more than 20 people still missing, the search operations had to be suspended due to a shift in the vessel's position that rendered the area unsafe. Operations were resumed the next day.[34] Four days later, 13 bodies had been recovered and another 19 were still missing and presumed lost.[35] On January 31, Italian divers ended their underwater search of the wreck, as the conditions inside had become too risky. The Italian Civil Protection Agency did add that they would continue their above-water search, using special equipment to search for bodies underwater.[36]

Carnival's Initial Response

Immediately following the incident, little was heard from Carnival as they left Costa to handle the situation. CEO Micky Arison failed to appear at the scene of the incident, instead expressing his condolences from Miami. It took five days after the incident before Arison tweeted the brief sentiment, "I gave my personal assurance that we will take care of each & every one of our guests, crew and their families" and included a link to a press release issued by Carnival on January 18.[37] It was not until a week after the crisis began that Howard Frank, a Carnival senior executive, was sent to Italy. However, it should be noted that he appeared to be only at Costa's headquarters in Genoa with no intention of making an appearance at the scene of the incident itself.

Shortly after the crisis began, Costa CEO Luigi Foschi offered an initial compensation consisting of a refund and discount on future bookings. A spokesman for the cruise line stated, "The company is not only going to refund everybody, but they will offer a 30 percent discount on future cruises if they want to stay loyal to the company." In response to this offer, passengers were quoted as stating it was "ridiculous and insulting."[38]

Financial Implications

Moody's – an American financial services and credit rating agency – estimated that total costs including the vessel, environmental, and passenger liability would easily reach $1 billion, but executives of the cruise line hoped many of those costs would be offset by the *Concordia*'s insurance. Costa Cruises's insurance deductible on the vessel itself was $40 billion. The reduction in Carnival's market cap greatly exceeded the direct costs to *Concordia*, suggesting that there were long-term concerns about the effect of the crisis on the industry in general and Carnival specifically.[39]

An Epilogue

While lawsuits are still moving ponderously about the Italian and U.S. courts and an entirely new set of names and faces now leads the two companies involved, it is not too soon to draw a few observations from what happened. First, both Carnival Cruise Lines and its subsidiary, Costa Cruises, were inexcusably late in making a public statement about the collision, capsizing, and the loss of life. The world at large, including friends and relatives of those aboard, learned of the disaster – detail by detail – primarily from British newspapers and broadcast channels. Those who could read Italian might have learned more from local papers in Italy. It took five days for the Carnival CEO to tweet out a message of condolence. Another two days elapsed before a corporate official arrived in Italy but not on scene. In the 19th century, that may have been acceptable but not in the 21st.

Second, the parent company accepted no responsibility in the days and weeks following the incident, claiming the subsidiary – separately incorporated – bore full responsibility for everything. And then, stunningly, the Costa CEO offered refunds on tickets purchased for the voyage and a 30 percent discount on future travel with the company.

The captain of *Concordia* blamed the company. The company blamed the captain. The Italian Coast Guard called it a "dereliction of duty" and "an unmitigated human tragedy." Thirty-two people lost their lives as a result of inattention and incompetence. The CEO of Carnival Cruise Lines, Mickey Arison, responded to criticism about his lack of visibility after the disaster. He released statements and posted tweets but said he did not feel he needed "to get in front of a camera." He continued, "Obviously, I am very sorry it happened." The Carnival chairman and CEO said to the *Miami Herald*, "When you have 100 ships out there, sometimes unfortunate things happen, but as I said, it was an accident."[40]

Three Ideas to Remember

As you anticipate and prepare for the next crisis in your organization, please do expect the best but plan for the worst. Both of the crises described in this chapter point directly to the value of three actions for any manager to consider:

- Commit to resolving the crisis and responding in a timely fashion.
- Pursue resolution with the expectation of success.
- Anticipate that it will get worse before it gets better.

References

1. Personal interview with Lou Cancelmi, VP Alaska Airlines Corporate Communications, February 25, 2004. By telephone.
2. Hein, C. and Tipps, T. *Alaska Airlines: Navigating Through Crisis Toward an Uncertain Future.* Notre Dame, IN: Eugene D. Fanning Center for Business Communication, Mendoza College of Business, University of Notre Dame. 2004.

3. "Transcript of Last 13 Minutes of Flight 261, Plus Context," Posted to corporate website, www.alaskaairlines.com, December 13, 2000.

4. "Key Moments of Flight 261: Alaska Pilots Analyze Cockpit Voice Recorder," Posted to corporate website, www.alaskaairlines.com, December 13, 2000.

5. "NTSB Hearing Q&A: Summarizing Key Points and Answering Employee Questions," Posted to corporate website, www.alaskaairlines.com, December 22, 2000.

6. CBS News, "Alaska Air Takes Blame for Crash." Posted to corporate website, www.cbsnews.com, June 3, 2003.

7. "Flight 261 Story a Challenging Test of Newspaper's Role," Seattle Post-Intelligencer, Posted to corporate website,www.archives.seattletimes.nwsource.com. January 19, 2003.

8. Shukovsky, P. and Johnson, T. "US looks into FAA's Alaska Air Oversight: Agency's Relationship with Airline Questioned," Seattle Post-Intelligencer, April 13, 2000.

9. Alaska Airlines, "Questions and Answers: Employees Inquire about NTSB Hearing, Recent Articles." Posted to corporate website, www.alaskaairlines.com, December 12, 2000.

10. Cancelmi. op. cit.

11. "Pilots Honored for Heroism During Crisis," Retrieved online: Seattle Post-Intelligencer, www.seattlepi.nwsource.com/local/air01.shtml, February 1, 2001.

12. "NTSB Witness Plan and Other Information," Retrieved online: Alaska World, www.alaskasworld.com, December 12, 2000.

13. Telephone interview with Lou Cancelmi, VP Alaska Airlines Corporate Communications, February 25, 2004.

14. Alaska Airlines, Alaska Air Group Almanac, 2002.

15. Telephone interview with Lou Cancelmi, VP Alaska Airlines Corporate Communications, February 25, 2004.

16. Federal Aviation Administration website, www.faa.gov, April 2004.

17. "Safety Last, FAA Inspectors Complain," Seattle Post-Intelligencer. Retrieved online: www.seattlepi.nwsource.com/local/alas05.shtml, March 5, 1999.

18. National Transportation Safety Board website, www.ntsb.gov, April 2004.

19. Air Line Pilots Association website, www.alpa.org, April 2004.

20. "Pilots Blame Alaska, FAA for Flight 261 Crash," Retrieved online: Seattle Post-Intelligencer. http://www.seattletimes/archives/nwsource.com, September 26, 2002.

21. Alaska Airlines website, https://newsroom.alaskaair.com, March 12, 2022.

22. Akwagyiram, A. "Italy Cruise Ship Costa Concordia Accident Eyewitness Accounts," BBC News. Retrieved online: January 14, 2012. http://www.bbc.co.uk/news/world-europe -16561382

23. Foster, J., Sorrentino, M. J. and Florance, C. Carnival Cruise Lines: Wreck of the Costa Concordia. Notre Dame, IN: Eugene D. Fanning Center for Business Communication, Mendoza College of Business, University of Notre Dame. 2012.

24. Squires, N. and Ward, V. "Cruise Disaster: Captain Was Bringing Crew Member Close to His Island Home," The Telegraph. Retrieved online: January 16, 2012. http://www.telegraph .co.uk/news/worldnews/europe/italy/9017767/Cruise-disaster-captain-was-bringing-crew-member-close-to-his-island-home.html

25. Agar, M. and Blenkinsop, A. "Concordia: How the Disaster Unfolded," The Telegraph. Retrieved online: January 16, 2012. www.telegraph.co.uk/news/interactive-graphics/9018076/Concordia-How-the-disaster-unfolded.html

26. "Cruise Ship's Cook Says Captain Ordered Dinner After Crash," CNN Europe. Retrieved online: January 20, 2012. http://edition.cnn.com/2012/01/19/world/europe/italy-cruise-cook /index.html

27. Beyette, B. "Costa Concordia Capsizing Spotlights Cruise Ship Safety," *Los Angeles Times*. Retrieved online: January 19, 2012. http://www.latimes.com/travel/la-tr-insider-20120122,0, 4033122. story

28. "History of Costa Cruises," Costa Cruise website. Retrieved online: www.costacruise.com/B2C/USA/Corporate/history/thehistory.htm

29. Dake, S. "A Short History of the Costa Concordia," Maritime Matters. January 22, 2012. Retrieved online: http://maritimematters.com/2012/01/a-short-history-of-the-costa-concordia/

30. Dake, S. "A Short History of the Costa Concordia," *Maritime Matters*. January 22, 2012. Retrieved online: http://maritimematters.com/2012/01/a-short-history-of-the-costa-concordia/

31. Squires, N. "Costa Concordia Captain Francesco Schettino 'Under Intense Pressure to Sail Close to Giglio,'" *The Telegraph*. Retrieved online: January 25, 2012. http://www.telegraph.co.uk/news/worldnews/europe/italy/9037602/Costa-Concordia-captain-Francesco-Schettino-under-intense-pressure-to-sail-close-to-Giglio.html

32. Ibid.

33. "Costa Concordia: Search resumes for ship survivors," *BBC News*. Retrieved online: January 19, 2012. www.bbc.co.uk/news/world-europe-16626640

34. Dake, S. "A Short History of the Costa Concordia," *Maritime Matters*. Retrieved online: January 22, 2012. http://maritimematters.com/2012/01/a-short-history-of-the-costa-concordia/

35. "Divers Abandon Search on Costa Concordia," *RTE News*. Retrieved online: February 1, 2012 www.rte.ie/news/2012/0131/italy.html

36. Walker, J. "Cruise Crisis Management FAIL: How Carnival is Ruining its Reputation Following the Costa Concordia Disaster," *Cruise Law News*. Retrieved online: January 22, 2012. www.cruiselawnews.com/2012/01/articles/social-media-1/cruise-crisis-management-fail-how-carnival-is-ruining-its-reputation-following-the-costa-concordia-disaster/

37. Russell, M. "Costa Offers Survivors 30% Off . . . A New Cruise," *Newser*. Retrieved online: January 23, 2012. www.newser.com/story/138046/cruise-survivors-offered-30-off-future-costa-cruises.html

38. Russell, Mark. "Costa Offers Survivors 30% Off . . . A New Cruise," Newser. Retrieved online: January 23, 2012. http://www.newser.com/story/138046/cruise-survivors-offered-30-off-future-costa-cruises.html.

39. "Arison on Costa Concordia Wreck: 'I Am Very Sorry It Happened.'" *NBC6 News South Florida*. Retrieved online: March 9, 2012. www.nbcmiami.com/news/local/arison-on-costa-concordia-wreck-i-am-very-sorry-it-happened/1918168/

40. Satchell, Arlene. "Update: Costa, Carnival Pledge Support to Concordia Passengers and Crew," *South Florida Sun-Sentinel*. Retrieved online: January 18, 2012. https://www.sun-sentinel.com/news/fl-xpm-2012-01-18-sfl-costa-concordia-more-deaths-link-20120118-story.html.

Crisis Communication

Chapter 13

Communication Is Your Primary Tool in a Crisis

Late in the afternoon of Friday, September 15, 2000, Laurie Gannon, Public Relations Director at Taco Bell Corporation, received a phone call from the company's government relations team. Gannon typically receives periodic phone calls from that department, bringing her abreast of Taco Bell's involvement with governmental agencies. When she picked up the phone, Gannon assumed it was another update; however, things swiftly took a turn for the worse. She was informed that a special interest group in Washington, D.C., would hold a press conference early the next week to discuss Taco Bell-labeled taco shells sold by Kraft Foods, Inc.

Inquiring further, Gannon learned that the product in question – Taco Bell *Home Originals*-branded taco shells sold in grocery stores – might contain a corn ingredient unapproved for human consumption. Although the report specifically targeted corn tortilla shells distributed and sold by Kraft Foods, the media and subsequent consumer reaction could potentially prove damaging to the Taco Bell brand.

Details were sketchy. Gannon discovered that the findings of a group known as "Friends of the Earth" would run in *The Washington Post* in its Monday print edition and that a press conference would follow. She quickly realized Taco Bell could be the subject of substantial negative media exposure. Although the work week was rapidly coming to a close, Gannon had to prepare a response – the phone call seemed perfectly timed so that Taco Bell would have minimal time to react. Nevertheless, she moved quickly, first notifying several key executives within Taco Bell, as well as those at Kraft, of this developing story. Her weekend was spent tracking down all available information on StarLink, the unapproved corn ingredient in question.[1]

In recent years, there had been much debate surrounding the side effects, if any, of genetically modified foods. Since these foods are a relatively recent creation, there were few comprehensive scientific studies of their long-term effects. Accordingly, some nations and a few non-governmental organizations took a hard stance on these so-called "frankenfoods" and had enacted or advocated for strict guidelines against their use.[2] Just prior to this incident, for instance,

DOI: 10.4324/9781003322849-17

the European Parliament imposed "tighter restrictions on the use of genetically-modified products."[3]

This debate was the central argument by mainly European nations and NGOs that publicly rallied against those supporting the use of genetically modified ingredients. In August 2000, corn-based products became the focal point in this debate as a series of tests had been conducted on 23 of the leading corn-based foods, including the Taco Bell *Home Originals* taco shells.[4] These tests had concluded that the taco shells contained the "Cry9c" protein – a pesticide that had not been approved for human consumption.[5]

The Taco Bell/Kraft License Agreement

Just four years earlier, Taco Bell and Kraft Foods announced the formation of a license agreement for Kraft to manufacture and distribute Taco Bell-branded taco shells in grocery stores.[6] Kraft had a strong reputation within this distribution channel, primarily through the many products the company currently offered.

Although terms of this deal remained confidential, many agreed that it was a standard license agreement, whereby Kraft, as the licensee, would produce and distribute Taco Bell products, including the *Home Originals* line. Taco Bell, the licensor, would oversee the use of its logo and trademarks to ensure the products would be held to the highest of standards. As described in an interview with Laurie Gannon, representatives from Taco Bell and Kraft would meet periodically to discuss, among other things, quality, financial, and operational aspects of the agreement. In addition, Taco Bell would have final say as to the use of its name in the marketing of all Taco Bell-branded products.[7]

With Kraft's superior distribution and national reach, that agreement was expected to help Taco Bell increase its brand reach without bearing the entire cost of the rollout.[8] Outsiders speculated at the time that Kraft would remit between 4 percent and 6 percent of the taco shell revenues on a graduated scale to Taco Bell.

The Challenge for Taco Bell Communicators

The challenge for Laurie Gannon and the communication staff at Taco Bell was multifaceted.

- Would Taco Bell executives allow her to take ownership of any portion of the problem, or does that belong entirely to Kraft Foods?
- Should Taco Bell visibly cooperate with Kraft in a recall announcement or in periodic updates to the press and public?
- Who explains to the public – and to wholesalers and retailers selling the Taco Bell *Home Originals* shells – what StarLink corn is, why it contains a modified gene to produce a pesticide protein, and how it got into those taco shells in the first place?

- Should Taco Bell consider abrogating the license agreement in order to protect its own brand? Is protective disinvestment a smart strategy here or simply a sign of panic at the Louisville parent, Yum! Brands?
- Further to the point, do you suppose Taco Bell has other genetically modified ingredients, even though vetted and approved, in other products on its menu board?
- Who talks with key stakeholders: customers, investors, franchise owners, suppliers, and business partners?
- Who communicates with interested observers, including the U.S. Food and Drug Administration, the Environmental Protection Agency, and the U.S. Department of Agriculture? Each of those agencies bears congressionally mandated responsibility for oversight on some part of the national food supply, genetic engineering, and the marketing of products intended for human consumption.
- How big a team and what sort of expertise will Gannon require? What kind of research should they begin? When the press begins calling, should she and her team have coordinated statements with Kraft in advance?

The Value of Communication in a Crisis

Given the goals we spoke about in Chapter 9, the Crisis Communications Team in any crisis situation must understand why communication is the central tool for resolving the problem and protecting the brand. Communication has three principal functions in such circumstances:

To Inform. The primary task of communicators in a crisis is to provide accurate, timely, easy-to-understand information. The challenge is in finding the information to begin with, assuring that it is right, and then crafting statements that people can read and easily digest. And, as you've seen, events move quickly, public opinion shifts with little notice, and no two stakeholders have exactly the same interests. In addition to messaging, communicators are faced with the challenges of channel selection and impact measurement. Subject matter experts and skilled writers will be essential.

To Counteract Misinformation and Disinformation. Some portion of the Crisis Communications Team must be devoted to monitoring news, information, public statements, and opinion surveys from the world outside of the company. It won't be long before they discover print, broadcast, and social media statements that are mainly opinion offered as fact. They'll also encounter deliberate attempts to control the narrative by people and interests entirely separate from the principal actors in the crisis. Simple, clear proof that what you're saying is true will be a continuing requirement until the situation is permanently resolved.

To Persuade. A subtle but important question will arise when stakeholders be-gin asking "what you stand for." Should Laurie Gannon and Taco Bell become *advocates* for genetically modified ingredients? Knowing that both lettuce and tomatoes – a substantial portion of their menu board – are almost entirely modified in much of the Quick Service Restaurant (QSR) industry, what should corporate spokespersons advocate for? How far beyond simple, inform-ative, factual briefings, and talking points should they go? Whose help will they require and why should their audiences believe them?

Sometimes Silence Is the Better Option

On February 26, 2012, George Zimmerman, a 28-year-old mixed-race Hispanic neighborhood watch captain, shot and killed Trayvon Martin, a 17-year-old Black student, near Zimmerman's home in Sanford, Florida. The night of the shooting, Zimmerman sustained wounds to his nose and the back of his neck, and he told au-thorities that he shot Martin in self-defense. Charges were not initially filed against Zimmerman because no evidence was found refuting Zimmerman's story.[9]

Nearly a week and a half later, the shooting gained national media atten-tion because of two key facts: first, Trayvon Martin was Black and George Zim-merman was not; and second, Trayvon Martin was unarmed at the time of the shooting. In an interview published by Reuters, Benjamin Crump, a lawyer for Trayvon Martin's family, said that on the night of the shooting police found "a can of Arizona ice[d] tea in [Trayvon Martin's] jacket pocket and Skittles in his front pocket."[10]

During the first few days following Martin's death, the story was covered at a local level and received only minor national attention. That changed soon af-ter Reuters published more details about the shooting, and news spread quickly across various blogs and social media websites. The public instantly became out-raged that a teenager carrying only a bag of candy and a can of iced tea was killed but no charges had been brought against the adult who pulled the trigger.[11]

Skittles as a Protest Icon

On March 8, 2012, the day after Reuters published a wire service article, the story began to appear on popular gossip blogs such as Gawker and news blogs such as the *Huffington Post*. These articles and numerous social media posts re-peatedly claimed that Martin had been carrying Skittles, rather than a firearm.[12,13] #Skittles was trending and became one of the top 15 Trayvon Martin-related hashtags on Twitter.[14] In April 2012, Skittles was mentioned in approximately 1,600 tweets, an increase of 1,200 percent compared to the 133 mentions the brand received in April a year earlier.[15]

The mere presence of the candy on the night of the shooting, however, was not the only factor that made Skittles a central symbol of the tragedy and subsequent public outrage. Trayvon Martin was also carrying Arizona-brand iced tea at the time, but Arizona did not receive the same recognition as Skittles. The candy's bright colors and slogan, "Taste the Rainbow," gave Skittles a natural connection to youth and innocence. The association became important because many supporters believed that Martin was an innocent child killed while walking home from the gas station.[16]

In addition to becoming a flag at protests for Zimmerman's arrest, Skittles were used in other ways to call attention to the case and to offer support Martin's family. Filmmaker Spike Lee used Twitter to encourage his followers to send bags of Skittles to the Sanford Police Department to protest the lack of arrest.[17] On Facebook, many supporters posted pictures of themselves on the ground pretending to be shot while lying next to a bag of Skittles. Spelman College, a historically black women's college in Atlanta, began buying Skittles in bulk and reselling the candy individually for fifty cents a pack to raise money for the Martin family.[18] Some people even used the association between Skittles and Trayvon Martin for their own gain, selling unlicensed merchandise with the images of Martin and Skittles.

In light of all the attention and exposure the Skittles brand received, Mars, Inc., parent company and owner of the Skittles brand, remained silent. Although Mars is not a publicly traded company, sources close to the company acknowledged a spike in Skittles sales in the months following the shooting, which continued to grow as the conversations surrounding the incident escalated.[19] Many people began to wonder if Mars was deliberately profiting from the tragedy, and they demanded that the company speak up and get involved.

Initial Response From Mars

The theory that Mars was profiting from a tragedy created significant public backlash for the company. Mars initially attempted to abstain from any response regarding the tragedy; however, as calls for its involvement grew louder, the company was forced to comment. On March 22, 2012, Jennifer Jackson-Luth, a spokeswoman for Mars, released a statement:

> We are deeply saddened by the news of Trayvon Martin's death and express our sincere condolences to his family and friends. . . . We also respect their privacy and feel it inappropriate to get involved or comment further, as we would never wish for our actions to be perceived as an attempt of commercial gain following this tragedy.[20]

Mars Inc.'s response was met with pragmatic acceptance by industry peers and experts. Amy Stern, President of Bender Hammerling Group, a public relations firm that works with food companies, said that Mars acted exactly as it should have. Stephanie Child, former crisis manager for ConAgra Foods, implied that there was not a right move for Mars, noting that any misstep could lead to further backlash. Beth Gallant, a marketing professor at Lehigh University and former brand manager for Nabisco, Kraft, Pfizer, and Crayola, also acknowledged that this was a most unusual situation that would be very difficult for any company.[21]

Others, however, were not satisfied with the response, calling Mars "tone-deaf" and oblivious to the reality of the outside world. Even before Mars responded, many were calling for the company to donate its excess profits. This sentiment only intensified after the company released a formal response. A petition posted on Change.org requested that excess profits be donated to a nonprofit organization of Trayvon Martin's parents' choice.[22]

Many threatened a boycott if Mars did not agree to the donation of profits. Rashad Moore, a student at Morehouse College, suggested donating to underprivileged communities. Weldon McWilliams, a professor of African-American studies at Cheyney University of Pennsylvania, also called for a boycott if Mars did not donate to less fortunate communities.[23] Some even suggested a boycott due to the association Mars had with the American Legislative Exchange Council, a nonprofit organization that assisted with the legislation behind Florida's "stand your ground" law.[24] These views caught on with the general public who echoed them via social media websites.

Did Mars, Inc. Do the Right Thing?

Should Mars have remained silent in the face of public outrage, particularly since its product was only incidental to the events in Florida? Or, should have it spoken up, defending or promoting the brand? Should the company choose to become an advocate for racial justice in this case? Corporate officials were reluctant to speak on the record, but one said in confidence to the authors, "There is nothing we could say that would satisfy everyone. Any actions we take will offend one group or another." That official said he thought it best that the company continue its charitable work, keep producing products people enjoy, and maintain a low profile.

When events as tragic and riveting as the Trayvon Martin shooting become the subject of a national conversation, people on every side of an issue are hoping for others to join them as advocates for their cause. Brands are occasionally hijacked into the verbal fray in such instances, while others are besieged by activists who want a globally recognized name attached to the position or cause they care about. Nearly every organization will, at some time, be approached by people who think it's your job to promote what they want.

Communication and Crisis Goals

The issues involved in the Trayvon Martin case did not involve misconduct or malfeasance on the part of Mars, Inc. or Hornell Brewing Company, Inc., owner and manufacturer of Arizona Iced Tea. They were not obligated to speak publicly, nor required to adopt a position in the debate. In many, if not most, instances that grow into a business crisis, however, the enterprise involved will have some explaining to do, not only about what it has done but also about what it intends to do in pursuit of a solution.

A key crisis management goal is to get "permission" to solve the problem. Organizational credibility and legitimacy are central to obtaining that permission. Those two qualities can be established only through accurate, consistent, honest communication. Absent credibility and legitimacy, the problem may no longer be yours to solve. A regulatory agency or government official may simply take that away from you.

Arthur W. Page was a vice president and director of AT&T from 1927 to 1947 and is often thought of as the father of modern corporate communication. In his extensive writings on the subject, Page observed, "All business in a democratic country begins with public permission and exists by public approval."[25] Page further wrote, "Real success, both for big business and the public, lies in large enterprise conducting itself in the public interest and in such a way that the public will give it sufficient freedom to serve effectively."[26]

His principles for ethical public communication are now espoused as a cornerstone of contemporary corporate practice. The Arthur W. Page Society, named in his honor, is today the leading professional association for senior public relations and corporate communications executives and educators. The society advocates on behalf of the corporate chief communication officer and seeks to strengthen that role. Page's seven principles are these:

- **Tell the truth.** Let the public know what's happening with honest and good intention and provide an ethically accurate picture of the enterprise's character, values, ideals, and actions.
- **Prove it with action.** Public perception of an enterprise is determined 90 percent by what it does and 10 percent by what it says.
- **Listen to stakeholders.** To serve the enterprise well, understand what the public wants and needs and advocate for engagement with all stakeholders. Keep top decision makers and other employees informed about stakeholder reaction to the enterprise's products, policies, and practices. To listen effectively, engage a diverse range of stakeholders through inclusive dialogue.
- **Manage for tomorrow.** Anticipate public reaction and eliminate practices that create difficulties. Generate goodwill.
- **Conduct public relations as if the whole enterprise depends on it.** No strategy should be implemented without considering its impact on stakeholders. As a management and policymaking function, public relations should encourage the enterprise's decision-making, policies, and actions to consider its stakeholders' diverse range of views, values, experience, expectations, and aspirations.
- **Realize an enterprise's true character is expressed by its people.** The strongest opinions – good or bad – about an enterprise are shaped by the words

and deeds of an increasingly diverse workforce. As a result, every employee – active or retired – is involved with public relations. It is the responsibility of corporate communications to advocate for respect, diversity, and inclusion in the workforce and to support each employee's capability and desire to be an honest, knowledgeable ambassador to customers, friends, shareowners, and public officials.

- **Remain calm, patient, and good-humored.** Lay the groundwork for public relations successes with consistent and reasoned attention to information and stakeholders. When a crisis arises, remember, cool heads communicate best.[27]

References

1. Hall, J. and Viola, M. *Taco Bell Corporation: Public Perception and Brand Protection (A)*. Notre Dame, IN: Eugene D. Fanning Center for Business Communication, Mendoza College of Business, University of Notre Dame. 2003.
2. "Banned Corn in Taco Shells" Retrieved online: January 21, 2003. www.more.abc-news.go.com.
3. "Europe Approves New GM Rules" Retrieved online: April 18, 2003. http://news.bbc.co.uk/1/hi/world/europe/1167511.stm.
4. "Banned Corn in Taco Shells" Retrieved online: January 21, 2003. www.more.abc-news.go.com.
5. "Shell Shocked," *ABC News*. Retrieved online: January 21, 2003. http://INK"www.more.abcnews.go.com"www.more.abcnews.go.com.
6. "Kraft Foods Acquires Taco Bell Grocery Products Line" *Kraft Foods, Inc. press release*. August 1, 1996.
7. Telephone interview with Laurie Gannon at Taco Bell corporate headquarters. April 18, 2003.
8. Bluth, Andrew. "Taco Bell Selling Its Grocery Line to Kraft" *The Orange County Register*. August 2, 1996.
9. "Trayvon Martin Shooting Fast Facts." *CNN*. Turner Broadcasting System, n.d. Retrieved online: February 11, 2015. www.cnn.com/2013/06/05/us/trayvon-martin-shooting-fast-facts/
10. Liston, Barbara. "Family of Florida Boy Killed by Neighborhood Watch Seeks Arrest." *Reuters*. March 7, 2012. Retrieved online: February 7, 2015. http://reuters.com/article/idUSBRE82709M 20120308?irpc=932
11. Boylan, M.; Gibilisco, J.; and McCallum, D. *Mars, Inc.: Skittles Becomes Part of a Controversial Shooting*. Notre Dame, IN: Eugene D. Fanning Center for Business Communication, Mendoza College of Business, University of Notre Dame. 2015.
12. Lee, Trymaine. "Trayvon Martin's Family Calls For Arrest Of Man Who Police Say Confessed To Shooting," *The Huffington Post*, March 8, 2012. Retrieved online: February 6, 2015. www.huffingtonpost.com/2012/03/08/family-of-trayvon-martin-_n_1332756.html
13. Gold, Danny. "Unarmed Black Teen Gunned Down By Neighborhood Watch Leader After Being Deemed Suspicious," *Gawker*. Gawker Media Group, March 8, 2012.

Retrieved online: February 6, 2015. http://gawker.com/5891805/unarmed-black-teen-gunned-down-by-neighborhood-watch-leader-after-being-deemed-suspicious

14. "Trending Zimmerman-Trayvon Martin Hashtags and Tweets on Twitter," *Tweeting.com*. Tweeting, March 27, 2012. Retrieved online: February 6, 2015. http://tweeting.com/trending-zimmerman-trayvon-martin-hashtags-and-tweets-on-twitter

15. Crain's Chicago Business Twitter account. *Twitter*, April 27, 2012. Retrieved online: February 6, 2015. https://twitter. com/crainschicago/status/195946764933664768

16. Severson, Kim. "For Skittles, Death Brings Both Profit and Risk." *The New York Times*. The New York Times Company, March 28, 2012. Retrieved online: February 1, 2015. www.nytimes.com/2012/03/29/us/skittles-sales-up-after-trayvon-martin-shooting.html?_r=0

17. Johnson, Craig. "Skittles, Arizona Iced Tea Speak Out About Shooting." *HLNtv.com*. n.p., March 29, 2012. Retrieved online: February 10, 2015. www.hlntv.com/article/2012/03/22/skittles-speak-out-trayvon-martin-deeply-saddened

18. Alexander, Blayne. "Spelman Students sell Skittles for Trayvon Martin," *11Alive News*. NBC Atlanta, March 30, 2012. Retrieved online: February 6, 2015. www.11alive.com/news/article/235856/3/Spelman-students-sell-Skittles-for-Trayvon-Martin

19. Severson, Kim. op. cit.

20. NewsOne Staff. "Skittles Releases Statement On Trayvon Martin's Murder." *NewsOne*. Interactive One, March 22, 2013. Retrieved online: February 6, 2015. http://newsone.com/1951455/skittles-releases-statement-on-trayvon-martins-murder/

21. Severson, Kim. op. cit.

22. Caldwell, Emily. "Donate excess profits since Trayvon Martin's Death." *Change.org*. n.d. Retrieved online: February 6, 2015.www.change.org/p/makers-of-skittles-and-arizona-iced-tea-donate-excess-profits-sincetrayvon-martin-s-death

23. Ghosh, Palash. "Trayvon Martin's Death And Skittles: A Peculiar Marketing Dilemma." *International Business Times*, July 15, 2013. Retrieved online: February 6, 2015. www.ibtimes.com/trayvon-martins-death-skittles-peculiar-marketing-dilemma-1346469

24. "Stupid Is as Stupid Does: People Who Flocked To Buy Skittles Helped Fund Law That Gave George Zimmerman Excuse to Remain Free for 46 Days," *Axiom Amnesia*. The Axiom Amnesia Theory, April 14, 2012. Retrieved online: February 6, 2015. http://axiomamnesia.com/2012/04/14/people-flocked-buy-skittles-helped-fund-law-george-zimmerman-remain-free-46-days/.

25. Block, E. M. "The Legacy of Public Relations Excellence Behind the Name." Historical Perspective, the Arthur W. Page Society. Retrieved online: March 5, 2022. https://page.org/site/historical-perspective.

26. Arthur W. Page Society. "Mission, Vision, Philosophy." Retrieved online: March 5, 2022. https://page.org/site/vision-misson-goals.

27. Arthur W. Page Society. "The Page Principles." Retrieved online: March 5, 2022. https://page.org/site/the-page-principles.

Chapter 14

The Importance of Being Earnest

Just as communication is the primary tool in a crisis, language is the primary tool for communication. Effective crisis writing is much closer to journalism than to writing for promotional public relations, marketing, sales, or advertising. Crisis writing succeeds using accuracy, objectivity, evidence, and empathy. It fails in the presence of slickness, euphemism, smugness, or spin. When George Orwell wrote in his famous essay "Politics and The English Language" that words are "an instrument we shape for our own purposes," he did not intend to praise our skill with language but to warn us to use honest words with clear intent.[1]

What types of writing are required in a crisis? Plenty, such as official company statements, CEO messages, apologies, executive remarks, news releases, briefings for executives, decision analyses, presentation slides, data analyses, fact sheets for the customer relations team, letters to employees, memos to business partners, HR policy changes, and congressional testimony. That's not all. Consider communications to stakeholders, internal Q-&-As, external FAQs, website copy, op-eds, letters to the editor, advertising copy, video scripts, photo captions, brief holding statements, Facebook posts, and of course, tweets. Each has its own technique.

Journalists are among the most important consumers of an organization's prose during a crisis. They are the lens through which an organization is viewed by the public. Organizations in crisis that speak and emulate the structure and language of journalism and understand its requirements for information will enable both reporters and crisis communicators to do their jobs more effectively, and that benefits everyone.

A company news release or statement should use basic journalistic structure and style. Newswriting must position and prioritize the key details in a form that journalists are accustomed to seeing and are, therefore, less likely to misinterpret. Journalistic writing is frequently structured as an inverted pyramid. At the top of the broad structure are the most important or newsworthy details (who, what, when, where, and why). A second paragraph is often a direct quotation from someone significant to the story or expressive of the main point. The next paragraph or two will detail the most crucial facts of the story, followed by less important detail and background right to the end.[2]

DOI: 10.4324/9781003322849-18

Journalists strive for simple and brief forms of expression so that their audiences can easily grasp their meaning in a single read. Short and simple words are the easiest to understand. Newswriting also employs short sentences and short paragraphs to maintain readers' interest. A paragraph containing a long and dense column of words is intimidating to readers, so most reporter's paragraphs are two or three sentences, sometimes just one. Another useful trait of journalism for organizations writing in a crisis is its emphasis on objectivity and facts. Objectivity is the lack of opinion or apparent bias. A company's news release that contains a description of the circumstances of its crisis should be presented matter-of-factly. Statistics and facts can serve as valuable objective evidence.[3]

In addition to writing with a journalistic structure and style, here are a few additional pointers for effective crisis writing.

When to Use Quotations

A newswriting style that emphasizes structure, simplicity, and objectivity is greatly strengthened by using direct quotations. While opinion and emotion have no place in a description of the facts of a crisis, a direct quote from a company leader in humble language can provide the feelings and thinking of the organization. Personal thoughts expressed by leadership – in quotation marks – can add context and enhance understanding of the company's viewpoint for employees and other insiders and for those outside who are evaluating its actions. Sentences in a news release's body copy such as, "We feel we have let our customers down. The company is working tirelessly through our dedicated team to make things right again for our customers as soon as humanly possible," are flat wrong for body copy. Instead, attribute these words to a company leader in the news release to add power. At the same time, keep facts and statistics in the body copy of a news release to maintain credibility and objectivity. Reserve quotes for insights, sentiments, and context.

Signed executive messages are, essentially, one big quotation. A signed piece adds personality and personal commitment. The downside is that providing the news media with an 800-word CEO message gives them too much to choose from. Accompany the message with a few important pull quotes, or put the top quotes in a complementary news release that explains the context of the message. For example: In a message to employees explaining the company's recent turnaround, CEO Bob Roberts said ". . . ."

Get It Right the First Time

In Chapter 3, "Set Up a Rapid Response Team Process," and later in this book, we recommend communicating with reporters during a crisis only via email. Email exchanges with a reporter remove any doubt about who said what and greatly reduce the chance that a spokesperson will be misquoted regarding a sensitive topic. Email allows a spokesperson to use approved language, which is especially important for legal matters. All emails should be meticulously proofread for errors in spelling and punctuation. An email is the written ambassador of the writer, and correct grammar and usage convey respect from the sender to the recipient.

Accuracy in crisis writing extends beyond proofreading to the facts used in any materials. Check and double-check the facts using experts and other resources that can validate them. Shortcuts cause mistakes. Considering the stakes in a crisis, the need for speed in the 24-hour news cycle is no excuse for a factual error.

Be Sincere. Be Brief. Be Seated

Rick Schostek, former Executive Vice President of American Honda Motor Co., Inc., was fond of admonishing his direct reports to be brief: "If I ask you the time of day, don't tell me how to build a watch."[4] Anything written by an organization in crisis is fair game for quotation by the news media. So, keep it brief. The fewer words used, the more likely the media will be to use the words they are given. Offering them too many choices to quote dilutes what little control one has in a crisis.[5]

Keep all your messages focused squarely on the central ideas you want to communicate and the outcomes you want to achieve. Eliminate any words, phrases, or sentences that do not directly support the points you want to make. Strunk and White's words about brevity and conciseness would make a good screen saver:

> Vigorous writing is concise. A sentence should contain no unnecessary words, a paragraph no unnecessary sentences, for the same reason that a drawing should have no unnecessary lines and a machine no unnecessary parts. This requires not that the writer make all sentences short or avoid all detail and treat subjects only in outline, but that every word tell.[6]

Your Authentic Voice

Effective crisis writing requires an honest voice that will put aside any corporate pretense and break through to the intended audience in a way that is relatable to them in human terms. If writing to employees in a crisis, tell them in real terms what is being done to fix the current predicament. Do not sugarcoat the negatives. Own up to customers that you made a mistake. Talk about your desire to restore trust and faith, and even ask forgiveness because you are determined that the problems you are facing will never happen again. Ask to be judged by your actions going forward. Transparency and candor go a long way to restoring confidence in your organization. Above all, no matter the audience, constantly reinforce that you are being true to the purpose and values of the organization, and repeat frequently that they are the foundation of every step you are taking to right the ship.

Empathy

Writing with empathy in a crisis starts with an understanding of your audience. What do they expect of us? Do we already have an established relationship? How does the crisis affect them? What questions do they have about our crisis? Do they still trust us? Empathy springs from an understanding of how your audience might think and feel about your actions and from your ability to acknowledge their viewpoint. An audience that cares about a company in crisis will expect that the company's leaders care as well. Allow that employees in a crisis may feel insecure about their compensation, job security, or even the future of their company. Acknowledge those sentiments in honest terms and express realistic confidence in the outcome. Recognize that customers may feel let down and tell them you understand why they may be angry.

Empathy can be reciprocal. A company in crisis that constantly communicates to its employees and that, at every chance publicly, thanks them for their efforts and patience may be viewed as compassionate and caring. Going to extraordinary measures to actively listen to customers' concerns 24/7 may be viewed favorably. Generosity in righting wrongs by providing fast refunds and offering substantial incentives to retain business may engender goodwill and even forgiveness. An organization under siege by the news media may elicit a *little* empathy from its customers if that media treatment appears unfair or too harsh.

The best way to achieve empathy from your audience is to keep working hard to solve your problem and keep communicating with them in a transparent, authentic voice. They may appreciate your seriousness of intent and give you some leeway because you are doing the best you can. But do not *ever* expect, or imply, that anyone should feel sorry for you. The best you can expect is the benefit of the doubt. Take it and be thankful.

Both empathy and authenticity are uniquely important to success in social media because of the conversational relationship between an organization and its customers and stakeholders. We'll discuss that dynamic in Chapter 19, "Social Media Has Changed the Crisis Communication Landscape."

Use Figurative Language – Sparingly

One of President Abraham Lincoln's slogans in his 1864 reelection campaign was "Don't change horses in midstream." During the turmoil of the Civil War, the reasoning went, it would be foolish to change leaders in such turbulent times. The 19th century voters got it. In fact, dismounting a horse in the middle of a river has nothing to do with keeping an incumbent president in office. Analogies compare something unfamiliar (presidential politics) with something familiar (crossing a fast-running stream on horseback), and that makes analogies persuasive. Analogies do not explain what something is, but rather what something resembles, and improve understanding of unfamiliar ideas.

Like most figurative language in crisis writing, analogies belong only within quotation marks. The CEO of a company that is losing market share might compare the market to "a field in need of cultivation." A company's long comeback from a crisis might be "running a marathon we are determined to win." Make sure that any analogy is a close match for the comparison being made and avoid trite and clichéd expressions. Remember, analogies prove nothing, but if they're fresh, they can make a complex point more understandable.

References

1. Orwell, G. "Politics and the English Language," April, 1946. Retrieved online: August 26, 2022. www.orwell.ru/library/essays/politics/english/e_polit/
2. "Journalistic Writing," The University of Arizona Global Campus Writing Center. 2022. Retrieved online: August 26, 2022. https://writingcenter.uagc.edu/journalistic-writing
3. Ibid.
4. Rick Schostek, via email. September 13, 2022.
5. "Be sincere, be brief, be seated." – Franklin D Roosevelt Book Browse. 2002. Retrieved online: August 28, 2020. www.bookbrowse.com/quotes/detail/index.cfm/quote_number/415/be-sincere-be-brief-be-seated
6. Strunk, W. and White, E. *The Elements of Style*. New York. The Penguin Press. 2005. p. 39.

Chapter 15

Put Your Employees First

Employees are, without question, the primary stakeholders of any organization faced with a public crisis. They can be both the most supportive ambassadors for an organization under fire or the most authentic of adversaries. Workers who vocalize their backing for a company during a crisis can create a groundswell of trustworthy grassroots support among neighbors and friends and on social media. At the same time, employees who are left uninformed by their organization about a controversial issue that is playing out in the media will feel mistrusted and alienated. Organizations in a crisis benefit from employees who are both informed and engaged, led by decisive and empathetic leaders, rallying around the prospect of a return to normalcy.

For Zenia Mucha, the recently retired Senior Executive Vice President and Chief Communications Officer of The Walt Disney Company, the number one asset needed by a company and its employees during a crisis is established trust.

"One of the most important things that our CEO Robert A. Iger stressed with all of us in leadership roles is the need to build trust with our employees," Mucha said.[1]

With more than 200,000 employees and 12 Disney theme parks located throughout the world, the potential for a crisis is high. Mucha said,

> The issues and potential problems that we faced daily as a company are somewhat similar to those of a midsized city. Operational issues such as safety, transportation, and first-rate service are important to employees and guests. A company needs to be nimble, and with so many moving parts, a strong relationship with your employee bases is critical.[2]
>
> When a situation develops that is out of your control, having employees work together with management to quickly address it can result in mitigating the issue quickly.[3]

Why are employees so important in a crisis? To Mucha, "Employees are your first line of defense. They are your frontline ambassadors that define the brand through their work and dedication. They are the personal connection that the brand has to the consumer."[4]

DOI: 10.4324/9781003322849-19

"Race Together"

Starbucks employees in green aprons everywhere found themselves in the glare of negative publicity as the Reuters wire service lede on March 18, 2015, reported:

> Starbucks Corp Chief Executive Howard Schultz has deftly navigated thorny issues such as gay marriage, gun control and Congressional gridlock, but his move to weigh in on U.S. race relations has brewed up a social media backlash.
>
> The world's biggest coffee chain kicked off the discussion when it published full-page ads in major U.S. newspapers earlier this week with the words "Shall We Overcome?" at center page and "Race Together" and the Starbucks logo near the bottom.
>
> Employees behind the counter were also given the option of writing "Race Together" on customers' coffee cups to help initiate dialog amid simmering racial tensions in the United States.[5]

The program directly engaged Starbucks employees in an issue important to the publicly minded CEO and was a bold initiative for such a high-profile company that backfired badly.

What is now the Starbucks Corporation began in 1971 as a roaster and retailer of whole bean and ground coffee, tea, and spices with a single store in Seattle's Pike Place Market. The company is named after the steadfast first mate in Herman Melville's *Moby Dick*, and the logo is inspired by the sea, featuring a twin-tailed mermaid. Starbucks offers more than 30 blends and single-origin coffees, hot and iced espresso beverages, and teas as well as pastries, sandwiches, salads, protein boxes, yogurt, and snacks. Starbucks operates more than 34,000 stores in 84 countries.[6]

The issue of race in America had been flaring since July 13, 2013, when George Zimmerman was acquitted of second-degree murder and manslaughter in the death of Trayvon Martin, an unarmed Black teenager who was shot during a scuffle in a gated Florida neighborhood.[7] The Black Lives Matter movement grew in prominence and was fueled in August 2014, when a white policeman in Ferguson, Missouri, shot an unarmed Black 18-year-old male. Additional police-involved shootings of unarmed Black men followed in Madison, Wisconsin, and New York City.[8]

Starbucks's CEO Howard Schultz had always worked hard to engage his employees and maintain their loyalty (Starbucks employees are referred to as "partners"). He extended full health benefits and a stock option program to part-time workers, refused to cut health benefits in the face of board pressure during lagging sales, and established a program to provide college tuition to full- and part-time partners who attend Arizona State University online.[9]

Schultz never shied away from taking positions on controversial social and political issues. He urged corporate leaders to cease political contributions when Congress became gridlocked over a deficit plan. Religious groups boycotted his products when he supported same-sex marriage, and he rejected states' open carry laws by asking customers to stop bringing guns into Starbucks stores.[10]

Motivated by the social justice movement sweeping the country in 2014, Schultz dove headfirst into the race issue by holding partner forums in Seattle, Oakland, St. Louis, and New York City. Kicking off the Seattle partner forum at Starbucks headquarters, Schultz told his employees, "If we just keep going about our business and ringing the Starbucks register every day, then I think we're, in a sense, part of the problem." Forum participants shared personal stories, experiences, heartbreak, hardships, and ideas. The partner forums were emotional, stimulating conversation, empathy, and compassion. Many partners appreciated the initiative and were grateful to their employer for engaging in collective dialogue over such an emotionally charged issue during a period of social upheaval.[11]

Based largely on the positive feedback from the internal partner forums, the "Race Together" public initiative was born to encourage a national dialogue about race at a time when civil unrest was dominating the news. Starbucks launched the campaign in full-page ads in *USA Today* and *The New York Times*. An internal memo urged its baristas to voluntarily write the words "Race Together" on the beverage cups they served customers and then engage them in conversations about race over the course of a week. Although there was no formal training, talking points were provided to the coffee servers to help facilitate the dialogue.

The Instagram hashtag #RaceTogether was initiated through @StarbucksPartners, which had more than 76,000 Starbucks employee and enthusiast followers. The hashtag #RaceTogether, however, was not launched on the main @Starbucks handle, perhaps signaling some internal sensitivity that the campaign was risky.[12] Advocating the campaign in an internal video to Starbucks employees, Schultz said the act of writing "Race Together" on coffee cups could "create and elevate a conversation in our stores that could go well beyond our stores."[13]

Negative reaction online to the Race Together initiative was immediate and enormous. Nearly three-fifths of the 79,000 social media first-day mentions of the campaign were negative. The commanding sentiment was that Starbucks was exploiting the complex issue of racism for the sake of publicity.[14]

Reuters reported that the campaign "has been met with snark and skepticism on social media, with many complaining the company was overstepping its boundaries with a campaign on sensitive cultural topics that had no place in the coffee shop's lines."[15]

"Honest to God, if you start to engage me in a race conversation before I've had my morning coffee, it will not end well," tweeted *PBS NewsHour* anchor Gwen Ifill. HBO's *Last Week Tonight* host John Oliver blasted the campaign for being tone-deaf and patronizing.[16] Writing in a *Time.com* column, former NBA star Kareem Abdul-Jabbar, a frequent commenter on racial matters, questioned Schultz's execution of the plan: "He's picked the wrong venue with the wrong audience using the wrong spokespersons."[17] Still other critics panned the company for urging its relatively low-wage partners to engage in such emotionally burden-some work.[18]

Scott Kleinberg, former social media editor at the *Chicago Tribune*, wrote, "There are certain conversations that, while important, are not meant to be started by baristas making a $5 drink for customers who are still wiping the sleep from their eyes while rushing to an early morning meeting."[19]

This tweet, purportedly from a Starbucks partner on the front lines, sums up the problem:

> Being a barista is hard enough. Having to talk #RaceTogether with a woman in Lululemon pants while pouring pumpkin spice is just cruel.
> ~ Ijeoma Oluo (@IjeomaOluo) March 17, 2015[20]

Unintentionally, Schultz had thrust Starbucks employees into an awkward and potentially charged situation. They might be at risk of offending or annoying customers. What if an employee chose not to participate? What does that say about them? In his 2019 autobiography *From the Ground Up*, Schultz reflected on partners' reaction to the Race Together program:

> "When we polled our store partners, many aired their displeasure, calling the effort divisive, embarrassing, and poorly explained," Schultz wrote. "It's true the execution was sloppy, not properly sequenced, and too swift, no question."
>
> "The truth is that I threw Starbucks onto the third rail of society in a way that put an unfair burden on baristas and store managers," he wrote. "These discussions needed to be had, but not in the way we had them."[21]

To his credit, however, Schultz was quick to assess the damage, and he managed the internal crisis communication with great skill and empathy. He immediately followed up with employees and owned the problem. On both the Starbucks internal website and the public website, he restated the goals of the Race Together effort. He thanked Starbucks partners for their efforts on the campaign and detailed other initiatives the company was taking to address racial inequality. He also reminded partners that writing "Race Together" on cups had been planned as a week-long initiative from the start, blunting growing speculation that the campaign had been dropped.[22]

"I want to offer my heartfelt thanks to every one of you for your fearless and energetic support of the Race Together initiative," Schultz wrote to his employees. "While there has been criticism of the initiative – and I know this hasn't been easy for any of you – let me assure you that we didn't expect universal praise."[23]

He added, "An issue as tough as racial and ethnic inequality requires risk-taking and tough-minded action. And let me reassure you that our conviction and commitment to the notion of equality and opportunity for all has never been stronger."[24]

Align and Time Your Messaging

By making the internal memo to Starbucks's partners public, Howard Schultz took a proactive approach to align his messages. In so doing, he lined up his communication strategies for handling the crisis both within the company and with outside stakeholders. Starbucks partners and the news media all received the same message, at the same time, a best practice in crisis communications that shows respect for employees and transparency to the public.

Auto plant workers commuting to their factory for the 7:00 a.m. morning shift should not be hearing for the first time about layoffs at their company from their AM drive-time radio station. Mid-level managers at a financial services firm should not be informed by the news feed on their smart phones that their CEO has been indicted. University professors should not be alerted by Twitter that all classes will switch to online in the fall. Bank employees should not first hear about their branch closing from a Google News feed. Hospital staff walking to work on a New York City street should not first see allegations of mismanagement at their facility on newsstand headlines.

Why give a heads-up about bad news to your employees? Why distract them with matters in which they may have no apparent stake? Why get everybody gossiping when they should be working? Besides, maybe nobody will hear about it. Better to keep a lid on it, right? That may well have been the case in the heyday of daily newspapers, radio, and television. But in the fast-moving digital age, with hyper-local information available and pushed out on social media and online platforms 24/7, failure to keep employees informed of bad news before they hear about it elsewhere is, well, bad news.

At Disney, as Zenia Mucha notes, trust is the most important part of the relationship between the organization and its employees. Trust is the intangible bond that leads people to have faith that others will act as they should and do what they say they will do. If you trust your doctor, you are more likely to benefit from their professional advice. If you trust your spouse, that will generate positive feelings and create self-assurance that they will behave in supportive ways. If you trust your employer, you will have confidence that its leadership will consider your welfare, even in tough times. Trust results in loyalty.

Leaving it to the news media or social media to inform your employees about a crisis in your organization can boomerang in several negative ways. Uninformed employees will immediately crank up the rumor mill. Why didn't they tell us? What are they hiding? Do they think we are children? Keeping employees in the dark breeds mistrust, which leads to skepticism, suspicion, low morale, and a lack of support.

A transparent approach has the opposite effect. Trusting your employees to hear bad news from you immediately establishes your credibility with them. Treating them like adults who can handle bad news will make them feel like insiders. Trusted with information and treated as members of a family in trouble, they may have an enhanced sense of belonging. Furthermore, being the first to inform your workers of a problem allows you to shape and influence the vocabulary, direction, and velocity of the public conversation. Certainly, this offers more control than you would have when trying to play catch-up, backpedaling with employees by having to explain a mischaracterization or factual error in media reports about your crisis.

A good rule of thumb concerning bad news is *get it out fast and get it out first*. At the very least, communicate with your employees about your crisis at the same time you release your first statement to the news media and other stakeholders. Preferably, give information to employees a little earlier but not too much in advance to allow an employee to leak it. As you post your initial statement to your media website, post it on your internal website as well. Employees should receive the same information you release to the news media. In some cases, employees may require additional details related to the crisis, such as company policies or the availability of counseling, and these can be included on your internal site as well. One caution: there is no such thing as a strictly internal memo, letter, or story on your internal website. Trust your employees, but do not be naïve. Avoid saying or writing anything to your employees that you would not be comfortable seeing on the front page of the *Los Angeles Times*.

As we have discussed earlier, quick communication is often required when reacting to a crisis, particularly in the early stages. While it is important to get information out fast, to both internal and external audiences, it should never be done at the expense of accuracy. Candor, transparency, and straightforwardness are essential, but if key information is missing, say so, and pledge to release it as soon as it's confirmed.

Put Leaders Up Front

A company in crisis should deploy its top leadership to communicate with employees both frequently and in several forms. If the CEO is the "face" of the crisis to news media and others, then the CEO should be the primary communicator with employees. Even if a different high-ranking company official is serving in that primary role, the CEO should still be visible with employees in some meaningful capacity, such as an early letter to employees on the organization's website, perhaps expressing assurance that the crisis will be resolved and expressing confidence in the executive who is serving as the "face."

Rather than relying on just one leader to communicate with employees, using several company leaders in this capacity will add to the perception of company transparency and openness for employees. A team of influential leaders can be used in various forms of communication to employees to give the accurate impression that the entire organization is committed to solving the problem. A straightforward written or video message on the company website from the CEO or other key leader is one obvious option. But how about an interview with the head of human resources about employment issues related to the crisis? Perhaps a signed article from the head of government relations could address how the crisis is playing out in Washington. A plant manager could produce a short video on production impact. A taped discussion between two leaders about the company's future could add yet another angle to the worrisome issue on everyone's minds.

Amy Edmondson is the Novartis Professor of Leadership and Management at the Harvard Business School, where she studies teaming, psychological safety, and organizational learning. Her most recent book is *The Fearless Organization: Creating Psychological Safety in the Workplace for Learning, Innovation and Growth.* Regarding the benefits of integrating numerous leaders into a crisis response, Edmondson said in an interview, "Involving several company leaders has the added benefit of modeling the kind of teamwork at the top that is needed by all – specifically teams that are aligned around purpose while allocating different roles to those with appropriate expertise."[25]

Think about messaging. Having decided to use the leadership team in a major way to address employees about a crisis, what do you want them to say?

- Leaders should convey a sense of urgency that the organization is committed to solving the problem and solving it quickly.
- As leaders, they should express both accountability for the ultimate outcome and complete ownership of the problem. Employees will view any finger-pointing or pleading "victim" as signs of weakness and a lack of commitment.
- Leaders should try to anticipate the concerns of the workforce and the questions they would ask and should attempt to address them before they are asked. In the same light, leaders should be empathetic (for example, Howard Schultz of Starbucks: "I know this hasn't been easy for any of you") and not hesitate to acknowledge employee anxiety and uncertainty about the crisis.
- Being appreciative of employees' efforts is an effective way to express a sense of togetherness and unity during difficult times. A thank you from the top goes a long way with employees.
- In her *TED Business* talk, Professor Edmondson advises leaders to "be transparent – about what you know and what you don't, as well as what you are doing to learn more."[26]
- Be hopeful. In the middle of a crisis – with an uncertain outcome and such concerns as unrelenting negative media coverage, nervous investors, and sagging sales – things can look pretty bleak to employees.

To this final point, just when things are looking dour may be the time for a leader to invoke Harvard Professor Rosabeth Moss Kanter's well-known "Kanter's Law," which states, in part, that "everything looks like a failure in the middle." In other words, it may look bad now, but it *will* get much better. With confidence and optimism, leaders should keep their employees up-to-date on progress toward solving the crisis and communicate their vision of what the organization will look like once the crisis is resolved.[27]

Another way to engender trust in leadership and maintain a sense of openness with employees during a crisis is to engage in two-way communication. Face-to-face leadership forums, along with Q-&-A sessions for employees, will require extensive preparation, but these are well worth the effort. We all know that not many employees will stand up and ask a question, and others will be especially reticent about a sensitive topic. But there is great power in the fact that they are given the opportunity to do so. Equally effective is leadership's willingness to stand on the dais and face the questions.

In addition to in-person forums, employees can be given the opportunity to ask questions about the crisis online or via email, which can then be consolidated by topic and answered by a key leader in a posted Q-&-A. An added benefit is that soliciting questions from employees may surface themes or employee concerns previously unknown by management. Differing viewpoints exist on whether such questions should be anonymous. Most (not all) employees who know their names will be attached to their questions tend to avoid submitting personal diatribes or craziness. However, anonymous questions give employees the opportunity to vent and express frustration or concerns without fear of retaliation.

Over-Communicate to Employees

An aggressive approach to internal communication during a crisis will help insure employees are at least well-informed and, preferably, engaged. With some exceptions, employees generally will not approach leadership to ask about the status of a crisis, out of shyness or just not wanting to interfere during a difficult time. But employee reluctance to step forward does not equal disinterest. The communication team's role is to provide solid, reliable, and consistent information and perspective, at a much more frequent cadence than during normal times. In crisis situations that involve operational matters, such as disrupted production or supply issues, establishing a standard cadence of crisis-related updates will allow employees to know when to expect the latest news.

The information overload threshold is far more forgiving during times of crisis, so organizations need not worry about continually repeating key messages to make sure they are understood and everyone is on the same page. A remote work environment and sense of detachment that can accompany it underscore the need to over-communicate. Field service workers can often feel out of the loop. Whether deploying key leadership or posting status updates on the internal website, a company must work hard to ensure that everyone is reached, and reached repeatedly, using all available internal channels to explain the organization's status and viewpoint.

What if there is no news? Don't go dark. An information vacuum feeds the rumor mill and causes distraction and loss of productivity. In the absence of information, employees may overreact and speculate that something is wrong. Such breaks in the action during a crisis can present opportunities for various members of the leadership team to step forward and communicate to reinforce the organization's key messages to employees.

In Case of Emergency

The unending operational and policy changes during the worst of the COVID pandemic taught many organizations the value of a mass employee notification system, along with the hazards of not having one. For urgent and fast-breaking matters, several mass notification services now exist that allow organizations to communicate proactively with their entire rank and file. Providers such as Everbridge, RedFlag, AlertMedia, Rave Alert, OnSolve and Hyper-Reach are among them. Look for a service that emphasizes simplicity, speed, and reliability.

Mass communication to employees concerning work delays or other disruptions to the normal flow of work should always include any changes to the pay status of workers. For example, if production plant workers are suddenly alerted to remain home because of severe weather, they should be informed whether they will be paid for their time. Employees left guessing about their pay status are likely to take to social media and start speculating, causing unnecessary worry.

Crisis Communication With Deskless Workers

Whether you operate a repetitive assembly line creating thousands of copies of the same product or a job shop producing made-to-order goods, most manufacturing environments share the challenge of how to effectively communicate with often thousands of employees who do not use computers at work. Exceptions are easy to find, but production workers generally do not have company email or company smart phones. Most have personal cell phones and private email at home; the practice of using these private channels to communicate with employees after work varies widely.

But what about during the work day? A production environment usually has quite a bit going on. In a bustling engineering and technical environment, communication often takes a back bench. With production quotas to maintain, time to read a letter about a business crisis from the CEO or watch a video is scarce. Many plants have prominently posted closed-circuit televisions throughout their facilities. Some plants maintain banks of computer kiosks that feature the company's internal website that workers can access during breaks. More sophisticated plants maintain a system of networked one-way monitors, including sound, that are used for technical training and special announcements. Such lineside training systems can be helpful for crisis communication as well.

None of these methods is perfect. The most effective crisis communication in a manufacturing environment is human interaction. At the top level, plant leadership should engage workers in two-way communication forums during work hours to make sure the company's crisis messages are heard and understood. Further down the chain, mid-level managers need to be well-equipped with updates, messages, and talking points so they can have informative discussions with their teams and smaller group leaders as they practice what some companies refer to as Management by Walking Around (MBWA). Manufacturing top leadership and mid-level management often have a distinctive technical skill set that does not include communication, and with such a challenging environment, interpersonal communication training for these leaders is strongly advised.

HR's Role

Whether in an office, manufacturing, or remote work environment, human resources plays a central role in effective crisis communication with employees. The HR team should be equipped with a robust and up-to-date Q-&-A document specifically focused on employee treatment and policy matters related to the crisis that can be used to answer employee questions. Working as part of the Crisis Communications Team, HR should serve as the voice and perspective of employees to those who are developing crisis communication materials.

Employees need a safe place to provide feedback and to express concerns and anxiety. HR's role in this respect also allows it to serve as a sensing function that can anonymously report employee morale issues and concerns to the Crisis Communications Team and to other company leadership.

Employees and Social Media

Conflicting opinions exist on whether to encourage employees to express their views on social media during a crisis involving their organization. It's a difficult question. On the one hand, the public may consider employees to be a more trusted and reliable source of candid information than pronouncements from the organization in crisis. Social media cannot and should not be blocked because employees will speak out. We would hope they will do so, consistent with the organization's social media policy. But that's different from encouraging and empowering them to do so. Arguably a well-informed employee who is encouraged by their organization to weigh in on social media and express the company's views might be publicly perceived as a truthful and dependable source of information or viewpoints.

On the other hand, legal issues and other delicate nuances are often layered within the complexities of crisis communication. The organization's designated spokespersons are aware of these subtleties and are schooled in how to handle them. A Master Q-&-A should be developed and updated daily, with each word carefully parsed by the legal team. Details and new developments often change daily. In a global organization, the occurrences can be market-by-market, and only the Crisis Communications Team is aware of, or should be aware of, the total picture. How can a member of the rank and file possibly be expected to stay current on all this?

With some frequency, an employee officially authorized by an organization to engage on social media about a crisis will get it wrong in one way or another, and their blunder could become a news story. On balance, our counsel is to never stop an employee from going on social media in a manner consistent with the organization's social media policy, which usually requires employees to stipulate that they do not officially represent the organization. At the same time, it is too risky to license or officially encourage them to do so.

We'll have more to say on this in Chapter 19, "Social Media Has Changed the Crisis Communication Landscape."

The Mouse and the Storm

Occasionally, a company and its employees are given the opportunity to work together to alleviate a crisis.

Hurricane Irma was a Category 1 storm when it reached Orlando, Florida, in September, 2017. Walt Disney World shuttered and closed its theme parks and water parks early on September 9 and kept them closed for the next few days. In the resort's 45-year history, it was only the 6th full-day park closure due to weather.

With the parks closed, many guests found themselves stranded in Disney hotels with their children. Some remained because they could not get flights out of Orlando in time to avoid the storm. Guests who lived nearby remained in their hotels because of the design strength of Disney's facilities and access to reliable supplies of electricity, food, and water. Some Disney employees hunkered down in Disney hotels because they felt unsafe in their own homes. Disney provided rooms to first responders as well. As the storm was approaching, some local residents were able to book rooms at Disney hotels because they believed them to be a safe haven.[28]

One such local resident felt lucky to book a room as she and her young family evacuated their home a few miles from Disney World and moved into a Disney hotel for the duration. She blogged that "Disney was a well-oiled machine."[29]

Zenia Mucha explained, "Senior citizens and other members of the community who were living in and around the area came to our hotels to ride out the storm. We had our own city, so to speak, our own generators, our own transportation system."[30]

Due to Walt Disney World's location in north central Florida, this was not Disney's first hurricane. Disney employees, known as "cast members," can volunteer to join the "Hurricane Ride Out Crew" and remain to help guests weather a storm. For Hurricane Irma, they stepped up to assist guests during a hazardous time, and even added a little Disney magic. Cast members helped quickly evacuate thousands from the parks on the first day. Hotel lobbies became gathering places for stranded guests as the winds and rain battered the property. For two days, cast members held impromptu singing and dancing sessions in lobbies full of children, did crafts, hula hooped, and played games with and entertained the stranded senior citizens. Disney characters always entertain families in the hotel lobbies during hurricanes, unless a shelter-in-place order is in effect. Hurricane Irma was no exception, and characters were out in force everywhere, interacting with families, dancing, and posing for photographs, much more so than on a normal Disney day.[31]

The young Orlando mother who sought shelter with her family wrote,

> I think the biggest thing needed during a crisis is compassion. And Disney compassion was beyond our dreams: staff went above and beyond to make guests feel at ease. To the cashier that let my husband have a free oatmeal in the morning to the greeters that never failed to call my daughter a princess, we felt like Disney's family.[32]

Mucha said,

> It was over and above on the part of our cast members. That kind of thing is not in their job description, right? But they were proud to be part of helping the community through that crisis and showing that their company has compassion for people within the community that they live and work in.[33]

On September 12, The Walt Disney Company committed $2.5 million to aid in humanitarian relief efforts across Florida and other areas impacted by Hurricane Irma, including a separate dollar-for-dollar matching gift program so cast members could donate as well.[34] As the storm passed on September 14, Walt Disney World Resort President George Kalogridis announced that every cast member who lost a shift due to the hurricane would be paid for the cancelled shift.[35]

"Those are the kinds of things that, as a company, you do that extend beyond your core mission. They define you to the employees and bond you in a way that you couldn't do in just an everyday situation," Mucha said.[36]

References

1. Interview with Zenia B. Mucha, via Zoom. July 7, 2022.
2. Ibid.
3. Ibid.
4. Ibid.
5. Baertlein, L. and Rigby, B. "Starbucks Brews Backlash with Debate on U.S. Race Relations." *Reuters.* March 18, 2015. Retrieved online: July 14, 2022. www.reuters.com/article/us-starbucks-ceo-race-relations/starbucks-brews-backlash-with-debate-on-u-s-relations-idUSKBN0ME2MQ20150318

6. Starbucks. "About Us – Company Profile." May 5, 2022. Retrieved online: July 15, 2022. https://stories.starbucks.com/uploads/2022/05/AboutUs-Company-Profile-5.5.22.pdf

7. "Trayvon Martin." *Wikipedia*. Retrieved online: July 14, 2022. https://en.wikipedia.org/wiki/Trayvon_Martin

8. Baertlein. op. cit.

9. Carr, A. "The Inside Story of Starbucks's Race Together Campaign, No Foam." *Fast Company*. June 15, 2015. Retrieved online: July 14, 2022. www.fastcompany.com/3046890/the-inside-story-of-starbuckss-race-together-campaign-no-foam

10. Ibid.

11. Ibid.

12. Meyer, K. "Crisis Management 101: Starbucks Stirs the Pot with #RaceTogether Campaign." *Medium.com*. January 14, 2016. Retrieved online: July 14, 2022. https://medium.com/the-social-reader/crisis-management-101-did-the-good-intentions-behind-starbucks-racetogether-pay-off-d39ffc6ece70

13. Ibid.

14. Parsi, N. "Communicating with Employees during a Crisis." *HR Today*. October 25, 2016. Retrieved online: July 14, 2022. www.shrm.org/hr-today/news/hr-magazine/1116/pages/communicating-with-employees-during-a-crisis.aspx

15. Baertlein. op. cit.

16. Ibid.

17. Abdul-Jabbar, K. "Starbucks' Flawed But Wonderful Plan to Tackle Race." *Time.com*. March 18, 2015. Retrieved online: July 14, 2022. https://time.com/3749633/kareem-abdul-jabbar-starbucks-racetogether/

18. Carr. op. cit.

19. Kleinberg, S. "Starbucks #Race Together campaign brews up bitter social media reaction." *Chicago Tribune*. March 18, 2015. Retrieved online: July 15, 2022. www.chicagotribune.com/business/chi-starbucks-race-together-social-media-20150318-htmlstory.html

20. Ibid.

21. Taylor, K. "Howard Schultz reveals how he decided to launch Starbucks 'embarrassing' and 'tone-deaf' 'Race Together' campaign despite internal concerns." *Businessinsider.com*. January 29, 2019. Retrieved online: July 14, 2022. www.businessinsider.com/howard-schultz-failed-race-together-campaign-2019-1

22. Parsi. op.cit.

23. Schultz, H. "A Letter from Howard Schultz to Starbucks Partners Regarding Race Together." *Starbucks.com*. March 22, 2015. Retrieved online: July 14, 2022. https://stories.starbucks.com/stories/2015/a-letter-from-howard-schultz-to-starbucks-partners-regarding-race-together/

24. Ibid.

25. Interview with Amy C. Edmondson, via email. July 27, 2022.

26. Amy C. Edmondson. "How to Lead in a Crisis—with Amy C. Edmondson | TED Business." *YouTube*. March 5, 2022. Retrieved online: September 6, 2022. www.youtube.com/watch?v=S2sxGUbTNpU

27. Moss Kanter, R. "Change is Hardest in the Middle." *Harvard Business Review*, August 12, 2009. Retrieved online: July 2, 2022. https://hbr.org/2009/08/change-is-hardest-in-the-middle

28. Mucha. op. cit.
29. Cristie. "What to Expect When You Stay at a Disney Hotel During a Hurricane." *Raising Whasians*. September 19, 2017. Retrieved online: July 18, 2022. https://raisingwhasians.com/what-to-expect-disney-hotel-hurricane/
30. Mucha. op cit.
31. "Hurricane Irma and Disney – What Really Happened." *Mickeyblog.com*. October 6, 2017. Retrieved online: September 12, 2022. https://mickeyblog.com/2017/10/06/hurricane-irma-disney-what-really-happened/
32. Mucha. op. cit.
33. Ibid.
34. News Release. "The Walt Disney Company Donates $2.5 Million in Humanitarian Aid to Support Communities Impacted by Hurricane Irma." September 12, 2017. Retrieved online: July 18, 2022. https://thewaltdisneycompany.com/walt-disney-company-donates-2-5-million-humanitarian-aid-support-communities-impacted-hurricane-irma/
35. Collins E. and Collins C. "Disney World's Hurricane Rideout Teams Have Been Activated for Hurricane Irma!" *Our Magical Disney Moments*. September 14, 2017. Retrieved online: July 18, 2022. https://collinsrace1.wordpress.com/2017/09/05/hurricane-irma-and-disney-worlds-hurricane-rideout-teams/
36. Mucha. op. cit.

Chapter 16

Engaging With Legacy Media

Few elements of strategic crisis communication are more crucial to get right than effective interaction with legacy news media. An organization in a crisis seeking to play either offense or defense against legacy media should know how these powerful and traditional organizations operate overall, what they need, what motivates them, what frustrates them, and what they value. Deeply relevant and influential within American culture, legacy media are the main lens through which organizations are viewed and judged by society. Legacy media and social media intersect in several significant respects, and we will discuss those junctures in Chapter 19, "Social Media Has Changed the Crisis Communication Landscape."

The Fourth Estate is a pillar of democracy in search of both the news and the truth. Our powerful and centralized political and commercial institutions require an independent third-party function that work to provide society with unbiased information, news, and analysis. Freedom of the press is a cherished Constitutional right, and the influence of newspapers, magazines, and television in our society is literally immeasurable. One key role of the media is to serve as a watchdog, conducting investigative journalism that may uncover illegal, illicit, or otherwise corrupt activity within our political, corporate, educational, religious, or other major institutions.

An Institution Under Siege

Legacy journalism, particularly newspapers, is also under heavy economic and social pressure and scrutiny from several sides. The digital age threatens the economic model of a newspaper traditionally supported by advertising and subscriptions. Advertisers have followed millions of Americans in the shift to getting news for free on the internet and on mobile devices from Google and other news aggregators. A number of metropolitan newspapers have either shut down or merged to survive. Others have drastically cut the size of their newsroom staff, laid off editors and reporters, enacted pay cuts, reduced the physical dimensions of the newspaper, or have become online-only publications.

DOI: 10.4324/9781003322849-20

Television viewership on cable news and traditional networks is cyclical, depending on world events. While trending steadily down for the past several years, viewership on both platforms surged to historic highs from audiences glued to televisions due to the COVID-19 pandemic and tumultuous 2020 presidential election. But a reversal of viewership since then appears to have plummeted below prepandemic levels.[1] News burnout may account for the steady decline. With interminable focus on grim news on every channel, viewers are exhausted by the unending bombardment of bad headlines, so it may just be easier for audiences to tune out. A perceived lack of objectivity and increased partisanship, mounting bias, and the lessening of civility on the various channels may also be reasons to switch off the small screen.

The public's trust in journalists and their news organizations is also declining. The 2022 Edelman Trust Barometer finds that only 50 percent of 36,000+ respondents trust the news media, ranking government, NGOs, and business as more trustworthy. Nearly one-in-two respondents view the news media as a divisive force in society.[2] Why might that be? "Gotcha" journalism? Sensationalism? Tabloid journalism? How about jumping to conclusions before all the facts are known and understood?

On August 28, 2009, California Highway Patrol Officer Mark Saylor and members of his family were killed in a crash in their Lexus sedan near San Diego. A call from a backseat passenger said the driver was unable to stop the vehicle, which was traveling at 120 miles per hour. The tragic incident thrust Toyota into a major crisis over potential sudden, unintended acceleration that would result in the recall of about 8 million vehicles.[3]

At the height of the Toyota sudden acceleration crisis in 2010, the driver of a 2008 Toyota Prius, James Sikes, also near San Diego, called 911 to claim his gas pedal was stuck, he was speeding faster than 90 miles per hour, and he could not get the car to slow down. A fast-thinking California Highway Patrol (CHP) officer pulled alongside Sikes's speeding car and coached him to a stop by having Sikes apply the brakes and emergency brake and then turn off the engine.[4]

That generated an archetypal media feeding frenzy. Fueled by California's ubiquitous news-chopper culture, dramatic overhead video footage of Sikes's Prius parked on the side of the road with a CHP patrol car led the national news on *every* major network. Sikes held a news conference and became a new kind of celebrity. The words "allegedly" and "claim" were hard to find in most of the news reports. Without a second thought, news anchors, commentators, pundits, and critics took to the airways to express indignation about the "runaway Prius." The news media wholeheartedly swallowed Sikes's story, hook, line, and sinker.

According to Christopher Scanlan, whose work has appeared in *The New York Times* and *The Washington Post*, "Generations of reporters have been raised on the journalistic bromide 'If your mother says she loves you, check it out,'" and with good purpose. "The principle behind it – careful journalism requires a dose of skepticism – can keep you and your news organization from making embarrassing mistakes." Did that happen in the case of James Sikes and his runaway Prius?[5]

The cavalry soon showed up in San Diego. On-the-spot investigations by both the National Highway Transportation and Safety Administration safety experts and Toyota engineers could not recreate sudden acceleration in the vehicle and found little-to-no evidence to support Sikes's claims.[6] Representative Darrell Issa (R-CA), ranking Republican on the House Committee on Oversight and Reform, the committee investigating the Toyota sudden, unintended acceleration matter, said the failure to duplicate the allegedly stuck accelerator, along with a vehicle design to prevent such occurrences, raised significant doubts about Sikes's story. "It doesn't mean it didn't happen, but let's understand, it doesn't mean it did happen," Issa said on the CBS *The Early Show*.[7] While not directly related to Sikes's claims, research by skeptical members of the automotive press uncovered that Sikes had declared bankruptcy in 2008, was more than $700,000 in debt – including owing $19,000 on his Toyota – and had a history of filing insurance claims for allegedly stolen property.[8] Although Sikes said he did not intend to sue Toyota, he wanted a new car. All good reasons to reserve judgment and determine the facts before reporting on nationwide television.[9]

Doron Levin is a veteran journalist who specializes in the intersection of social media and journalism. Currently Editor-In-Chief of *BetterInvesting* and a talk show host on Sirius XM Radio, Levin has been a major contributor to *Fortune* magazine, *The New York Times*, *The Wall Street Journal* and *Bloomberg News Service*.[10]

Regarding professionalism and accuracy in news reporting, Levin says that a combination of training and experience from the ground up are the formula for success as a journalist. In terms of training for the big time, he says,

> So how did I get to be a reporter at *The Wall Street Journal*? By a very rigorous vetting process. I went to Columbia and graduated with a master's. I had my first job at *The St. Petersburg Times* and did well enough there to get an interview with *The Wall Street Journal*. They vetted me the first few months and gave me very inconsequential stories to cover to make sure that I was on the up and up. They saw I knew how to be accurate, and I knew how to be fast. And then as things changed, they gave me more and more important stories.[11]

Levin said the hiring standards for journalists have changed due to economic pressure on newspapers and the effect is lower quality:

> There is no vetting process anymore. Anybody who comes out of . . . I was going to say anybody who comes out of school . . . but you don't have to come out of school anymore. You don't even really have to go to school. You just have to be fluent enough to persuade somebody that you can put an English sentence together, and boom, you're out there.[12]

With fewer editorial staff to serve as filters, less experienced staff, and fewer legacy media reporters required to file more and more stories, bias can creep into the newsroom. Levin said,

> You're not really being supervised by an editor these days whose job it is to caution the reporter and open the reporter's minds to the biases that we all have about everything, so that news reporting can be more empirical toward the goal of making news reporting as objective as possible.[13]

Jayne O'Donnell, who wrote for *USA Today* for 28 years, agrees with Levin. "Journalists just starting out need to develop their experience by writing basic news stories and learning the fundamentals. Instead, some of these inexperienced journalists are asked to take on complex social issues and they're not yet really equipped to do that."[14]

Zenia Mucha, formerly of Disney, believes that another potential reason for mistrust of the media is the "clickbait" mentality of reporters who are evaluated by the number of clicks their stories get as well as editors who demand sensational headlines to attract readers. "They know it's not necessarily fully accurate, but they write it for clickbait. The headline is likely to be more nefarious and alarming than the full story," Mucha said.[15]

Mucha recalled a 2013 story reported on CNN and several other media outlets about a vacation villa that partially collapsed into a sinkhole in central Florida, about 30 miles northwest of Walt Disney World. No one was hurt. The *US News* headline shouted, "Massive Sinkhole Causes Disney World-Area Resort to Collapse."[16] Many other media followed the leader, putting Disney into their headlines and ledes. "What?" asked Mucha. "How does this justify putting Disney into the headline? The sinkhole was nowhere near us. And the story got picked up everywhere. You would have thought that the entire Magic Kingdom fell into a sinkhole. That's clickbait," Mucha said.[17]

Develop Mutual Regard

Despite its many woes, the news media are undeniably influential and important. How fairly or critically an organization in crisis is depicted by the news media can greatly influence the public's perception of that organization and the outcome of the crisis. Understanding the media's processes, needs, motivations, frustrations, and values is an essential knowledge set for professionals in crisis communication. Waiting until a crisis develops to personally connect with the media that cover you is a critical mistake. If the first time you hear a reporter's name is when he or she is on the telephone with a tough question, you are already off on the wrong foot. If young and inexperienced journalists calling you about a problem in your organization are total strangers, they will likely perceive you as just another palace guard and a barrier to doing their job.

On the contrary, take time to build strong and authentic interpersonal relationships with journalists who cover you and that first crisis-driven phone call becomes more of an initial conversation than a showdown. Intentionally establishing a trusting relationship with the journalists who cover you is not manipulation. On a day-to-day basis, journalists need information from organizations, and communications professionals should be their initial and primary conduit. Let them know you are an approachable and honest human being. Bring them into your operation. Let them speak with your executives in a calm environment to understand your strategies and thinking. If you have production plants, take them onto the plant floor. If you are an exporter, take them to the loading docks. Introduce them to your experts who can educate them on complex matters. Take the time to establish your credibility, integrity, and transparency with the journalists who matter to you; all this interaction may pay off in the future if the going gets rough.

Veteran *USA Today* journalist Jayne O'Donnell is now founder and CEO of the nonprofit Youthcast Media Group, which trains diverse groups of high school students to do multimedia reporting and social media. On the importance of providing training and guidance to young journalists, she said, "Reporters, particularly the younger inexperienced ones, need so much help." She explained that as a young automotive reporter in Washington, D.C., trying to cover a highly complicated industry, one of the major U.S. automakers took the time to help her better understand the issues. O'Donnell said,

> The communications guys from one of the Big Three gave me background interviews with their policy people. I wasn't well-sourced yet, but I really started to understand how Washington works on the inside. And they introduced me to their experts on Corporate Average Fuel Economy so I could develop my expertise on a very complex political and regulatory issue that I had to write about. Granted, it was from their own perspective, but I could sort out the spin. It was very helpful, and I learned a great deal.[18]

She said, "When I was a little nobody reporter with *Auto Age* magazine, most of the PR people, including one from a big European maker, didn't have anything to do with me." She added, "I've never forgotten that."[19]

From the corporate side, Mucha agrees on the need for solid relationships with legacy media:

> It is important to take reporters who are new to the beat in to speak to management and to executives and to creators, so they can develop a better understanding of the business, of how you run that business, what your priorities are, and what is important to you.[20]

In today's social media, anybody can pretend to be a reporter for whatever reason and make a baseless allegation. Their goal is usually to get the legacy media to pay attention and pick up their story, even though they know it has zero merit. That's one example of when having relationships with legacy media can come into play. You can have an exchange with your legacy media contact and, based on your credibility and established sense of trust, point out that an assertion on social media has no validity.[21]

Understand the Media's Needs

In a public health crisis or natural disaster, the news media are an invaluable emergency broadcast service for people affected by the incident and who need it most. The media serve up policy updates from public officials and, at times, seek clarity on behalf of the public in the face of confusing reports. Public officials frequently hold regular news conferences to keep the media and their audiences up-to-date. What happened, how to stay safe, weather information, and emergency shelter information are the media's top priorities. Investigative journalism plays a secondary role to providing reliable, updated information.

Media relations during an organizational crisis shares one similarity: the media's incessant desire and need for information. Once a major company crisis breaks, no matter the cause, the fierce competitiveness of news organizations will kick in to get the story first and beat the competition, even for a matter of moments. Communications practitioners should be aware of the competitive pressures within the news business and, in the interest of fairness, be careful to provide information and updates to all interested media at the same time via email or on their media websites or on private wire services such as PR Newswire or BusinessWire.

You will find exceptions. On occasion, it may be advisable to grant an exclusive interview or give select information to a single news source, if you are clear on your goals – such as increasing the likelihood that your story will be published – and are aware of the risks. If your story angle is sufficiently strong, an exclusive is a powerful incentive to a reporter because it gives them a one-up on their competition, enhances their sense of ownership of the story, and boosts the chances of it being published. It is risky in that exclusives can alienate and even offend competitors who were not so favored – so, proceed with caution.

O'Donnell says competition among journalists is intense:

I used to get *The Wall Street Journal* at home, and I used to walk out to the driveway with knots in my stomach. I was afraid to pick up the paper to see if I'd been scooped. I just hated getting beat.[22]

Move Swiftly

To do their jobs in a crisis, reporters need information quickly to remain competitive and keep up with the 24-hour news cycle, often updating their stories several times a day.

Alan Ohnsman should know. A senior staff reporter for *Forbes* who tracks technology-driven changes in transportation, he previously reported for *Bloomberg News* and *Business Week* and has covered several companies in crisis. He also dealt directly with crisis communications during a stint running the public relations team for a Los Angeles startup. As a wire service reporter, Ohnsman said he was under more time pressure to get news out promptly than other types of media. He explained,

> When a bad thing happens, we quickly reach out to the company for reaction. If we don't get one right away, the standard practice would be to write that the company did not "immediately respond." I will follow up and let them know I need an answer as soon as possible. If an inordinate amount of time passes, the "immediate" goes away, replaced by "The company did not respond."[23]

When asked his definition of "immediate," Ohnsman said,

> I think it really depends on the issue. Is it an automotive accident? A recall? A fatality? Is it an executive engaged in terrible behavior? Is it sexual? Does it involve criminal behavior? There is a whole range of issues, and the more serious, the more immediate.[24]

Ohnsman advocates a frank and direct attitude on the part of corporate communications:

> There may be something bad that has happened where there are not enough facts, so there's an inability to say anything of value. In a case like that, a company should avoid saying "no comment." The best thing the company can say is "We don't have enough information to give you a meaningful comment right now. As soon as we have more of the facts, we will be able to share more in detail." It might be more effective if a company was more honest in that way, and the reporter will be more likely to give them the benefit of the doubt.[25]

O'Donnell concurs with a candid and straightforward approach to response time and offers some valuable advice. "The best PR people always asked my deadline because then they knew how much time they had to get back to me, and that is smart and helpful to both sides."[26]

"These days there is so much pressure to publish quickly, especially when you have something exclusive. It's important to get back to us very quickly because otherwise we'll publish and say you were not available for comment." She added,

> It's scary for PR people. I empathize sometimes when I see a story that says a company was not immediately available for comment. That might just mean

we didn't pick up the phone in the newsroom or look at our email because we were so busy getting the story out because of the tremendous competition.[27]

And that's why you communications people have to be looking at your darn phone all weekend and evenings.[28]

So true.

Stay Out of the Bunker

Some journalists have an inherent mistrust of corporate communication staff, who they may view as an obstruction. Compounding this viewpoint, relations between a journalist and an organization in crisis can quickly become adversarial if the organization appears to be hiding something, if the organization is untruthful, or if the organization is not responsive to the media's need for information.

Mark Rechtin, an automotive industry journalist with 30 years' experience writing and editing at such publications as *Motor Trend, Consumer Reports,* and *Automotive News* and a recipient of the Jesse H. Neal National Business Journalism Award, characterizes the playbook of panicked or overwhelmed crisis communications staff as "The Five Ds."

1. **Delay:** Buy time for the company to organize initial response messaging. Depending on the magnitude of the crisis and the media interest in it, this request for patience for a corporate response can be hours or days.
2. **Deflect:** Engage in "whataboutism" or other distracting tactics to minimize the issue while marshalling resources to defend the company from accusations.
3. **Deny:** Many companies issue categorical denial statements until presented with deeper detail of the accusations presented by the media or plaintiff attorneys.
4. **Discredit:** While the media attempt to find further details to circumvent the denial, the communications team airs any potential weaknesses in the original claims. This often takes the form of an on-background whisper to a trusted, sometimes-influential media resource, who publishes it as a "scoop" – not knowing they have been manipulated.
5. **Defame:** A last-gasp attempt – usually an *ad hominem* attack against the entity making the accusation – in hopes that the media will lose interest in an issue raised by someone labeled as a "crackpot who just doesn't understand."

"The final PR Hail Mary is threatened legal action," Rechtin said. "That can throw a scare into smaller media entities to stop chasing the story. However, if the media have strong evidence of corporate wrongdoing, and its own pit bull attorneys, that threat usually falls flat." Rechtin recalls *Automotive News* publisher Keith Crain being summoned to a boardroom meeting where an automaker warned of legal action in response to an article Rechtin wrote. Crain's confident response:

"We welcome discovery." The automaker's lawyers quietly shuffled out of the boardroom minutes later. No legal action followed.[29]

Sources

In the Watergate scandal of the 1970s, *The Washington Post* reporters Bob Woodward and Carl Bernstein leaned heavily on an anonymous source within the government they dubbed "Deep Throat" for their investigative journalism that ultimately led to the resignation of President Richard Nixon. In a crisis, journalists' sources can be officially approved spokespersons and experts within an organization who are designated to speak to the media. Communications professionals should know who their resident experts are, train them to speak with the media, and sit in on any interviews that are granted. Sources can also include a company insider who speaks on the record to the media without any authorization and discloses sensitive material, intentionally or not. Or an employee or ex-employee who speaks anonymously to avoid retaliation. Journalists who use such anonymous sources often uncover compelling facts but risk entanglement with the law.

According to the Society of Professional Journalists,

Anonymous sources are sometimes the only key to unlocking that big story, throwing back the curtain on corruption, fulfilling the journalistic missions of watchdog on the government and informant to the citizens. But sometimes, anonymous sources are the road to the ethical swamp.[30]

Levin is candid, and a little scary, about the value of journalists' having good sources inside an organization:

Even though you have to operate with the media relations people, you need other sources inside the company. It's your job to meet people and to develop relationships with trust and then to use those relationships to report on what's happening in the company.[31]

Rechtin once received confrontational phone calls from an automaker's executives, complaining about his articles describing the company going through a rough patch. "My response was straight from the teen-slasher film *When A Stranger Calls* in that my story tips were coming from within the headquarters of the automaker. Disgruntled employees were my main sources."[32]

Targeting Target

In a landmark exposé titled "How Companies Learn Your Secrets," published in *The New York Times Magazine* on February 16, 2012, author Charles Duhigg described how some retailers profit by predicting major changes in people's lives.

Specifically, the retailer Target had developed a "pregnancy prediction model," using predictive analytics to deduce when women customers were likely to be pregnant and then send them coupons and advertisements for products they would need before and after childbirth.[33]

Currently writing at *The New Yorker Magazine*, Duhigg was an investigative reporter at *The New York Times* in 2012 when his story blew the lid off Target's practice of using big data to forecast the reproductive cycle of its women customers. Duhigg is a Pulitzer Prize winner and the author of *The Power of Habit* and *Smarter Faster Better*. Duhigg's provocative article about Target was excerpted from *The Power of Habit* and was published two weeks in advance of the publication of his best-selling book.[34]

The core element of predictive analytics is the selection of the predictor (such as the products we buy or the types of movies we watch), that is measured to predict future outcomes. For example, if we enjoy action movies, Netflix will tee up Tom Cruise or Chris Pratt films on our smart TV. If we buy golf balls on Amazon, we'll get ads for golf clubs and colorful pants on our desktop.

Such data-gathering technology is commonplace, and even welcomed by many consumers because of the discounts, but Duhigg's *The New York Times Magazine* article was so powerful because he hit a raw nerve by exposing Target's ability to spy on pregnant women for commercial purposes.

To get the facts for his story, Duhigg relied heavily on Target employee Andrew Pole, a statistician who created algorithms that identified customer trends and habits using predictive analytics.[35] Pole was astonishingly candid with Duhigg about Target's inner workings and gave Duhigg extraordinary access to the skunk works within Target's marketing operations. That is, until he suddenly and unaccountably stopped talking to Duhigg.[36]

Before he clammed up on the reporter, Pole admitted that if Target was able to determine the due dates of pregnant women before other retailers, it would have a significant advantage over competitors who did not know the women were expecting. "We knew that if we could identify them in their second trimester, there's a good chance we could capture them for years," Pole admitted to Duhigg.[37]

Pole said he and his team used a sample of women whom they knew to be pregnant and tracked their buying habits, resulting in a "pregnancy prediction score," which identifies, with 87 percent accuracy, whether women are pregnant or not. The analytics can also predict the woman's probable due date.[38]

With Pole giving Duhigg the silent treatment, Duhigg approached Target to discuss Pole's work. In an email exchange for this book, Duhigg said that Target "declined to speak with me about the data analytics operation."[39] Instead, Target's representatives gave him a statement, which stated in part: "We've developed a number of research tools that allow us to gain insights into trends and preferences within different demographic segments of our guest population."[40]

Duhigg then sent Target a list of fact-checking questions and a thorough summary of his reporting. This time he received a more brusque reply: "Almost all of your statements contain inaccurate information and publishing them would be misleading to the public. We do not intend to address each statement point by point." The company did not identify the information that they claimed was inaccurate or misleading. They did point out that Target "is in compliance with all federal and state laws, including those related to protected health information."[41]

When Duhigg offered to fly to Target's headquarters to discuss its concerns about the accuracy of his story, a spokesperson emailed him that no one would be available to meet him. When he flew there regardless, a security guard said, "I've been instructed not to give you access and to ask you to leave."[42]

Duhigg's *The New York Times Magazine* story caused a sensation and was itself the subject of numerous news stories and programs. A YouTube video complained that Target could "data-mine its way into your womb."[43] The cover story of *The Week* reported, "It's time we all were more aware of how companies can crunch data to unlock the most intimate details of our lives."[44] In popular media, comedian Stephen Colbert dedicated his "The Word" segment to the Target story, with a segment subtitled "Surrender to a Buyer Power."[45] A skit on a popular Australian TV comedy program depicted a pregnant woman staggering through a Target store. Her water breaks and she is approached by a store employee wanting to sell her diapers.[46]

Some Reflections

The relationship between Duhigg and his key source at Target raises compelling questions about how organizations should engage with legacy media. We may never know if Andrew Pole was authorized by Target to speak so extensively with Charles Duhigg. However, it is difficult to fathom that Target was fully aware of the magnitude of sensitive and possibly confidential information he was disclosing. Pole's sudden silence followed by Target's bunker-like behavior thereafter could indicate that Pole was acting independently from corporate policy, in other words, freelancing, at least until Target found out about it and shut him down.

In an email exchange for this book, Duhigg was asked about his interaction with Target's corporate communications staff, and he offered an instructive answer. Duhigg wrote,

> I had access to many, many sources within Target (Andrew Pole and numerous others), and so, to be honest, I didn't really need cooperation from corporate communications to write my article. And all of the information in that article was verified by multiple sources, and so I don't know how much corporate communications could have swayed what appeared in print.[47]

Organizations have an obligation to be open, responsive, and helpful to reporters, to tell the truth, and to provide accurate, factual information so that journalists can do their job. When Target finally decided to pull the plug on Andrew Pole, responded to Duhigg with terse statements, and then refused to discuss its allegation that Duhigg's facts were wrong, it undermined any chance it may have had to help shape the story. At the same time, organizations also need clear, and clearly communicated, internal policies specifying who is authorized to disclose information to the news media. An organization's corporate communications team should always be thoroughly aware of what is being said and who is saying it.[48]

The Journalist and the Bank

On September 20, 2016, before the Senate Committee on Banking, Housing, and Urban Affairs, Wells Fargo CEO John Stumpf was in the hot seat.[49] As millions watched, Senator Elizabeth Warren (D-MA) drilled into the bank executive with one pointed question after another about Wells Fargo's perfectly legal "cross-selling strategy" – selling additional accounts and bank services such as credit cards to existing bank customers. The senator railed on the CEO for his "gutless leadership."

How did Wells Fargo's cross-selling practices go so dreadfully wrong that the Senate committee summoned Stumpf to testify about what would become a years-long crisis and reputational disaster for the company?

Wells Fargo & Company boasts a storied past tied to the evolution of the American West. Today, Wells Fargo is one of the "Big 4" U.S. banks, along with JPMorgan Chase, Bank of America, and Citigroup. As of July 2022, the company had approximately $1.9 trillion in assets, served one in three U.S. households, and was ranked No. 41 on *Fortune's* 2022 rankings of America's largest corporations.[50]

What is cross-selling? Simply put, the more services and types of accounts a bank can offer, the more lucrative services and accounts it can "cross-sell" to its customers. A banker looking to cross-sell customers would urge them to also open a new credit card account to supplement the checking account they just opened. How about a savings account, too? Need a Platinum credit card? Bundling such products means increased fee revenue and customer loyalty; the more bank products a customer uses, the less likely they are to switch to a competitor, making them more "sticky."

When John Stumpf rose to CEO in 2007, Wells Fargo averaged 5.5 of these various banking products per household. It touted its cross-selling strategy to investors as evidence of its customers' deep loyalty and was popular on Wall Street because of the industry-leading practice. It reached more than 6 products per household in 2012.[51]

With publication of his December 21, 2013, front page *Los Angeles Times* investigative story titled "Wells Fargo's Pressure-Cooker Sales Culture Comes at a Cost," reporter E. Scott Reckard kicked in the door on a crisis for Wells Fargo that would eventually cost the bank billions of dollars in fines.[52] Reckard, now retired, was a staff writer who covered mortgage, housing, and banking for the *Los Angeles Times* business section.

"To meet quotas, employees have opened unneeded accounts for customers, ordered credit cards without customers' permission, and forged client signatures on paperwork. Some employees begged family members to open ghost accounts" so they could hit their sales targets, Reckard wrote in his opening salvo story. Reckard had doggedly reviewed "internal bank documents obtained by the *Times*" and scoured court records as well as interviewed current and former bank employees at branches in nine states.[53]

According to Reckard's story, a former Wells Fargo personal banker said that his branch manager would greet the staff at the beginning of every day with a daily quota for products such as direct deposit accounts and credit cards. Failure to meet the goals meant employees needed to stay and work after hours, often begging family and friends to sign up for additional services.[54] "He would say: 'I don't care how you do it – but do it, or else you're not going home,'" the former employee said.[55]

Reckard reported that another former Wells Fargo branch manager said her employees convinced a homeless woman to open six checking and savings accounts. "It's all manipulation. We are taught exactly how to sell multiple accounts," the former manager said.[56]

In response to the *Times*'s investigation and Reckard's story, Wells Fargo officials stated that ethical conduct is a priority at the bank and that the bank's strong focus is on selling products and services that benefit customers. Chief Financial Officer at the time, Timothy Sloan, said that he was "not aware of any overbearing sales culture." Wells Fargo denied any wrongdoing.[57]

On May 4, 2015, a lawsuit by the city of Los Angeles claiming that Wells Fargo drove employees to open unauthorized accounts for customers, increased the pressure for action by two federal regulators: the Consumer Financial Protection Bureau (CFPB) and the Office of the Comptroller of the Currency (OCC) – who were already looking into the problems at the bank. A later analysis by CFPB concluded the bank may have opened as many as 1.5 million checking and savings accounts and more than 500,000 credit cards without customers' authorization or knowledge.[58]

Tip of the Iceberg

On September 8, 2016, Wells Fargo announced a massive $185 million settlement in response to the growing allegations of sales pressure and false accounts. Wells Fargo would also pay refunds to customers who paid fees on accounts they did not want. Again, the bank did not admit any wrongdoing but apologized to customers for giving them products they did not request and announced steps to change its sales practices.[59]

Media coverage of the Wells Fargo settlement and crisis was intense, unrelenting, and coast-to-coast. Beginning with Reckard's initial revelations in 2013, the *Los Angeles Times* alone published 65 major feature stories and columns on the crisis through July 2017.[60] At the peak of the crisis in early October 2016, Wells Fargo attracted more than 9,000 negative online and print headlines per week. During the same period, social media lit up as well, with some 600,000 Wells Fargo stories shared on Facebook, Twitter, and LinkedIn.[61]

Less than one month after the company settled the first lawsuit, Wells Fargo announced an independent investigation into its own retail banking sales practices. Three weeks later, after continuing pressure from the media, the public, and lawmakers, Stumpf resigned.[62] His successor, insider Timothy J. Sloan, said he regretted the lack of urgency within the Wells Fargo rank and file in bringing the problems with cross-selling to top leadership. "When I think about the retail sales practices issues we've had at the company, I wish that the business had escalated the issue sooner" to Wells Fargo's top management.[63]

The company launched a new nationwide advertising campaign called "Re-Established" to put the massive crisis in the rearview mirror and reassure customers that it was taking steps to improve. Costing millions of dollars, the advertising ran on nationwide television, in print publications, and on digital platforms. Superbly produced, the centerpiece TV spot features the iconic Wells Fargo stagecoach and is a visual timeline of nostalgic images. The gravelly voiced narrator intones: "We know the value of trust. We were built on it. . . .. We always find the way, until we lost it." The ad concludes "It's a new day at Wells Fargo, but it's a lot like our first day." Cue the stagecoach. "Wells Fargo. Established 1852. Re-established 2018."[64]

Sloan's tenure continued to be swamped in controversy and criticism for being an insider ill-equipped to change the company's culture because he had been there all along. Fines, lawsuits, and settlements piled up under his leadership totaling more than $3.8 billion.[65]

Capping off the steady stream of multimillion- and billion-dollar fines and settlements that resulted from this crisis, on February 21, 2020, the U.S. Department of Justice announced that Wells Fargo had admitted wrongdoing and would pay $3 billion to resolve its criminal and civil liability from its undue cross-selling practices.[66]

Wells Fargo's newest CEO since late September 2019, Charles Scharf, who has significantly cleaned house at the bank and who is known inside the bank as "Chainsaw Charlie"[67] for his cost cutting and staff reductions, said of the settlement, "We are committing all necessary resources to ensure that nothing like this happens again."[68]

Seeds of the Story

In a *Fraud Magazine* article in 2017, Reckard recalled that the Wells Fargo story had its origins with a call to the *Times*'s newsroom from a former employee describing immense pressure to meet sales goals.[69]

The fired banker's story resonated with Reckard, and he decided to write about it. He wrote a small story after checking with Wells Fargo, which confirmed the firings but characterized them as evidence that it did not tolerate employee dishonesty. "After our newspaper published the first article, no one could have foreseen the volume of emails and phone calls that started coming in," Reckard recalled.[70]

Within days, Reckard's editor approved a major investigation, and he started compiling stories and calling Wells Fargo for comment.

> Almost immediately, I was asked to talk to the top corporate PR guy at the bank, Oscar Suris; this was a change from the usual policy of talking to lower-ranking flacks, . . . That too, seemed to indicate we might be onto something big.[71]

In his past investigative stories, Reckard frequently relied on employees as sources. In a 2016 interview with the *Columbia Journalism Review*, Reckard said that employees are the holy grail of sources. "If you want to really know what's going on, you have to go out and talk to people who are out in the field."[72]

A Few Observations on Sources

In an email exchange for this book, Reckard reflected on how the bank's attitude toward him changed from warm to cold as he dug more deeply into the story:

> For the most part, the relationship with the company as I investigated the sale troubles remained fairly cordial. However, as the reporting began to reveal what appeared to be a national problem the commenting dried up, no top executives were made available, and the company continued its attempts to portray the bad practices as limited. Toward the end of the process, certain conversations became tense verging on hostility as the horror stories added up. . . . I think the bank continued to suggest that everything was under control and the sales practice issues overblown.[73]

The Wells Fargo crisis is instructive on several counts. The appointment of long-time insider Timothy Sloan to replace the embattled CEO, John Stumpf, telegraphed the bank's unwillingness to change and kept the public spotlight on the company as media and public officials remained skeptical and expressed their outrage. That said, Sloan's regret over the lack of urgency within Wells Fargo about escalating the problems with cross-selling to top management is a teaching moment for communications professionals. Problems that arise within a company should not remain in someone's inbox because they are too hard to solve. Every organization should have a strong internal sensing function and a process for quickly escalating issues, particularly those originating in remote field offices, to top leadership for analysis and decisive resolution.

Reckard's practice of relying on employees to source his stories is notable. Not unlike Charles Duhigg's reliance on Target employee Andrew Pole for the red meat in Duhigg's exposé on Target's marketing practices, Reckard ignited the Wells Fargo crisis based on a phone call from a single upset former employee. Later, he followed the journalism rule of thumb that reporters should use multiple sources, especially when reporting on controversy, and he also relied on court records and leaked internal documents. But it was primarily the employees, both former and current, who exposed Wells Fargo's cross-selling practices and served as the nucleus of the crisis throughout. Certainly not in all cases, but an organization's relationship of trust with employees, combined with a process of evaluating employee engagement and morale, can help organizations avoid problems. An environment of trust should be strengthened by a clearly communicated policy requiring that all media inquiries and contact be referred to corporate communications.

One small but important note: once Reckard started his major investigation and began speaking with numerous sources, including employees, customers, and lawyers, he began calling Wells Fargo corporate communications for comment, as he should. Almost immediately, he was referred to the top corporate PR officer at the bank's headquarters, Oscar Suris. Normally, Reckard would have been put on the phone with lower-ranking PR specialists. For Wells Fargo to put so much corporate firepower on the line was an unmistakable red flag that gave Reckard the notion that there was something significant afoot. Journalists are trained observers who take notice of everything you say and everything you do. Corporate communications practitioners should always carefully assess the level of spokesperson they offer to answer a reporter's questions. A journalist will often draw a correlation between the level of spokesperson and the relative importance of their news story.[74]

Stealing Thunder

When a crisis first emerges within an organization, for example, when a product defect is identified internally, an executive exhibits bad behavior, or environmental damage occurs such as a spill or chemical release, the organization faces an important choice. Should it say and do nothing publicly and hope it blows over, or should it proactively disclose the issue to the news media? Often, organizations are hesitant to take the proactive approach for fear of provoking negative media coverage and unwanted attention from stakeholders that could have been avoided had the issue never been made public. Why disclose a problem if there is an even chance no one will ever know about it?[75]

But what if someone does find out? The BP oil spill in 2010 was not revealed by the company until it had become a full-blown disaster. Volkswagen leadership was alerted to its emissions cheating a year before it was uncovered by the U.S. Environmental Protection Agency and the California Air Resources Board. In both cases, the companies faced huge and long-lasting waves of negative publicity and public and governmental outrage, not only because of the environmental impact of their actions but also for failing to come forward in a timely manner with the truth.[76]

A communicator's task of convincing the C-suite to take a proactive and transparent approach to disclosing a major problem before the media or someone else discovers it may be a very challenging conversation. But it is one that must be had, and important research backs up the argument for self-disclosure. One might start the C-suite discussion with the number one Page Principle, rooted in ethical behavior, to "Tell the Truth."[77] The option of self-disclosing a crisis is also supported by many more reasons beyond a basic ethical imperative to do the right thing.

The theory behind self-disclosure involves the concept of "stealing thunder." In other words, an organization preemptively discloses major problems or crises before the news media become aware of them. Stealing thunder means breaking the news before the media have a chance to do so. It means taking away (stealing) the media's element of surprise (thunder) by intercepting and somewhat neutralizing the provocative "gotcha" appeal of a breaking investigative story.

This approach has several advantages. Important and compelling research on the stealing thunder concept reveals four strong reasons for an organization to self-disclose before a crisis unfolds.

- **First,** the research shows that organizational spokespersons who steal thunder and self-disclose are found to have more credibility than those who do not.[78] This is a big advantage because transparency will be perceived and interpreted as honesty.
- **Second,** if a company self-discloses bad news, the resultant crises can appear less serious or severe.[79] If the crisis appears to be no big deal because the organization was forthcoming about it, it is less interesting.
- **Third,** organizations that steal thunder from the media by revealing negative and potentially damaging news may appear more trustworthy and consumers are more liable to continue buying their products.[80] In this respect, openness is a virtue and customers will be more forgiving because of it.
- **Fourth,** one recent study finds that consumers of news will sense that the bad publicity generated about an organization that stole thunder is actually "old news" and will be more likely to disregard it.[81] If the organization was transparent enough to offer up the information, maybe it's not so bad, and it's already been covered by the media, so why do I need to care about it?

Any degree of message control whatsoever in a crisis is difficult enough to achieve. Both legacy media and social media are more complex and multifaceted than they once were, and the opportunities for information to be leaked or divulged in an uncontrolled manner, against an organization's wishes, are unlimited. Stealing the thunder from all this potential noise is a tactic that may mute likely antagonists both from within the organization and without, by beating them to the starting line. An organization that gets the news out first, even if it is unpleasant news, is in a much stronger position than one offering a back-footed reaction to an unexpected headline in *The Wall Street Journal* exposé.

Concealing a major crisis in the hopes that no one will notice it may be a tempting option. Don't do it. Solid research backs up the notion that such a choice is both risky and ill-advised. The BP and Volkswagen cases are clear proof that hiding a bad situation only makes matters worse once the truth comes to light. Stealing thunder can reduce the amount of attention paid by the public and limit damage to the organization's bottom line, reputation, and image.[82] Former U.S. Secretary of State Henry Kissinger captured the essence of stealing thunder when he said, "Any fact that needs to be disclosed should be put out now or as quickly as possible because otherwise the bleeding will not end."[83]

Some Nuts and Bolts for Legacy Media Relations

In Writing

Prepare a Concise Standby Statement

The moment you become aware of a crisis in your organization, prepare a brief time-buying, standby statement for media as soon as they reach out. You may not have all the facts yet, but an email stating, "We are aware of this situation and are taking steps to determine the causes of the problem and correct it. We will have more details as soon as they become available" is preferable to "no comment," which will appear to the media and the public that you are hiding something.

A Good Formal Statement Is a Short Formal Statement

The fewer words you use, the greater the chance the media will quote you verbatim – which is what you want. Give them a long statement and they will summarize it and may lose your main point. Don't give them a choice of your words.

Deploy Your Spokesperson and RRT

Once the trigger event occurs (even if you have stolen thunder) have your spokesperson ready to go and arm them with your Master Q-&-A. Deploy your Rapid Response Team to develop your facts and message points and obtain approval from the crisis team before any interaction beyond your standby statement. (See Chapter 3, "Set Up a Rapid Response Team Process").

Use Email With Journalists During a Crisis

Companies in crisis need to decide whether they will speak with journalists on the phone or rely exclusively on interaction via email, which is the safer alternative because it allows some semblance of message control and helps to avoid costly mistakes. Doron Levin said he prefers email because it creates a written record of what was said. He added,

> I don't mind posing written questions and I don't mind getting written answers. I think it builds up credibility when you can put quotes around something and both sides agree on what was said. Having quotes in stories is much better than using unidentified sources which raises all kinds of other problems.[84]

For Alan Ohnsman, however, email-only responses make him dubious: "Our guard goes up and suspicion increases. I would naturally assume we are on to something here. This company has something to hide. It's like pleading the Fifth. It's like you've just admitted that you're guilty."[85]

On balance, we recommend email-only responses in a crisis. Reporters who grouse about it will get over it, as long as they get the information they need.

Attribute Statements to Your Organization, Not Yourself

Your CEO is your most powerful communication tool in a crisis, and a statement over their name carries great authority and conviction. However, attribute other general statements and updates to your organization rather than to a communications staffer so the statements will not be seen as personal opinion. To avoid personal liability, formal statements attributed to an organization, rather than a person, are always preferable in instances where litigation or interaction with law enforcement is involved.

In Person

Follow Rumsfeld's Rules for Spokespersons

The late Donald Rumsfeld, twice Secretary of Defense and adviser to several presidents, was a master at the microphone during his frequent news conferences, often sparring with the media and seeming to enjoy it. His clear rules for spokesmanship let the media know what to expect. He is widely thought to have told a group of journalists, "Here's how this is going to work. One, I know, and I am going to tell you. Two, I know, and I am not going to tell you. Three, I don't know. That's it."

If You Go "Off the Record," Go Carefully

A good practice when going "off the record" is to ask yourself if you would be comfortable seeing your private comments on the front page of *The New York Times*. There is always the risk that the information you provide in confidence will be too juicy for the reporter to resist, so proceed with caution and be sure you have a trusting relationship with the journalist. Jayne O'Donnell said she always appreciated off-the-record comments:

> My goal is to be as accurate as possible. There have been times when I may have been heading in the wrong direction and 'off the record' guidance from a company has helped me get the story right. I very much value that kind of assistance.[86]

As a corporate spokesperson, Zenia Mucha agreed that such guidance is helpful but only if there is mutual trust between the spokesperson and the reporter:

> Providing guidance is important because it allows you to provide context to a situation or to a crisis. And that context is vital to journalists, particularly when it comes to reporting something that's complicated. I always believe in giving journalists the benefit of the doubt. If they prove that they don't deserve your trust, then that's the end of that.[87]

Rechtin urges communicators to establish their formal definition of "off the record" with every journalist they interact with – since there as different interpretations of the term. He said,

> Depending on your personal definition, "off the record" can mean, "You can write about it, but don't attribute it to me." It can mean, "You can't print this as fact unless you get second, independent corroboration, and you still can't attribute it to me." And it can also mean, "This conversation stays between the two of us and is not for publication under any circumstances." Not establishing those ground rules with a journalist upfront can lead to harrowing misunderstandings.[88]

Use the 10/3 Rule to Your Advantage

Spokespersons, particularly on television and radio, should develop their three most important talking points about their crisis and then work hard to express them in no more than ten seconds – the time a television news editor will allow for your sound bite. If you can't fit all three points into ten seconds, then only say the top two. Practice and time yourself until you can accomplish it.

Block and Bridge

A common error in interviews is to become focused on the questions being asked and neglecting to convey your key talking points. Don't become fixated on answering each question directly, but, instead, confidently block and bridge to the information you want to convey. Blocking means avoiding a contentious or hostile question or one that you do not want to answer. Bridging means making the transition away from the adverse topic to the points you want to drive home. Blocking and bridging techniques use smooth transitional phrases, such as "That's a good question, but the most important thing is . . .," "I appreciate your question, but let me point out . . .," and "I am unable to answer that because it's proprietary information, but what I can tell you is . . ."

Don't Repeat the Negative

A common mistake when answering questions is to repeat negative words or hypotheses used by the reporter. When former president Richard Nixon said, "I am not a crook," he left the impression that he was a crook. You have positive talking points to convey, and if you repeat the reporter's negative words, you will likely be quoted in a bad light. For example: Reporter: "Are you aware of the allegations of fraud and other criminal activity at your company?" The wrong answer is, "We deny any fraud or other criminal activity at our company." Better to say, "Our company culture is based on integrity and any claims to the contrary are without merit." Back in 1974, a magazine published a list of the 10 dumbest members of Congress, with Virginia Senator Bill Scott (R-VA) topping the list as the very dumbest. How did he respond? He called a news conference to deny that he was stupid, pushing the story into national headlines and proving that the magazine had been right.[89]

Never Lie to a Journalist, No Matter What

On this point, Levin is unequivocal:

> If you really want to have a relationship of trust between a reporter and a media relations representative for a company, the first thing you have understand is to never mislead or never lie to the reporter, because once you do that, it's just over.[90]

Mucha said in her role as a corporate spokesperson,

> My rule dealing with the press is I don't lie to you. I make it a point that they know that. Now, I don't tell you everything either because some of it I can't and some has to hold until the proper time. For disclosure and competitive reasons, it's important to understand what can be disclosed and when.[91]

Don't Take Negative Coverage Personally

Accept that reporters are out to achieve their goals. Their purpose is to understand what has happened and then interpret and report it. Equally, a communications practitioner's job is to defend and promote their organization. Both sides need to acknowledge their respective roles and not internalize the motives and actions of the other. Bill Koenig, formerly of *Bloomberg News*, said, "My best advice for PR people is you can't take it personally. Most of the time the journalists involved don't really have a personal stake in the outcome of a story. We are just doing our jobs."[92] Levin said the nature of the news business leans toward the sensational, and that is a simple fact of life:

> We don't write about the 90 million people who cross the street safely every day. We write about the guy who got hit by a truck. That's the nature of what gets in the newspaper. We're focused on things that go wrong. Human failures, mechanical failures, business failures, things that people would rather not publicize.[93]

Forget the News Conference (Unless You Can't)

News conferences are good for telling good news and emergency communications and little else. When was the last time you saw a company in crisis hold a news conference that went well? Unless there is a compelling story to tell or an injustice that needs to be corrected, stay off the podium in a room full of reporters – it is a perch fraught with peril and risk.

Set the Television Interview Ground Rules

With so many ways to communicate your organization's messages in a crisis, the riskiest, right up there with a news conference, is a televised interview. So much can go wrong with the visual medium. An executive wiping a sweaty brow under hot lights, or shifting their eyes, or hesitating just for a moment telegraphs anxiety. Everything you say can and will be edited in an unflattering manner. However, if good reasons exist to consent to an interview, establish the ground rules, and set a time limit of no more than 10 minutes. One corporate communications executive who asked not to be identified recalled that *60 Minutes* wanted to interview them when their company was in hot water. The Chief Communications Officer agreed to the interview but stipulated that it had to be live. *60 Minutes* went away, unable to claim that the company refused to be interviewed.

Beware the Luncheon Club

Company officials are frequently invited to speak at service organizations, business groups, and conferences. Know that for a company in crisis that such speakers are fair game for enterprising journalists who can ambush a company official and ask uncomfortable questions about the crisis. Coordinate closely with any official company speakers who may encounter media anywhere. Decide in advance if they are prepared to address the crisis. It might be better to suspend such appearances until the crisis is behind you.

References

1. Rothschild, N. and Fischer, S. "News Engagement Plummets as Americans Tune Out." *Axios.* July 12, 2022. Retrieved online: August 1, 2022. www.axios.com/2022/07/12/news-media-readership-ratings-2022

2. "Edelman Trust Barometer 2022." Edelman. January 24, 2022. Retrieved online: August 22, 2022. www.edelman.com/trust/2022-trust-barometer

3. Bunkley, N. "Toyota Settles Over California Deaths." *New York Times.* September 18, 2010. Retrieved online: October 12, 2022. www.nytimes.com/2010/09/19/business/19autos.html?searchResultPosition=6

4. YouTube. "Man Described Runaway Prius." *CNN.* March 9, 2019. Retrieved online: August 2, 2022. www.youtube.com/watch?v=qP9rIIfYUnk

5. Scanlan, C. "If Your Mother Says She Loves You: A Reporter's Cautionary Tale." *Poynter.* The Poynter Institute for Media Studies. April 17, 2003: Retrieved online: August 3, 2022. www.poynter.org/reporting-editing/2003/if-your-mother-says-she-loves-you-a-reporters-cautionary-tale/

6. Evans, S. "Toyota Releases Preliminary Report on Runaway Prius, Finds No Problems." *Motor Trend.* March 15, 2010. Retrieved online: August 2, 2022. www.motortrend.com/news/toyota-releases-preliminary-report-on-runaway-prius-finds-no-problems-7009/

7. YouTube. "San Diego Runaway Prius: What's Next? Issa's Here with the Answer." *CBS' The Early Show.* March 15, 2010. Retrieved online: August 2, 2022. www.youtube.com/watch?v=k_kFUiyneF0

8. Hardigree, M. "Did Bankrupt Runaway Prius Driver Fake 'Unintended Acceleration?'" *Jalopnik.* March 11, 20109: Retrieved online: August 2, 2022. https://jalopnik.com/did-bankrupt-runaway-prius-driver-fake-unintended-acce-5491101

9. Lopez, K. "FOX40 Investigates: Internet Speculation of Hoax Surrounds Prius Driver James Sikes." *Fox 40.* March 11, 2010. Retrieved online: August 4, 2022. https://web.archive.org/web/20110724075041/www.fox40.com/news/headlines/ktxl-news-jamessikesinvestigated0311%2C0%2C4677651.story

10. Interview with Doron Levin, via Zoom. July 22, 2022.

11. Ibid.

12. Ibid.

13. Ibid.

14. Interview with Jayne O'Donnell, via Zoom. June 29, 2022.

15. Interview with Zenia Mucha, via Zoom. July 7, 2022.

16. Bidwell, A. "Massive Sinkhole Causes Disney World-Area Resort to Collapse." *U.S. News.* August 12, 2013. Retrieved online: August 2, 2022. www.usnews.com/news/newsgram/articles/2013/08/12/massive-sinkhole-causes-disney-world-area-resort-to-collapse

17. Mucha. op. cit.

18. O'Donnell. op. cit.

19. Ibid.

20. Mucha. op. cit.

21. Ibid.

22. O'Donnell. op. cit.

23. Interview with Alan Ohnsman, via Zoom. July 20, 2022.

24. Ibid.

25. Ibid

26. O'Donnell. op. cit.

27. Ibid.

28. Ibid.

29. Interview with Mark Rechtin, via email. July 28, 2022

30. Farrell, M. "Anonymous Sources." Society of Professional Journalists. No date available. Retrieved online: August 5, 2022. www.spj.org/ethics-papers-anonymity.asp

31. Levin. op. cit.

32. Rechtin. op. cit.

33. Ibid.

34. Charles Duhigg. *Wikipedia*. Retrieved online: July 22, 2022. https://en.wikipedia.org/wiki/Charles_Duhigg

35. Duhigg, Charles. "How Companies Learn Your Secrets." op. cit.

36. Ibid.

37. Ibid.

38. Ibid.

39. Interview with Charles Duhigg, via email. July 20, 2022.

40. Duhigg, Charles. "How Companies Learn Your Secrets." op. cit.

41. Ibid.

42. Ibid.

43. 'How Target Figured Out a Teen Girl Was Pregnant Before Her Father Did." YouTube. July 17, 2022. Retrieved online: September 12, 2022. www.youtube.com/watch?v=wYw6roXhJxs

44. Staff Report. "Issue of the week: When companies know you too well." *The Week*. January 8, 2015. Retrieved online: July 21, 2022. https://theweek.com/articles/477852/issue-week-when-companies-know-well

45. *The Colbert Report*. Comedy Central, Feb. 22, 2012. Retrieved online: July 22, 2022. www.cc.com/video/dv9iqc/the-colbert-report-the-word-surrender-to-a-buyer-power

46. *The Checkout*. ABC 1. April 11, 2013. Retrieved online: July 21, 2022. www.youtube.com/watch?v=f2Kji24833Y

47. Interview with Charles Duhigg, via email. July 20, 2022.

48. Belock, B., Fasheh, F. and McKeever, A. *Target Corporation: Predictive Analytics and Customer Privacy*. Notre Dame, IN: Eugene D. Fanning Center for Business Communication, Mendoza College of Business, University of Notre Dame. 2013.

49. Kostry, N., Malloy, T. and Wang, M. *Wells Fargo & Company: Accusations of Illegal Customer Account Management*. Notre Dame, IN: Eugene D. Fanning Center for Business Communication, Mendoza College of Business, University of Notre Dame. 2017.

50. Wells Fargo News Release. July 15, 2022. "Wells Fargo Reports Second Quarter 2022 Net Income of $3.1 billion, or $0.74 per Diluted Share." Retrieved online: July 26, 2022. https://www08.wellsfargomedia.com/assets/pdf/about/investor-relations/earnings/second-quarter-2022-earnings.pdf

51. Reckard, E. Scott. "How the wheels came off the Wells Fargo stagecoach." *Fraud Magazine*. November/December. 2017. Retrieved online: July 27, 2022. www.fraud-magazine.com/article.aspx?id=4294999811

52. Reckard, E. Scott. "Wells Fargo's pressure-cooker sales culture comes at a cost," *Los Angeles Times*. December 21, 2013. Retrieved online: July 27, 2022. www.latimes.com/business/la-fi-wells-fargo-sale-pressure-20131222-story.html

53. Ibid.
54. Ibid.
55. Ibid.
56. Ibid.
57. Ibid.
58. Corkery, Michael. "Wells Fargo Fined $185 Million for Fraudulently Opening Accounts." *The New York Times*, September 8, 2016. Retrieved online: February 19, 2023. https://www.nytimes.com/2016/09/09/business/dealbook/wells-fargo-fined-for-years-of-harm-to-customers.html
59. Corkery, M. "Wells Fargo Fined $185 Million for Fraudulently Opening Accounts." *The New York Times*. September 8, 2016. Retrieved online: September 23, 2022. www.nytimes.com/2016/09/09/business/dealbook/wells-fargo-fined-for-years-of-harm-to-customers.html
60. "Full Coverage: Wells Fargo Scandal." Story Gallery. *Los Angeles Times*. September 27, 2016. Retrieved online: July 28, 2022. www.latimes.com/business/la-wells-fargo-story-gallery-20160927-storygallery.html
61. Arenstein, S. "Wells Fargo Doing Well Pushing Good Stories, Yet Overall Theme Lacking as It Counters Crisis." *PR News*. January 30, 2017. Retrieved online: July 28, 2022. www.prnewsonline.com/wells-fargo-doing-well-pushing-good-stories-yet-overall-theme-lacking-as-it-counters-crisis/
62. "John Stumpf." *Wikipedia*. Retrieved online: July 27, 2022. https://en.wikipedia.org/wiki/John_Stumpf
63. Peltz, J. "As Wells Fargo's Earnings Fall, New CEO Wishes Crisis Was Handled Earlier." *The Los Angeles Times*. October 14, 2016. Retrieved online: July 28, 2022. www.latimes.com/business/la-fi-wells-fargo-earnings-20161014-snap-story.html
64. Peltz, J. "Wells Fargo Launches Ad Campaign to Leave Accounts Scandal behind. Not Everyone Is Buying It." *Los Angeles Times*. May 9, 2018. Retrieved online: July 28, 2018. www.latimes.com/business/la-fi-wells-fargo-ad-campaign-20180509-story.html
65. Wolff-Mann, E. "Wells Fargo Crisis: The Complete List." *Yahoo Finance*. March 12, 2019. Retrieved online: July 28, 2022. www.yahoo.com/now/wells-fargo-crisis-the-complete-timeline-141213414.html
66. News Release. "Wells Fargo Agrees to Pay $3 Billion to Resolve Criminal and Civil Investigations into Sales Practices Involving the Opening of Millions of Accounts without Customer Authorization." U.S. Department of Justice. February 21, 2020. Retrieved online: July 29, 2022. www.justice.gov/opa/pr/wells-fargo-agrees-pay-3-billion-resolve-criminal-and-civil-investigations-sales-practices
67. "Charles Scharf." *Wikipedia*. Retrieved online: July 29, 2022. https://en.wikipedia.org/wiki/Charles_Scharf
68. Flitter, E. "The Price of Wells Fargo's Fake Account Scandal Grows by $3 Billion." *New York Times*. February 21, 2020. Retrieved online: July 29, 2022. www.nytimes.com/2020/02/21/business/wells-fargo-settlement.html
69. Ibid.
70. Ibid.
71. Ibid.
72. Vernon, P. "Q&A: Former *LA Times* Reporter on Story That Led to $185 Million Wells Fargo Fine." *Columbia Journalism Review*. September 12, 2016. Retrieved online: July 27, 2022. www.cjr.org/q_and_a/wells_fargo_la_times_accounts.php

73. Interview with E. Scott Reckard, via email. August 13, 2022.
74. Kostry, N., Malloy, T. and Wang, M. "Wells Fargo & Company: Accusations of Illegal Customer Account Management." op. cit.
75. Claeys, A., Cauberghe, V. and Pandelaere, M. "Companies Fare Worse When the Press Exposes Their Problems Before They Do." *Harvard Business Review.* August 22, 2016. Retrieved online: July 31, 2022. https://hbr.org/2016/08/companies-fare-worse-when-the-press-exposes-their-problems-before-they-do
76. Ibid.
77. Arthur W. Page Society. "The Page Principles; Seven Proven Principles that Guide Our Actions & Behavior." Retrieved online: July 31, 2022. https://page.org/site/the-page-principles
78. Arpan, L. and Pompper, D. "Stormy Weather: Testing 'Stealing Thunder' as a Crisis Communication Strategy to Improve Communication Flow between Organizations and Journalists." *Public Relations Review.* Volume 29, Issue 3. September 2003. Retrieved online: July 31, 2022. www.sciencedirect.com/science/article/abs/pii/S0363811103000432
79. Arpan, L. and Roskos-Ewoldson, D. "Stealing Thunder: Analysis of the Effects of Proactive Disclosure of Crisis Information." *Public Relations Review.* Volume 31, Issue 3. September 2005. Retrieved online: July 31, 2022. www.sciencedirect.com/science/article/abs/pii/S0363811105000809
80. Fennis, B. and Stroebe, W. "Softening the Blow: Company Self-Disclosure of Negative Information Lessens Damaging Effects on Consumer Judgment and Decision Making." *Journal of Business Ethics.* February 14, 2013. Retrieved online: July 31, 2022. https://link.springer.com/article/10.1007/s10551-013-1647-9
81. Claeys, A., Cauberghe, V. and Pandelaere, M. op. cit.
82. Ibid.
83. Kissinger, H. *Brainy Quote.* 2022. Retrieved online: September 23, 2022. www.brainyquote.com/quotes/henry_kissinger_117426
84. Levin. op. cit.
85. Ohnsman. op. cit.
86. O'Donnell. op cit.
87. Mucha. op. cit.
88. Rechtin. op. cit.
89. Heil, E. "History's Most Cringe-Inducing Presser? It Wasn't Cohen's." *The Washington Post.* April 17, 2013. Retrieved online: August 6, 2022. www.washingtonpost.com/blogs/in-the-loop/post/historys-most-cringe-inducing-presser-it-wasnt-cohens/2013/04/17/dd98eba4-a77c-11e2-a8e2-5b98cb59187f_blog.html
90. Levin. op. cit.
91. Mucha. op. cit.
92. Interview with Bill Koenig, via Zoom. June 10, 2022.
93. Levin. op. cit.

Chapter 17

Responding to News Media Inaccuracy

All media outlets make mistakes, and with remarkable frequency. In 2019, *The New York Times* reported that in the prior year it published more than 4,100 corrections on digital articles and estimated that hundreds more corrections ran on various graphics packages, podcasts, and videos. Still other corrections appeared only in print editions. However, in context, consider that the *Times* published more than 50 million words and 55,000 articles in the same period.[1]

When mistakes happen, most news organizations issue printed and online corrections. However, some errors and their corrections are better than others:

The *San Carlos Enquirer Bulletin*: "A headline on an item in the Feb. 5 edition of the *Enquirer Bulletin* incorrectly stated, 'Stolen groceries.' It should have read, 'Homicide.'"

The Brazilian magazine *Veja*: "The candidate likes to spend his time reading Tolstoy, and not watching *Toy Story*, as originally reported."

The Guardian: "A reader noted that our recipe called 'Spaghetti with radicchio, fennel and rosemary' didn't include spaghetti, fennel or rosemary."

The Washington Post: "An earlier version of this story incorrectly located Brooklyn in the Canadian Province of Quebec. It is in New York."

The Economist: "In our article about the death of Kofi Annan on August 23 we said that he wore a goatee. An alert reader has pointed out that he sported a Van Dyke, which is a goatee plus moustache. Sorry to split hairs."[2]

In the 1948 presidential election, Democratic incumbent President Harry S. Truman was in a too-close-to-call reelection race against Republican Governor Thomas E. Dewey of New York. The *Chicago Daily Tribune*, a notably pro-Republican newspaper, had once called incumbent candidate Truman a "nincompoop." On election night, the newspaper double-checked with its Washington correspondent and other political experts who all assured the editors of a clear Dewey victory by the next morning. The first edition of the *Tribune* went to press and was delivered to the streets before all the results were counted, sporting the banner headline "DEWEY DEFEATS TRUMAN" across the front page. A few

DOI: 10.4324/9781003322849-21

days later, after his surprising upset victory over Dewey, President Truman stood on the rear platform of his train and grinned for reporters as he held the newspaper aloft with the embarrassing *Tribune* headline.[3]

While the "DEWEY DEFEATS TRUMAN" headline may be the most infamous of such blunders, numerous examples abound over the years of newsrooms predicting the wrong outcome of an election in a rush to outpace their competition. With Senator Hillary Clinton (D-NY) predicted to win the 2016 United States presidential election against Donald Trump, *Newsweek* magazine printed Clinton's face on the cover with the caption "Madam President" and sent them to newsstands.[4]

Why Do Journalists Make Mistakes?

Journalism at its best is an honorable profession that aspires to excellence and ethical behavior in the interest of getting at the truth. According to the National Public Radio *Ethics Handbook* on the importance of accuracy,

> Our purpose is to pursue the truth. Diligent verification is critical. We take great care to ensure that statements of fact in our journalism are both correct and in context. In our reporting, we rigorously challenge both the claims we encounter and the assumptions we bring. We devote our resources and our skills to presenting the fullest version of the truth we can deliver, placing the highest value on information we have gathered and verified ourselves.[5]

Nevertheless, the *Tribune* made its mistake out of wishful thinking, deliberate political bias, and poor judgment. Today, while favoritism and partisanship certainly exist in the media, the accelerated pace of journalism and declining newsroom resources are probably the root causes of most errors. Busy newsrooms, full of many inexperienced journalists on deadline to outdo the competition, race against time to publish their stories online, then again on social media, and yet again in print for the morning edition. Fewer editors, less time, and more pressure are the culprits. Errors inevitably slip through. Speed eclipses accuracy. Fact-checking often takes a back bench in the last few minutes before hitting the "publish" key. Names, dates, places, and events regularly get misidentified in the hubbub of meeting deadlines and frequent story updates.

Types of Errors

Three types of journalism errors are the most common. First, simple factual errors are the most frequent, such as an incorrectly spelled name or a wrong name, state, county, town, street, body of water, or other detail. Similarly, a source might be misidentified, or too many pronouns may lead to vagueness about exactly who is being referred to. All can be easily corrected, and journalists are usually happy to do so immediately in the online version of their story, then on social media, and then in the morning paper.

A second category of errors is more serious because they can influence accurate understanding of the news and what happened. One egregious error, particularly if intentional, is the use of images that express a bias, favorable or negative. For example, two photographs of the same hypothetical CEO tell different tales. In one warmly lit photo, the CEO appears on stage in front of employees, confident, robust, action-oriented, and in charge. In a second photo, more starkly lit, the same CEO hunkers in the backseat of a limousine, appearing weak, vulnerable, tired, and anxious. Which photo of the CEO does the news organization use in a story about the company during a crisis?

Also, in this category of serious media errors are inaccurate or incomplete quotes that distort the meaning of the person being quoted. In the same way that everyone in prison claims they are innocent, everyone with a regretful quote in an article claims they have been misquoted. When calling the media outlet to complain about a misquote, the burden of proof often falls to the person making the complaint. This reality is another reason we recommend using only email when communicating with the news media during a crisis. There can and should be no ambiguity about what was written or who wrote it.

To prevent quotation problems during a live interview, be sure to record it, first asking the journalist's permission to do so. Limit the time of the interview to no more than 10 minutes; the fewer quotes, the less chance of error. If recording is not an option during an interview (and it almost always is), ask the journalist to read back any direct quotations being attributed to you. Eager to secure their quote and move on, reporters may impatiently signal that your request is annoying or inconvenient. Do not fall for it. Their compliance with your request is standard journalistic practice. Ask them for a read-back in the interest of accuracy and your commitment to everything being right. Be firm but avoid an insistent tone.

Print and online journalists will generally correct such serious misquotation errors themselves, once proven. Television is not as inclined to admit mistakes. Television time is highly prized, short-form, and condensed. A mixture of fast-moving bites, images, commercials, graphics, talking heads, and maps, television's structure makes it more challenging to insert a correction into a TV news broadcast than into a newspaper or online article. Several examples exist of television news networks apologizing for the inappropriate comments of their commentators or guests. However, devoting costly airtime to correcting factual errors is much less common.

In 2012, George Zimmerman was on trial in Florida for the murder of 17-year-old Black high school student Trayvon Martin, who Zimmerman claimed he had shot and killed in self-defense in a Florida suburb. The Zimmerman trial was considered by many to be a test case for America's racial divide as the nation watched on television and Martin's family sat in the courtroom for weeks of emotional testimony.

During media coverage about Zimmerman's 911 call to police saying he had spotted Martin in his neighborhood, NBC's *Today* edited the clip of Zimmerman's call this way:

This guy looks like he's up to no good . . . . he looks black.

However, this is what the recording said:

[Zimmerman] This guy looks like he's up to no good. Or he's on drugs or something. It's raining and he's just walking around, looking about.
[Dispatcher] O.K., and this guy—is he white, black or Hispanic?
[Zimmerman] He looks black.[6]

David Carr, media writer for *The New York Times* called the *Today* edit "a remarkable lapse in editorial process that inflamed a highly emotional issue, and it created suspicion that journalists and media outlets were picking sides."[7]

Carr pointed out that NBC news management fired the producer, disciplined staffers, held meetings to discuss best practices, and issued apologies for making it appear that Zimmerman had made racist comments in what Carr called "the trifecta of being misleading, incendiary, and dead-bang wrong." Carr also pointed out, however, that *Today* never corrected the error on the air. No one explained to *Today's* millions of viewers exactly what happened and how it was corrected.[8]

"Clearly, broadcast news time is precious, and it would be impractical to correct every small error. But this was no misdemeanor. This was a deeply misleading compression in editing about an event that has taken on national significance,"[9] Carr wrote, adding,

Somewhere in the four expansive hours of *Today* – perhaps between the segment about a loud peacock that was bothering neighbors and the preview of Eva Longoria's show about "hunky bachelors" – somebody could have looked into the camera and set the story straight.[10]

Misleading or inaccurate headlines – those giant-font banners that draw our interest – also fall into this second category of potential media errors. News organizations handle headline-writing differently, but all headlines have the same purpose – to attract attention to the story and prompt the reader to read on. For the most part, headlines are not written by the journalists who write the story and are usually written by a copy editor, by other editors, or by those responsible for laying out the newspaper's pages.

Headlines can certainly be catchy, and that is their job. Companies in crisis may cringe at some headlines, but if the oversize bold font type is directly relevant to the story, complaints to the newsroom will likely go unheeded. Pure clickbait, however, designed solely to seduce the reader to click on a total nonstory, is worth complaining about. On June 29, 2022, headlines by the *New York Post, Fox News,* and several others shouted that a bust of President Abraham Lincoln and a copy of the Gettysburg Address had been "removed" from the Cornell University library in Ithaca, New York. Really? Abraham Lincoln? Removed? With so many historical figures being cancelled, I must read this, right? *Click!* Drilling down a little below the headline, a university spokesperson explained that the removal of the Lincoln bust was always planned because it was part of a temporary exhibit on the 150th anniversary of the Gettysburg Address that ended in 2021.[11]

The third category of media inaccuracies is the most difficult to correct because the media might not acknowledge or believe they have committed an error. Reporting or editorializing that contains subjective judgment, assumptions, cynical tone, lack of context, and opinions, rather than facts, can rarely be corrected, much less retracted. Imagine that a company uncovers a complex cyberattack within its organization, then takes a week to figure out exactly what happened, and then steals thunder by self-disclosing? What is to stop the media from writing, "The company tried to keep the problem from the public for far too long before reporting it"? What exactly is too long? Subjective observations that a spokesperson appeared "nervous" in an interview or "looked down at their hands" during an interview are impossible to refute.

The naturally skeptical media's constant quest to answer the questions, "What did they know and when did they know it?" leaves wide room for interpretation of timelines, accounts by sources, and other details unfolding in a crisis. Here again is an instance in which standing relationships of trust with a journalist may at least get you a fair hearing and the opportunity to explain additional context or background. Even so, a wholesale reversal or retraction by the news organization is rare. The best you might expect would be a follow-up story that repositions some of the details, with no admission of any type of correction. Ultimately, you may wholeheartedly disagree about how your organization is characterized in a story, but sometimes editors and reporters may close ranks and reason, "We are standing by our story. We did an extensive investigation, checked multiple sources, and we believe we were accurate. That is the end of that."[12]

How to Correct Inaccuracy (or Try to)

All news organizations handle corrections differently, but most make corrections, usually visible in the same place online and in print, so readers can find them. As a rule, let the nits and small stuff go. Minor errors mean nothing. However, any error of real substance should be corrected if possible. In the digital age, a major uncorrected error can spread across media platforms like a California canyon fire and remain online to haunt an organization forever, years after a crisis has passed. Future journalists coming to a beat will discover such uncorrected historical claims online and consider them part of the news record to be reported in forthcoming stories. So, such mistakes should be found and purged, quickly.

A crisis requires relentless monitoring of all media platforms. Aggressive monitoring should be thought of conceptually as both radar and sonar. Radar is monitoring everything coming your way, all expected inbound coverage on all the media channels you anticipate. For correcting errors, designate a media-savvy member of your Rapid Response Team, preferably your day-to-day spokesperson who has relationships with journalists who cover you. Once an error is found, have them contact the journalist with a sense of urgency about the need for correction. Sonar is proactively monitoring (pinging) beyond the reaches of your normal channels to capture coverage of your crisis on blogs and social channels you might not normally monitor. Look everywhere.

A common knee-jerk mistake that indignant communications practitioners make when seeking to correct a media error is to immediately call a reporter's editor. Don't do it. Always start with the reporter. Always. They have the most knowledge of their own story and are the straightest line to a correction. Jayne O'Donnell, formerly with *USA Today* says, "You should be talking to me first because if I really made a mistake I can explain it to you, and I'm going to fix it." She adds that contacting her first "is also a chance to develop a relationship." She explains,

> If you're going to debate with somebody, debate with me, because I know everything about the story. It doesn't help to go to my editor first because the editor and the reporter will talk regardless. Going to the editor first is like a little kid telling on his brother, and the editor doesn't want to bother unless you have spoken with me first.[13]

O'Donnell also notes a recent new presence in the modern newsroom:

> If the debate turns into an argument and if I say I am not going to budge, then you could say you're going to need to speak to my editor. In that case, the lawyers are probably going to get involved as well.[14]

Letters to the Editor

If your request for correction goes unheeded and you want to go on record with your viewpoint, consider sending a Letter to the Editor (LTE). Your strategic goal is to get the letter published, so know the rules that will help you do that. If responding to a newspaper or online article, timeliness is key, so submit your letter as quickly as possible, preferably within 24 hours after the article was published. In your first sentence, mention the date, title, and author of the article. This sentence may also convey the theme of your argument, perhaps that the article "contained several clear errors in fact" or "failed to consider key events." If the authority of the letter's author is clear from the signature, that is sufficient. If not, establish the author's standing early on. If you desire to "set the record straight," then say so, but be sure to follow through with clear and persuasive facts. A weak LTE is worse than no LTE at all.

As always, do not repeat any negative allegations that were written about you, but instead, stick to the facts you wish to refute. Avoid opinion words like "unfair," "dishonest," "unreasonable," and "biased." Self-righteous or indignant copy that makes you feel good about your complaint will be ignored. Bright copy that prompts the Letters Desk editor to say "Okay, this is reasonable and succinct" is on target. Find out the publication's length requirements for an LTE (usually between 150–300 words) and write it shorter than the maximum. Brevity will improve your chances. Know that you will likely be edited, so the more concise and to-the-point, the better.

To get an LTE published in a major publication, you will need to squeak. Most big publications will not admit it, but they get thousands of LTEs, usually through an online portal set up for this purpose, and most of them are consigned to what overwhelmed editors call the "slush pile." The volume is just too much to handle, and many worthy letters are never printed. So, your letter will likely get lost if submitted in this manner. If your organization is in crisis and in the news and you want to submit an LTE to right a perceived wrong, you fortunately have an immediate leg up with the news organization covering you. Contact the reporter writing about you, even though they may be the source of the complaint and tell them you want to submit an LTE. If no help is forthcoming, now is the time to contact the reporter's editor about bringing your LTE to the attention of the Letters Desk. Most news organizations who have been covering your crisis will at least consider your letter, but they have no obligation to publish it.

Op-Ed

Convincing a newspaper to publish an article about your crisis, authored by your CEO or other top leader, and printed opposite the editorial page (op-ed) of a newspaper, is a longshot but not impossible. The op-ed page is usually reserved for persuasive guest articles about political or social topics currently in the news about which people care to have an opinion. Therein lies one of the problems with your organization's chances of securing an op-ed spot that competes for precious space with childhood education, tax increases, social justice, and other issues people care about. You may be convinced that you have been wronged or misunderstood enough by a publication to boil your blood, and you want to reshape public opinion in your favor, in your own words. But who cares? Try to obtain some assurance up front that the publication will even consider your op-ed, or you may be wasting your time preparing one.

If you proceed, timeliness is again paramount. Length is about 500 to 800 words. Like an LTE, clearly state the date, title, and author of the offending article up front. Do not repeat the negative and state your main point right away. To convey that you are not being unfair in your complaint, acknowledge a few points that the publication got right before detailing the things that are mistaken. Use concise sentences and short paragraphs. Persuasively make your case that a wrong has been done to you by the publication and state the clear evidence that supports your assertion. Include a human angle, if possible, like empathy for your employees who have been hurt by the paper's claims. End with your commitment to put the crisis behind you by stating your positive goals for the future. Do not spend time coming up with a clever title because the newspaper will do that for you, like it or not.

Self-Publish

The newspaper has refused both your LTE and your op-ed. The analog-age chestnut that it is never a good idea to declare war on someone who buys ink by the barrel may be valid, but you do have ways to tell your story and defend yourself against a perceived wrong committed by a news organization. Think twice, however, and consider doing nothing more. The big downside of airing your grievances on self-publishing sites and your own internal and external websites and other platforms is that you will likely draw bigger audiences to your crisis than you intended. Two of the biggest self-publishing content sites are Medium, and LinkedIn, where you can self-publish your complaint, and there are many more similar (but all a little different) self-publishing platforms like Blogger, HubPages, WordPress, and NewsBreak.

Corporate Advertising

A full-blown nationwide crisis like the Wells Fargo cross-selling scheme (see Chapter 16, "Engaging with Legacy Media") prompted the banking giant to mount a nationwide image-repair campaign that included full-page newspaper and magazine ads and prime-time television commercials for untold millions of dollars. A crisis so widespread requires extensive damage repair. However, what if your beef is with a particular news outlet that published a damaging and unfair article about you, and they refuse to publish your LTE or your CEO's op-ed? Based on the premise that the readers you care about are the ones that read that paper, you might consider some localized corporate advertising to tell your story in your own words. You will need to swallow hard and commit resources to advertise in a newspaper that is attacking you. A full-page "open letter" from your CEO to the newspaper's readers would have similar content to the op-ed refused by the paper. But keep in mind, "Who Cares?" as you make your case for fairness. Avoid the temptation to draw undue interest to a crisis few are paying attention to other than you.

References

1. Moore, L. "The News in 2018 Was Memorable. So Were These Corrections." *The New York Times*. January 3, 2019. Retrieved online: August 8, 2022. www.nytimes.com/2019/01/03/reader-center/new-york-times-corrections.html

2. Mantzarlis, A. "The funny, the weird and the serious: 33 media corrections from 2018." *Poynter*. December 18, 2018. Retrieved online: August 8, 2022. www.poynter.org/fact-checking/2018/the-funny-the-weird-and-the-serious-33-media-corrections-from-2018/

3. Dewey Defeats Truman. *Wikipedia*. Retrieved online: August 8, 2022. https://en.wikipedia.org/wiki/Dewey_Defeats_Truman

4. Ibid.

5. National Public Radio Ethics Handbook. "Accuracy." 2022. Retrieved online: August 8, 2022. www.npr.org/about-npr/688139552/accuracy

6. "NBC Producer's Editing of 911 Call in Trayvon Martin Case Misleads Viewers." *YouTube. Flackcheck.org*. April 10, 2012. Retrieved online: August 11, 2022. www.youtube.com/watch?v=Xf_AtDnVhyA

7. Carr, D. "TV Corrects Itself, Just Not on the Air." *The New York Times*. April 22, 2012. Retrieved online: August 9, 2022. www.nytimes.com/2012/04/23/business/media/tv-news-corrects-itself-just-not-on-the-air.html

8. Ibid.

9. Ibid.

10. Ibid.

11. Rogers, Z. "Cornell Removes Gettysburg Address, Bust of President Lincoln From school Library." *ABC News Channel 12*. June 29, 2022. Retrieved online: August 10, 2022. https://wcti12.com/news/nation-world/gettysburg-address-bust-of-president-lincoln-removed-from-cornell-university-library-abraham-randy-wayne-rebecca-valli

12. Mallary, J. "Why Journalists Make Mistakes & What We Can Do About Them." *Poynter*. July 7, 2010. Retrieved online: August 11, 2022. www.poynter.org/reporting-editing/2010/why-journalists-make-mistakes-what-we-can-do-about-them/

13. Interview with Jayne O'Donnell, via Zoom. June 29, 2022.

14. Ibid.

Chapter 18

Deploy Your Websites

Dedicated Crisis Microsites

A dedicated, crisis microsite can become a primary communication tool for reaching the audiences you want to reach and controlling the message you want to convey in a crisis.

The village of Brightwaters, New York, is on the southern coast of Long Island, a 119-mile, densely populated sandspit extending east from New York City. Many of Brightwaters's affluent homes are perched on a canal that leads to the Great South Bay. Brightwaters is also where the big red warning arrow on NBC meteorologist Al Roker's weather map often points as the next landfall for hurricanes headed up the Atlantic Coast, once finished with points southeast. The residents are accustomed to evacuations, power outages, and fish in their basements.

When the water rises, Brightwaters's families rely on the Suffolk County Office of Emergency Management website and its "Suffolk Alert" emergency texting system to contact residents and keep them updated. Burghs almost everywhere have similar sites, as do many police and fire departments and utilities, with differing levels of function and usefulness – but with the common purpose of being the centralized source of information in an emergency.[1]

In a business crisis, the purpose of a crisis microsite is much the same. A dedicated crisis microsite has several advantages. First, providing your information to the news media before you post it on your own microsite makes it subject to misinterpretation; a crisis microsite allows you to disperse information and messaging in language of your choosing. Additional background from you on the microsite can provide valuable context. Journalists, customers, stakeholders, and your employees converging on your microsite will see information, facts, and your company's perspective on the situation. Second, a microsite gives you the power to set your own schedule for updates, and if you do so regularly, your stakeholders, including the news media, will know where and when to go for the latest information. Next, establishing a microsite shows your organization's dedication to open and transparent communication about your crisis. The nature and extent of the information you choose to post is up to you. Finally, a crisis microsite gives

DOI: 10.4324/9781003322849-22

your main website some breathing room; visitors who have no awareness of the crisis or no interest in it will want to engage with your main site as they wish.

The Withdrawal of Vioxx From the Market

On September 30, 2004, pharmaceutical giant Merck & Company announced a voluntary withdrawal of its worldwide supply of Vioxx, its blockbuster arthritis medication that had brought in $2.5 billion in sales the prior year. Merck & Company executives said the recall was driven by a study that found patients taking the popular drug for at least 18 months suffered more strokes and heart attacks. At the time of the recall, about two million people were taking Vioxx. Since the drug's approval in 1999, more than 100 million prescriptions had been written for the medicine.[2]

With only two-and-a-half days between the decision to withdraw the drug and the forthcoming announcement, Merck & Company's communications team had to figure out how to reach Vioxx users worldwide, the news media, physicians, patients in clinical trials, researchers, regulators, employees, and sales representatives globally who were calling on doctors and clinics to promote the benefits of Vioxx.

The team prepared a special website, *www.vioxx.com*, to supplement its *www.merck.com* website, and a toll-free number for medical professionals and the general public with questions. The company's *www.vioxx.com* website traffic grew from about 4,000 daily visits the day before the recall announcement, to 234,000 visits on October 1. By early December, the *www.vioxx.com* website had attracted more than two million visitors, while the company's *www.merck.com* website had an additional one million visitors. The team's toll-free telephone number received more than 120,000 calls in the first 6 days following the announcement.[3]

Light Up Your Crisis Microsite

In Chapter 2, "Be Strategic in Your Planning," we advised you to create a stand-by website in advance of a crisis that will lie dormant until it needs to be up and running in an instant. A stand-by website is your ready-made, hidden website on the ready 24/7, that you will activate when a trigger event occurs. Copy is written in advance and preapproved, and it should have the capacity to be updated quickly and easily. Ideally, you will create a stand-by site for each major potential threat that can be anticipated. Large manufacturers will experience delays in production. Supply chains will bottleneck. Big corporations will be cyberattacked. Pharmaceutical companies will have product recalls. Ships will sink. Unionized labor forces will strike. Planes will crash (the airline industry makes extensive use of stand-by sites).

Crisis microsites operate most effectively as parallel sites to an existing main website. All traffic and questions about the crisis are directed to the crisis microsite, but the main site remains accessible from it. In the same way, a navigation button may be placed on the main site that links directly to the crisis microsite. However, it need not be a major presence on the main site's homepage. A subtle navigation button linking to the crisis microsite is a transparent acknowledgment that the organization takes the matter seriously and has complete crisis-related information offered elsewhere. The search function on the main site should be populated with an exhaustive list of crisis-related keywords that link directly to the crisis microsite. Anyone looking for crisis-related information should be able to find it on all platforms via links to the crisis microsite. Be sure to include a team from IT to manage the technical interface between the crisis microsite and the main site.

Looks matter. Your crisis microsite should avoid the sophisticated look and branding of a marketing site. Crisis communication and transparency are the objective, not sales. Even though you are proud of your brand and want everything branded appropriately, according to high company standards, a crisis microsite with too much window-dressing telegraphs the message "they knew this was coming."

A crisis microsite landing page followed by subject-specific tabs should be sufficient. Put the most important information up front, no matter how distressing. The homepage is a good place for a message from the CEO and is where an apology would be positioned, if required. The homepage's top priority should be easy links to information specifically for those most affected by the crisis. An automobile safety recall homepage would include how customers can determine if their car is included in the recall and link to the most convenient place to have it repaired. Similarly, a faulty home gym equipment homepage would explain to customers how to return it and receive a refund. In more serious cases, the homepage for a transportation accident would focus on survivors and their families and help those affected find assistance. Consider a multilingual site, at least for the main sections, if that is appropriate for your target audience.

Include a series of visible tabs on the homepage, each dedicated to separate elements of the crisis. Design the simple site so that tabs can be easily added or deleted by the communication team. Some tabs on your crisis microsite might include:

- **Our Viewpoint**. Include your organization's official, succinct, and quotable position on the crisis, leading with the main points you want your audiences most to understand. Use your company statement, which may be more effective in the words of a senior executive. Add a statement of company purpose.
- **What Is Next?** Detail the plan and goals of specific actions your organization has taken, and is taking, to mitigate the crisis for anyone affected by it. Add a timeline for resolution, if available.
- **We Disagree.** If you have been treated unfairly by the news media in a significant manner, post your response and correct the record. You might reprint your letter to the editor, an op-ed, or a statement outlining the factual reasons you believe the coverage was in error.

- **Customer Support.** Provide ways for customers to seek relief from effects of the crisis and to contact your organization on the channels you designate, such as social media, phone banks, or email.
- **Active Links.** Provide easy-to-navigate crosslinks between the crisis microsite, main site, and social media channels and post a toll-free number for questions. Let people know if you are providing updates via social media and how they can follow you.
- **News Media Information.** Include all published official statements and updated operational information. Provide news media with the option of subscribing to an RSS feed. For an ongoing crisis that has daily or frequent updates, such as production changes, temporary layoffs, or product shortages, post the updates at the same time each day in a prominent manner so that news media can accurately discern the changes day-over-day. Inform key media of this recurring practice to save time and reduce individual inquiries. List all designated spokespersons available globally, 24/7, but let consumers know these contacts are for news media only; link to the *Customer Support* tab for consumers who have questions.
- **News Media Coverage.** If news media coverage is all negative, better to leave out this tab. If balanced, include it, in the interest of transparency, even the uncomfortable stories. Link to *We Disagree* tab if applicable.
- **Corporate Social Responsibility.** In a low-key manner, recognize charitable or other cause-related actions you may be taking in response to the crisis. Explain how the public can donate, if applicable.
- **Relevant Background.** Provide useful narrative and factual background to help people understand in greater detail what happened and why. Resist using your basic statement for this purpose.
- **Company Purpose, Footprint, and History.** People coming to your crisis microsite may not be familiar with your organization. This should be straightforward and brief. Avoid advertising jargon and self-praise. Link to your main site.
- **Separate Stakeholder Tabs.** If you have a regulatory or NGO component to your crisis, consider tabs for these or other key stakeholders who require specialized information. This section could include congressional testimony or scientific data.
- **Contact Us.** Even though direct contact links have been provided in several places throughout the tabs, this catch-all can be a dropdown menu with links to *Customer Support, Active Links, News Media Information* or to ask a general question.

Unrelated to your crisis, your organization most likely hosts a general media newsroom site for day-to-day company announcements, statements, product introductions, editorial, executive biographies, and high-quality photographs and videos. Place a navigation button to your crisis microsite on the homepage of your media newsroom, and likewise, provide a link from your crisis microsite to your media newsroom.

Deciding if and when to activate a crisis microsite is one of your most important judgment calls, and there is no one-size-fits-all answer. Overestimating a crisis of relative low severity, affecting few people, not drawing much media attention, and unlikely to get much worse, or last for a long time, probably does not merit a crisis microsite. Posting a crisis microsite for such a short-term matter could make matters worse by drawing undue attention to your problems. An informative media newsroom website is adequate for posting statements in such an instance. But a severe crisis, one that is inspiring media inquiries and is likely to get worse and be drawn out over time, requires a robust response and a crisis microsite.

In the interest of quick action, a crisis microsite should be simple and very easy to update on a technical level. Before your crisis microsite is activated, determine who will be responsible for updating the information. Crisis communication is not in marketing's usual wheelhouse, so shift that role to the Rapid Response Team or corporate communications exclusively for the microsite. Crisis information changes quickly and frequent updates must be made promptly and easily by the team on the ground, without waiting for review by marketing and its agency, which can take undue time.

A Note on Your Employee Website

In a crisis, it is imperative that you communicate with your employees at the same time you post to your microsite, to other internal channels, or release statements to the news media or other stakeholders. Employees should receive identical information to whatever you release externally, and likely more. In some instances, employees will need additional details related to the crisis, such as company policies that have changed as a result of the crisis, work schedule changes, compensation impacts, or the availability of counseling. Remember that anything communicated to your employees or suppliers can easily make its way to the news media or social media.

Talc in Baby Powder: A Case in Point

On August 11, 2022, Johnson & Johnson Consumer Health announced that it would change to an all cornstarch-based baby powder formula and discontinue its popular but controversial talc-based Johnson's Baby Powder globally in 2023.[4]

Johnson & Johnson is the subject of more than 40,000 lawsuits, many from women battling ovarian cancer or mesothelioma. The plaintiffs have alleged that Johnson & Johnson continued selling baby powder containing talc while being aware of its health risks, such as potential contamination from asbestos. The company stopped sales of its talc-based baby powder in North America in 2020.[5]

The company did not reference the litigation in its announcement but said it had made a "commercial decision" that "will help simplify our product offerings, deliver sustainable innovation, and meet the needs of our consumers, customers, and evolving global trends."[6]

It reiterated its long-held stance on the safety of its powder. "Our position on the safety of our cosmetic talc remains unchanged. We stand firmly behind the decades of independent scientific analysis by medical experts around the world that confirms talc-based JOHNSON'S® Baby Powder is safe, does not contain asbestos, and does not cause cancer."[7]

The company has a robust presence on the web concerning the asbestos-in-talc issue.

While its main site, *www.jnj.com* does not have any navigation buttons directly addressing talc, the search function links to 18 separate scientific studies, news releases, and a strongly worded rebuttal to a December 14, 2018, Reuters article that Johnson & Johnson labeled "one-sided, false, and inflammatory."[8] A search on the homepage for Johnson's Baby Powder leads to 557 articles, and the distinct product page for baby powder is focused on talc safety. While the homepage does not invite a reader to research the issue, anyone interested can easily find it.

The separate, dedicated sites are where the transparency is notable. Johnson & Johnson is not hiding from this issue. Optimized with a Google ad "Johnson & Johnson – Get the Facts About Talc" and labeled *www.factsabouttalc.com*, the site is organized into talcum powder safety information, a news media information center, news coverage of the talc issue, and litigation news coverage. The section on the litigation itself is extensive and includes more than 5,000 court documents that have been admitted into evidence over the years, inviting the reader "to review the evidence and make up your mind." The site also contains a portal that allows consumers to ask the company questions. Separately, the company supports an optimized and dedicated link to "5 Important Facts About Talc Safety," for a condensed treatment of the issue.[9]

Even though Johnson & Johnson has decided to discontinue its sale of talc-based baby powder on a worldwide basis, its robust web presence on the talc issue will continue to work hard for the company as a useful consumer and media communication resource as the litigation carries on and the company continues defending its interests in court and in the public eye.

References

1. Suffolk County Office of Emergency Management Website. 2022. Retrieved online: August 23, 2022. www.suffolkcountyny.gov/Departments/FRES/Office-of-Emergency-Management
2. Gust A. and Bartucci, G. "Merck & Company, Inc.: The Recall of Vioxx® (B)." Notre Dame, IN: Eugene D. Fanning Center for Business Communication, Mendoza College of Business, University of Notre Dame. 2005.

3. Ibid.
4. News Release. "Johnson & Johnson Consumer Health to Transition Global Baby Powder Portfolio to Cornstarch." August 11, 2022. Retrieved online: August 23, 2022. www.jnj.com/johnson-johnson-consumer-health-to-transition-global-baby-powder-portfolio-to-cornstarch
5. Hsu, T. and Carin-Rabin, R. "Johnson & Johnson Will Discontinue Talc-Based Baby Powder Globally in 2023." *The New York Times.* August 11, 2022. Retrieved online: August 23, 2022. www.nytimes.com/2022/08/11/business/johnson-and-johnson-talc-corn-starch.html
6. Johnson & Johnson News Release. op cit.
7. Ibid.
8. News Release. Statement on Reuters Talc Article. December 14, 2018. Retrieved online: August 23, 2022. www.jnj.com/statement-on-reuters-talc-article
9. "Facts About Talc." Johnson & Johnson. 2020. Retrieved online: August 23, 2022. www.factsabouttalc.com/safety

Chapter 19

Social Media Has Changed the Crisis Communications Landscape

The basic principles of effective crisis communication apply equally to both legacy and social media. Social media's evolving form of information-sharing, however, creates both new risks and new openings for organizations in a crisis. The rules keep changing as new players enter the game, expanding the meaning of audience, stakeholders, and what constitutes news. One truth is certain for crisis communicators working in this disruptive environment: it is going to get harder.

Social media has revolutionized business marketing. Many global brands heavily weight their social media activation in advertising and marketing to reduce costs. They also generate meaningful customer engagement as the consumer interacts with its products and services through the company's platforms and with other customers, on their own terms. Companies recognize that customer advocates are a powerful marketing tool because people trust and listen to what others think and say. Social media also provides internet forums and chat rooms for customer fan communities to develop. Company-sponsored Facebook pages full of positive comments and photos of happy customers showing off their new products are gold to the marketing department.[1]

Vigorous company outreach on social media also provides the opportunity to learn more about a company's customers. As engaged consumers become more involved with a company's multiple social media channels, information volunteered by the consumer can help compile a customer's profile. With more complete information, marketers are better able to group and target customers according to their preferences.[2]

That is the good news.

The Arsenal of Disapproval

Andrew Winston, a consultant on sustainable business strategy and author of the books *Green to Gold*, *The Big Pivot*, and *Net Positive*, wrote,

> The speed of shame is as fast (and as ruthless) as the internet. When will companies realize that everyone now has a video camera on them, and that they

DOI: 10.4324/9781003322849-23

can broadcast live on Facebook within minutes? People can now destroy brand trust at the speed of light, with consequences that are far-reaching.[3]

Before social media, unhappy consumers, frustrated by what they judged to be an unresponsive company, could gripe to the local TV news consumer watchdog. Or they could complain to a newspaper reporter about their ill-treatment by a business. Today, social media presents many options for individuals or groups to publicly express displeasure, complaints, or concerns about a business or other organization.

Unintended Consequences

An organization's own social media channels can be turned against it. Initially set up to forge relationships with customers and others, a company's social channels can become forums for displeased people to flood them with grievances.

Website Clones

Clever search engine optimization allows individuals to create troublesome blogs, websites, and Facebook pages that appear in searches next to an organization's official website. Worse, an organization's branded graphics, including photos of its executives and products can easily be stolen to create a fake site that appears legitimate.

Chatterboxes

Although Facebook has cut into the popularity of message boards, consumer disapproval of an organization can still be posted on thousands of internet forums and chat rooms of several types, some moderated and requiring registration, and others anonymous and uncensored.

#HeadsUp

Hashtags are among the more common and powerful communication tools for expressing support or discontent and publicizing it. Hashtags such as #DeleteUber or #BoycottToyota or #antiChevronDay can be used on social media to rapidly distribute complaints or allegations against a targeted organization and also track and recruit supporters. In the women's rights and social justice movements, the hashtags #MeToo and #BlackLivesMatter became symbols of the causes they represent.

Video Wild West

YouTube and TikTok are two video sharing sites with unprecedented social influence, for good and for bad. Video content is uploaded to these sites by consumers, advertisers, politicians, educators, news media, entertainers, and others. Add to this, conspiracy theorists, swindlers, pranksters, impostors, and numerous other bottom-feeders with a cell phone. YouTube videos are uploaded at a rate of more than 500 hours of content per minute by more than 2.9 billion monthly users. TikTok has more than one billion monthly active users. Companies preparing for a crisis, or in the middle of one, need robust capabilities well beyond their standard YouTube and TikTok marketing practices to plan how most effectively to deploy these sites in defense of their brand and reputation.[4]

A Plucky Response

Many British fans of Kentucky Fried Chicken were not feeling much love for the Colonel around Valentine's Day 2018. More than three-quarters of the popular franchise's 870 restaurants were shuttered because they had run out of an essential item on their menu: chicken. The shortage was caused by a perfect storm in the supply chain. For years, KFC had used a distributor that maintained six refrigerated warehouses from which they delivered fresh chicken to the stores. A new distribution contract went to German-owned DHL, which operated only a single warehouse in what is known as the "golden rectangle" of central England, where many warehouse operations stage products for just-in-time overnight delivery throughout the U.K.[5]

On February 14, two separate multiple-vehicle collisions on major access roads to the rectangle, including one fatality and two injuries, caused the police to shut down key intersections in the area, resulting in massive traffic jams. The DHL chicken delivery trucks could not get into or out of their single supply depot. The combination of gridlocked traffic, a brand-new logistics contract, DHL drivers unfamiliar with their routes, a new IT system, and lack of a contingency plan caused a chicken shortage that dragged on for nearly two weeks and kept hundreds of KFC stores closed.

Chicken farmers complained that their freshly slaughtered chickens were going bad. Chicken spoiled in unrefrigerated DHL trucks and, in one instance, was dumped roadside. Customers complained to the police on Twitter, only to be tweeted back that it was not a police matter. Politicians in the Bristol area were urged to call for nationalization of the chain to prevent problems like this in the future.[6]

Both legacy media and social media lit up across the U.K. and across the ocean in the U.S., including on CNN and the *Today Show*, fueled by the irony of a chicken restaurant without any chicken. The hashtags #ChickenCrisis, #KFC Crisis, and #KFCClosed were born.[7] The *Daily Mail* called it "the great KFC chicken shortage," while social media jeered "Fowl Play!" and "Holy Cluck!" Sarcastic YouTube videos compared the shortage to a pub without beer or a florist without flowers. Others vented that they were taking their families to McDonald's. British comedians got laughs at KFC's expense. KFC tweeted a tongue-in-beak statement saying that their newly hired delivery partner "had a couple of teething problems" getting chicken to its restaurants, which one hangry customer on Instagram called "a poultry excuse."[8]

The best word to describe KFC's social media presence is charming. The words young, hip, international, irreverent, lighthearted, and cool also fit. With 58 million Facebook followers and 2 million on Twitter, KFC fans all over the world share their devotion to Colonel Sanders's fried chicken, famously made up of the Colonel's secret recipe, consisting of 11 herbs and spices – a closely guarded trade secret that has never been revealed. Add clever to KFC's social media descriptors. Fans had fun sleuthing over the big online mystery about why KFC only followed 11 people on Twitter. One enterprising fan discovered that KFC only followed the five former Spice Girls and six guys named Herb – an homage to the secret recipe. The revelation was liked on Twitter 715,000 times and retweeted more than 322,000 times.[9]

KFC's response to the chicken shortage crisis was both immediate and imaginative. The company issued constant and droll updates online such as, "The chicken crossed the road, just not to our restaurants." The tone of all the statements was humble and conversational, and every social post gave a "[s]hout out to our restaurant teams who are working flat out to get us back up and running again." KFC immediately established a dedicated microsite where customers could check the location of the nearest open restaurant and the status of other ones nearby, noting, "We're updating this as regularly as we can."[10]

The company's next move was a full-page ad in two major newspapers with a combined readership of more than six million readers throughout the U.K. and posts on social media platforms.[11] Set against a bright red background, the iconic white and red chicken bucket with a sketch of Colonel Sanders face lies on its side, empty, with a few fried crumbs tumbling out. The bold letters **FCK** stand out, rearranging the usual KFC. In other words, we messed up, and we own this problem. Below the near-expletive bucket were the words:

We're Sorry

A chicken restaurant without chicken. It's not ideal. Huge apologies to our customers, especially those who travelled out of their way to find we were closed. And endless thanks to our KFC team members and our franchise partners for working tirelessly to improve the situation. It's been a hell of a week, but we're making progress, and every day more and more fresh chicken is being delivered to our restaurants. Thanks for bearing with us. Visit kfc.co.uk/crossed-the-road for details about your local restaurant.[12]

The cheeky ad was an immediate success and a breakthrough for the brand – a wide-scale apology for the inconvenience and disruption caused to both KFC customers and franchisees and a straightforward and clear explanation of what was being done to solve the crisis. On social media, PR consultant Andrew Bloch tweeted, "KFC apologizes with a full-page ad in today's Metro. A masterclass in PR crisis management." Twitter was brimming over with similar sentiment, such as, "How could you not forgive them?," "How cool," "Apology accepted," and "Perfectly pitched apology ad."[13]

The ad, which appeared in just two U.K. newspapers, generated more than 700 news articles and TV reports, for a combined global reach of 797 million people. An additional 219 million social media users saw the branded "FCK" image, meaning that the campaign generated a total earned media reach of more than one billion. All from a single ad on a single day.[14]

A few months later, Meghan Farren, Chief Marketing Officer of KFC for the U.K. and Ireland and the executive who greenlighted the ad, was in Cannes to receive an award for the campaign. She said, "At that time, our business was, to be honest, on its knees." She explained that irate customers came into the few open stores, most of which served very limited menus, and berated and abused KFC employees over the shortages:

> After we ran the advert, I think our team members felt supported and felt valued. And they felt that their customers understood that it wasn't their fault and that their abuse shouldn't be directed at them, but at the brand, and that's what we wanted.[15]

Farren said she was shocked when her ad agency first came up with the idea. But it grew on her because she felt KFC should avoid a more standard corporate response and needed something very different that would appeal to people's humanity. She explained that she nervously brought the ad into the KFC corporate lawyer for review, and, to her surprise, the lawyer smiled. "Allowing people to empathize with you can really go a long way to rebuilding trust and to forgiveness," she said. "We allowed people to empathize with us through being human and allowing them to see how we were feeling."[16]

"Brands are like people. They are run by human beings. And if you want people to connect with other people, you are authentic and open and honest and humble, and we just acted like that," Farren said.[17]

KFC moved quickly (the ad was developed in 24 hours) and transparently, answering questions and posting updates on social media daily. The company was able to reverse the narrative with its funny and nearly obscene advertising, even as it was grappling with its logistics problems. The ad was a humble apology to KFC customers, provided cover and showed appreciation to KFC employees, and accepted clear ownership of the problem and a commitment to work hard to fix it. The humble tone of the ad demonstrated a shrewd understanding of the brand's core customer and remained consistent with how it had been communicating with its young and hip audience on social media and elsewhere.

Social Media Crisis Levels

Grouping social media crises into three basic levels can help an organization determine the nature and extent of its response. Assessing the level of a crisis and correlating that with the scale of the response is a difficult judgment call. Overreacting may draw unnecessary attention to a relatively minor situation. Underreacting may allow a problem to grow beyond control. Ask: "What is our pain tolerance for negative posts? What is our threshold for differentiating a few negative comments from a true crisis? What level of crisis would merit targeted engagement with individuals or groups, and what level would merit a robust public campaign from our organization?"

The social media team should have an advance plan of action specifically designed for crisis response. As a key member of the Rapid Response Team, they should have in place a quick process for getting their messaging approved. Understanding the level of a crises they may encounter can help inform the protocols they develop. A social media crisis level can be determined based on an analysis of:

- The severity of the trigger event.
- The potential for the problem to grow.
- The likelihood of the crisis being resolved within a reasonable amount of time.

The analysis should also include a deep understanding of an organization's audiences, including key stakeholders, and how they might react to negative news about the organization on social media. Based on these observations, companies can create operational standards for each one of these three levels:

Level 1: Multiplatform Social Media Crises. An organization that finds itself under assault from several social media channels at once, attracting coverage from legacy media on both its traditional and social channels, and criticism from government officials and other stakeholders, faces the highest potential for reputation damage. If a multiplatform crisis grows big enough, legacy media will also start double reporting on the extent of the social media spread as well as the cause of the crisis itself. Problems like this will not go away on their own. Multiplatform crises usually involve serious matters with high potential for big publicity. Full-scale mobilization is likely required.[18]

Level 2: Emergent Social Media Crises. Emergent crises are problems in the formative stage that have the potential to expand into a significant crisis if not handled right away, with speed and precision. Social media-savvy customers who are unhappy with their treatment by a customer relations department know that it is a good strategy to complain on social media. Companies act quickly because they want to keep such complaints contained, to avoid them growing into any kind of widespread customer insurgency. Many companies, particularly airlines and automobile companies, monitor their social media sites with collaborative teams from marketing and customer relations and work to take complaining customers offline to quickly resolve their issue one-to-one.[19]

Level 3: Guilt by Association. If a supplier to a global name-brand corporation gets into hot water on social media over an employment issue at their plant, someone is going to connect the dots and try to drag the big company into the discussion. If a major competitor has a safety recall, say for infant car seats, most infant car seat manufacturers may receive questions on social media about the safety of their seats as well. For example, when Toyota was experiencing its alleged unintended sudden acceleration crisis in 2010 (See Chapter 16), all major automakers were deluged by customers wanting to know if their products had any of the same problems.

In such an instance, a curated and empathetic social media response is not the best course of action. Instead, one-size-fits-all communication is advised. Once the facts are known, and it is confirmed there are indeed no direct ties to the other organization's crisis, issue a strong proactive statement across-the-board that clearly distances your company from the problem. Do not engage on behalf of another company. Monitor both your and the other company's social coverage to make sure there is no runoff onto your brand. Keep your distancing statement visible until the crisis subsides.[20]

Where Legacy and Social Media Intersect

When Queen Elizabeth II of the United Kingdom died on September 8, 2022, the palace put into action a long agreed-upon plan to simultaneously alert news outlets around Great Britain, Northern Ireland, and the world of the queen's passing. Reflecting a new dynamic, however, the news was first broken on the Royal Family's Twitter feed and on its website, before being issued to global news organizations by the British Press Association.[21]

Legacy and social media are codependent. The old and new media forms interact, prop up one another, and compete with one another. The landscape of legacy media is now proliferated with social media, and the social media environment is now flush with journalists and former journalists.

Doron Levin, a veteran journalist who has written for *Fortune Magazine*, *The New York Times*, *The Wall Street Journal* and *Bloomberg News*, reflected on the rapid dawn of social media:

I was working for *Bloomberg* in about 2010, and suddenly we were beginning to understand how consequential everything was on social media, because of Twitter, Facebook, Instagram, Snapchat, and the cell phone. So, the cell phone, along with social media, has really changed the reporting of news, because everyone is connected now. Everyone is a reporter.[22]

In the analog age, C-Suite discussion of handling the media during a looming crisis centered on the question: "What is *our* stance going to be on this, and what are *we* going to say to the media and the public about this problem?" With social media, the question is: "What stance are *others* going to take on this, and what are *they* going to say to the media and to *each other* about *us*?"[23]

A fundamental shift in thinking about crisis communication has occurred in many businesses, away from robotically issuing canned media statements, news releases, and interviews, to proactive listening and then preparing to engage in conversation. On social media, a story can virally accelerate from nothing-to-crisis in just a few hours, spreading faster than an actual virus. Consequently, an organization needs the mindset to open its ears and challenge its conventional approaches, listen deeply across all platforms to understand what is being said and by whom, and accept that control is not what it once was.

Similarly, legacy media's traditional role as society's primary voice of one-way news and information has evolved. We rely on professional journalists as storytellers who make judgments about what constitutes actual news. We rely on them to investigate perceived wrongs and to help us make sense of political and social activities and trends.

The New Fountain of Breaking News

Brandon Borrman served as Vice President of Global Communications at Twitter from 2017 until 2021. With the informed perspective of having been the CCO of one of the world's largest social networking services, he said one effect of everyone being a reporter is the way leads are first developed and crises are uncovered. He said,

> What has happened is the dynamic has flipped such that social media is usually where the crisis starts. I think it is very rare for a company to get a phone call from a reporter, and that is the first time they are hearing that something is wrong. So, it is no surprise that one of Twitter's biggest customer bases happens to be journalists, because they can see what's happening. Journalists will often see something start to bubble up from people tweeting about it, and then the media pick up on it and take it to the company in question.[24]

Borrman sees the issue of breaking news becoming more complex with the proliferation of social media sites.

> What's becoming the challenge is you must understand how all these different platforms work together. TikTok is now the place where much of this stuff starts. People start putting out videos on TikTok, then people on Twitter start tweeting about it. Then journalists notice those tweets, and then they call corporate and say, "I want to talk to you about it. What's happening?"[25]

Alan Ohnsman, of *Forbes* and a former wire service reporter at *Bloomberg News*, is also active on both legacy and social media. While he acknowledges the profound impact of social media on the way news is now broken, he also considers social media "a double-edged sword." Ohnsman said,

> Every reporter is addicted to Twitter because Twitter is an amazing live news feed. It is truly a nonstop source of information. Twitter is where everything is happening in terms of breaking news and live information, and as a source of new and critical information, it's terrific.

Yet, according to Ohnsman, the other edge of the sword is that "Twitter also has many shortcomings, and there's a lot of stuff that gets going on Twitter that's just complete garbage that builds up into a sort of frenzy."[26]

Looking at the way news breaks on social media from the corporate standpoint, Zenia Mucha, recently retired CCO of The Walt Disney Company, said that social media in general is "an asset and a major problem, and it depends on how you utilize it." Defining Disney's approach to breaking news she said, "Early on we made a determination to use our social media and become our own news source. So instead of always relying on a press release or statement, we posted the news on our social media sites."[27]

Mucha explained that because the Disney brand has millions of followers on its several social media channels, self-publishing was a more governable course of action. "You control your own narrative to a greater degree, rather than relying on traditional or other social media to interpret your messaging."[28]

Offering up valuable counsel for crisis communicators, Mucha said that Disney's strategy of breaking its own news applied across-the-board, to both good news and bad:

> Even if it was an upcoming price increase or a change or postponement on an upcoming parks project, we controlled the information and became an authentic news source. I think that helped enormously to reduce media outlets writing negative, screaming headlines for clicks.[29]

Jayne O'Donnell, formerly of *USA Today*, agrees with Bormann's belief that companies are rarely shocked or surprised when bad news about them surfaces. An auto reporting colleague of O'Donnell's from *The Wall Street Journal* advised her early in her career not to let anyone be surprised by what is in a story:

> Why not let them know beforehand? You don't want to listen to whether it's bad or good, but you do want to know if it's accurate. Because once the story comes out, you do not want to be dealing with the angry calls and the lawyers the next day.[30]

Where Will the Story First Appear?

In the highly competitive, fast-moving news environment, on what platform is a crisis story from a legacy news organization likely to break first? On a wire service, in a print edition, on a digital stream, or from a single reporter's Twitter feed? The answer may help communicators monitor more precisely for breaking stories before or during a crisis.

Levin said news organizations' policies on where to break stories were not always clear when social media first appeared:

This is an issue for reporters and news organizations together. Initially there was not any kind of company policy. You had reporters discussing their stories on social media before they were vetted by the newspapers. But if you talk or respond to something on social media, you are telegraphing your biases. You are showing the world that what you think in a way that can either undermine or reinforce what it is that you are reporting. So, the papers had to come up with specific policies to affect who could talk about what.

In the end, however, big news organizations asserted themselves in this area. "Most reporters understand if you're working for *The New York Times*, the *Times* wants to be able to break the story in their own way."[31]

About the practice of reporters posting their stories on social media before their news organizations have the chance to publish, Ohnsman said,

That's really dumb. I am astonished that reporters will tweet out something that they haven't published yet. It's a generational thing with many reporters who are focused on the volume of content they throw out on Twitter. But what they write will be much less, because that is the world we live in now. Their audience is not who is going to read their article. It is who is following them on Twitter. There are different incentives for different groups.[32]

Ohnsman, who has more than 22 years of experience as a journalist for major news organizations, said it is his own practice to be "more concerned with the quality of the work, to make sure that this is the way I want it to be, and that I've written it well." In respect to breaking news on social media before his employer does so, he said,

Especially if it's something heavy, if it's breaking, I'm not going to scoop myself. Why do I want to give a competitor information? If a competitor tells me what they are going to publish, I'm going to jump on that real fast. So, for competitive reasons, I think going out first like that is boneheaded. Moreover, for legal reasons, if it is something controversial, and your news organization's legal team has not signed off on what you're Tweeting, you're a fool.[33]

Turning the Tide

What happens when adults tell teenagers not to do something? This became the communications challenge for Proctor & Gamble (P&G), for public health officials, and for both legacy media and social media when people, mostly teenagers, started eating poisonous Tide laundry detergent pods on YouTube and Facebook and daring others to do the same.

The colorful and popular Tide Pods, a self-contained packet of laundry detergent wrapped in a dissolvable coating, were introduced in 2012. Like most detergents, Tide Pods can be harmful or fatal if ingested, and there were several reports of children and adults with dementia accidentally consuming the pods. The Centers for Disease Control and Prevention listed them as a health risk and *Consumer Reports* called them a health hazard.[34]

Responding to the dangers and criticism, P&G issued warnings about consuming the pods, altered the packaging of Tide Pod containers from clear plastic to solid tubs, and added tamper-resistant lids, prominent warning labels, and an unpleasant tasting chemical to the pods.[35]

The genesis of the crisis may have been a 2015 opinion article in the satirical newspaper *The Onion*. Supposedly written by a child, the headline read "So Help Me God, I'm Going to Eat One of Those Multicolored Detergent Pods." The alleged author, who appeared to be a 4-year-old boy, wrote, "From the very second I saw those blue and red detergent pods come out of that shopping bag last week, I knew immediately that, come hell or high water, I would eat one of those things."[36]

In 2017, an internet meme got rolling with several images of Tide Pods depicted as breakfast cereal, pizza topping, and pastry fillings. Several of the faked photos depicted celebrities like Donald Trump, Mike Myers, Hillary Clinton, and Oprah eating the detergent pods. The ever-helpful *Onion* weighed in again with a phony news release from P&G unveiling a "New Sour Apple" Tide Pod – "Like a trip to the laundromat and the candy store all at once."[37]

By 2018, on the heels of the meme's wide popularity, the media began writing stories about people on social media engaging in the Tide Pod Challenge. People, mostly teenagers, would record themselves biting down on Tide Pods, gagging, and spitting or swallowing the pods, and then daring others to accept the challenge and repeat the behavior – a severe health risk that can cause serious burns to the mouth and respiratory tract.

Social media challenges were not new. The ALS Ice Bucket Challenge of 2014 involved recording a bucket of ice water being poured over a person's head and then circulating the video on social media to raise money for research on amyotrophic lateral sclerosis (ALS), also known as Lou Gehrig's disease. The challenge raised $220 million.[38] Less charitable social media-driven challenges circulating around the same time included the Banana Sprite Challenge – quickly drinking a can of Sprite and then eating two bananas without vomiting, and the Cinnamon

Challenge – swallowing a spoonful of ground cinnamon in less than one minute without anything to drink.[39]

The Washington Post headline read: "Teens are daring each other to eat Tide pods. We don't need to tell you that's a bad idea." The *Post* reported that "videos circulating on social media are showing kids biting into brightly colored liquid laundry detergent packets. Or cooking them in frying pans, then chewing them up before spewing the soap from their mouths."[40]

As an immediate internet sensation, boosted by the hashtag #TidePodChallenge, the dangerous fad caused an alarming increase in sickness from people ingesting the detergent.[41] That usage spiked dramatically in early 2018 with *USA Today* reporting that the American Association of Poison Control Centers (AAPCC) listed 86 cases of intentional exposure to detergent packets before the end of January.[42]

P&G issued statements to CNN and several media outlets warning of the hazards of ingesting Tide Pods. Every major television network and cable channel covered the Tide Pod Challenge on its news and morning programs and on social media channels, warning potential participants. As a social media-bred crisis, the challenge also received heavy coverage on popular online media like Engadget, Mashable and CNET. At the height of the crisis, the Tide Pod Challenge was mentioned every six seconds on social media.[43]

Early in the crisis, P&G CEO David Taylor urged parents to warn their teenage children about the serious dangers of participating in the social media challenge. "The possible life-altering consequences of this act, seeking internet fame, can derail young people's hopes and dreams and ultimately their health," Taylor wrote in a statement. "Even the most stringent standards and protocols, labels and warnings can't prevent intentional abuse fueled by poor judgment and the desire for popularity."[44]

In a game-changing move, P&G petitioned both Facebook and YouTube to immediately remove the "videos that glorify harmful behavior."[45] Facebook agreed to remove #TidePodChallenge content from both Facebook and Instagram. YouTube also agreed to remove any videos of people eating the potentially toxic detergent packets. "YouTube's Community Guidelines prohibit content that's intended to encourage dangerous activities that have an inherent risk of physical harm. We work to quickly remove flagged videos that violate our policies," the company said in a statement.[46]

P&G flooded Twitter, Facebook, YouTube, and *www.tide.com* with the message: "What should Tide PODs be used for? DOING LAUNDRY. Nothing else. Eating a Tide POD is a BAD IDEA." The company also posted meme-looking humorous posts with serious safety messages that people could share. It also produced a 60-second advertisement with popular NFL star Rob Gronkowski and ran it heavily across social media. "Gronk Knows that Tide PODs are for DOING LAUNDRY, nothing else. What the heck is going on, people? Use Tide Pods for washing. Not eating. Do not eat. NO, NO, NO, NO, NO, NO, NO,"

Gronkowski wagged his finger and warned. P&G was also active on its @tide Twitter account, offering advice if the pods are swallowed and warning people not to consume them.[47]

The company partnered with advocacy and industry groups like the AAPCC and with the U.S. Consumer Products Safety Commission, both of whom issued media statements and went on social media to help spread the word that the behavior should stop. As part of a reverse peer-pressure grassroots movement, young people on social media who opposed the practice also started posting their own memes and other content ridiculing and shaming anyone stupid enough to eat a Tide Pod. The challenge became uncool, and there were no more videos to encourage it, so it soon stopped.

Analysis

When young people started recording themselves eating laundry detergent and daring others to do the same on social media, P&G correctly assessed that it had a "Level 1: Multiplatform Social Media Crises" on its hands. The trigger event was as severe as it could get. The problem had a high potential for growth, and it was getting worse. The dangerous behavior would likely continue if not resolved in a short period of time.

Some crises are self-inflicted, but, in this instance, P&G was not culpable for the reckless behavior of consumers. While the public's concerns were certainly justified, the responsibility did not belong to P&G. Most crises of an organization's own doing require an apology. In this case, P&G notably did not apologize for the behavior of others, and that was the right decision because it had done nothing wrong. However, P&G did immediately own the problem and let the public know that it was working hard to solve it.

When potential problems with its laundry pods were first raised, P&G took several preventative steps to help deter accidental ingestion, including changing the packaging and adding warning labels and a bitter-tasting coating. What it could not prevent was unexpected and foolish behavior on the part of its customers. From reckless driving in an automobile, to using spray glue as hairspray (this happened), to using duct tape to silence unruly grade school students (so did this), companies cannot be sure that their products will always be used as they intended. Millions of people on social media make the unexpected more likely to happen. Even more reason to conduct strategic crisis planning and war-game numerous scenarios in anticipation of an inevitable crisis.

P&G's quick and comprehensive response was both reactive and proactive. The company went on social media to express its concerns and offer help, establishing two-way engagement with consumers. P&G moved quickly to issue statements to news media and got its CEO involved up front, with an emotional and engaging appeal to customers and parents. Its successful request that YouTube and Facebook remove the videos and other #TidePod Challenge content reflects both the severity of the issue and increased openness on the part of social media companies to police offensive content on their sites. Deploying a popular influencer like Rob Gronkowski to carry the message in a rather juvenile advertisement reflected a solid understanding of P&G's target audience for the campaign.

To Engage or Not to Engage?

Zenia Mucha, formerly of Disney, and Brandon Borrman, formerly of Twitter, have both been on the corporate frontlines when something started snowballing on social media that required them to decide whether to engage. What goes into that decision-making process? What tips the scales to make companies jump in, or remain silent, or wait and see?

Borrman said,

> First is getting an agreement internally on the level of pain tolerance that everyone is comfortable with. Sometimes the answer is simply just let it go. It will burn itself out. It may take a couple of weeks and we must be comfortable with that. Just getting that in place and getting everybody on the same page is step number one.[48]

> Much of this is going to come back to your instincts and experience. Ironically, I used to tell my management team that although we are Twitter, we cannot manage this company based on what we see on Twitter. As a communications person, you need a solid understanding of your audience and what they're being influenced by. Then you can go to your leadership and say, yes, I see this tweet. I know it is incredibly annoying. I know 1,000 people have retweeted it. It is not going elsewhere. Employees are not talking about it. I am not getting calls from journalists about it. We are not seeing it picked up on other platforms.[49]

> If you can come in with an understanding of your audience and how they interact with one another, you can help leadership understand that Twitter is really a tiny subset of the bigger world, and you can put it in context and help them control their angst. That will help them understand what they should respond to and what they do not need to worry about.[50]

Like Borrman, Mucha said there is no single factor that helps a company decide whether to engage when something is blowing up on social media:

> First and foremost, you have to go back and ask, how is this story going to impact our brand or our business? My management team? My CEO? Is this something that will matter to the consumer? To our employees? What does this do to investors? You have multiple constituencies to process before you decide whether it's impactful. Maybe it's just a few people screaming on their Twitter feed. With social media moving so fast, this analysis is absolutely

necessary. Some feel it's critical to respond immediately. I feel that is a much more dangerous path, especially when you do not have all the facts or fully understand the repercussions.[51]

Most likely, what's screaming at you from Twitter now and for the next ten minutes nobody will care about in 25 minutes. If you don't have all your facts, and you say the wrong thing, or you create a bigger story out of it than it needs to be, then that's on you. Communications people sometimes feel like they must respond right away. And I always say, no, actually, you don't.[52]

Once in, Take a Different Approach

Once organizations decide to engage, Borman said,

> They must go into it with is an understanding that so much of our jobs as communicators over the last 20 something years has been about controlling the situation and putting up walls between our companies and the outside world. That is not a successful approach on social media, because it's a conversation, it's a dialogue.[53]
>
> Many companies want to just put out a statement and let that be the end of it. With traditional media, that has been right. You do the interview, you put out the statement, and then you're done. Maybe they'll do a follow-up piece in a week. That kind of dynamic doesn't work on social media. If you're going to put out a statement, people are going to respond to it, and they're going to ask questions, and they will expect you to continue to engage and answer those questions.[54]

As such, Borrman recommends against using a traditional corporate approach to posting on social media under the corporate mantle:

> You need to have a face associated with your social media. People think they are talking to people, not companies. You've got to figure out who are the right people who are going to engage. It can't really just be the corporate handle or the corporate account that does it.[55]
>
> There is a level of transparency and discomfort that you have to bring to the table. If something happened with one of your products, you must be willing to acknowledge that something's happened and then share some detail on what went wrong. What are you doing to fix it? In some ways it's kind of like Crisis 101. It's just accelerated on social media, and you have to be willing to some extent to let go and understand you can't control it in the same way you could when it was just sharing a couple of statements with the news media.[56]
>
> If you go into it with honesty and a little bit of humility, I think you can have some success and turn the tide. And if you do it well, what you will find

is that in the first couple of days you start to have other people saying, hey, they've been open about this. Let's give them a chance to try and fix this.[57]

Some Best Practices for Social Media Strategic Crisis Communications

Organizations facing a crisis on social media, that either unfolded there or is spreading because of it, will want to arm themselves with these proven practices.

Use an authentic voice in all your communication. The term "authentic" is overused in communications for good reason. Social media engagement is a conversation that requires a voice that will express the values of the organization in terms that are genuine, human, fallible, empathetic, sincere, and honest. Ann Handley is *The Wall Street Journal* bestselling author of *Everybody Writes: Your New and Improved Go-To Guide to Creating Ridiculously Good Content* and was named by *Forbes* as the most influential woman in social media. Handley advises,

> Lead with empathy, and use the right tone of voice. Address people's emotional concerns: not "this is overblown" but "we're heartbroken, too." This is your opportunity to be relatable and human, not corporate and stiff. You can't address an emotional issue with a rational argument.[58]

"Approach any crisis with humility," she said. "It's OK to express vulnerability. Engaging directly and honestly will strengthen relationships and build goodwill. Share facts, but don't lead with them." Carefully choose the people who will represent you on social media. Select your most talented writers who understand your organization's principles and philosophy.[59]

Determine the crisis level based on your analysis of the severity of the trigger event, the potential for the problem to grow on social media, and the likelihood of the crisis being resolved within a reasonable amount of time. You want to match the social media protocols you have planned for in advance with the level of the crisis you face. Understand the difference between a true crisis and a problem that can be solved by a targeted response to an effected group or individual, or by an offline conversation.

Quickly acknowledge the problem if you are facing an issue that you have determined is legitimate, and not a rumor, fake, or bait, even if you do not yet have all the details. Staying quiet for too long on social media telegraphs that you are fearful or hiding something. Let your audience know you are aware of the issue and are working hard to learn more. Tell them you will keep them updated and let them know where to find information once it becomes available.

Apologize, if appropriate, and do so sincerely and deliberately if your organization has done something wrong that affects others. Express regret or remorse for whatever happened and accept responsibility, blaming no one else. Focus foremost on the victims of your actions. If one of your products has caused fatalities or injuries, center your apology around the victims and express sympathy and heartfelt condolences to the victims and their families. If your actions have resulted in a violation of the trust your customers placed in you, focus on your desire to renew that trust with concrete actions. Pledge to prevent a recurrence and promise to make things right. If your organization is in a major crisis, it will likely affect your employees, who must face their friends and neighbors every day, and may be embarrassed or blamed. Acknowledge and thank them for their continued service and make it clear that the responsibility lies with the organization's leadership, not them.

Be *the* authoritative, credible source of information in a sea of misinformation. Rumors, speculation, and allegations will fly. But you know more about your crisis than anyone on social media, so be forthright from the start that you will be as transparent and forthcoming as possible. Make it clear where your official statements and information will be posted, link to those places, and post it at the same time every day if practical.

Engage but do not confront social media trolls. Social media is full of trolls who have a need for attention and will seek it by trying to provoke you and lure you into a public conflict. They are the bullies of social media. Before acting, be sure not to mistake an upset customer venting their anger for a troll. Once you determine you have a troll, the most clear-cut option is to ignore them and remove their annoying posts. But that may incite them to complain even more loudly of being suppressed. Consider a single, diplomatic, and nonconfrontational reply that also corrects any misinformation the troll may have posted. But not more than one post. You want the troll to go away, and it will not if you keep feeding it attention.

Direct your audience to your website. If you are not engaging individually regarding your crisis, use all your social platforms to clearly direct interested social media users to your general or crisis-specific microsite, where all your statements and updates are posted.

Pause your scheduled social media posts and postpone any planned product updates. If your organization is in a major crisis, or in the event of a high-profile tragedy affecting many people, suspend your scheduled social media marketing activity – it is likely to be inappropriate, insensitive, and even offensive. Be sure you have systems in place that allow you to shut off all scheduled social posts, across all platforms, at a moment's notice. Regarding posts during a large disaster, Handley said, "If it's a tragedy that's dominating every news outlet, brands should keep mum. It's partly an issue of respect, and partly one of coming across tone-deaf if they continue with business as usual."[60]

Coordinate closely with customer relations and everyone else who posts incoming and outgoing social media communications. Customer relations and social media need to operate hand in glove and be fully aware of what one another are posting. Ideally, a customer who jumps on a general Twitter handle to complain can be intercepted and engaged with privately by customer relations.

On the larger topic of the need for coordination of all social media posts, Borrman said,

> Having a high-level of coordination between anybody who touches social media is critical. They can have whatever level of independence each company determines is correct. But when it comes to crisis, there has got to be a way that somebody can pull the red tag and halt everything for the time being.[61]

Maintain a Strong Social Media Policy for employee guidance and communicate it throughout the enterprise. All organizations should have a clear position on employees' obligations and responsibilities regarding their use of social media and should insist that employees draw a clear distinction between official communications and personal views. Confusion can arise when employees post on company social sites and are mistaken for company spokespersons, so the distinction must be very sharp. Statements like, "I work for Company A and this is my opinion, not Company A's" and "I work at Company A, but I am not an authorized spokesperson the Company A, and my personal view is . . ." may be helpful.

Borrman said there is no guarantee that employee statements with such disclaimers will not be used against a company during a crisis: "Your employees are all on social media, and when times get rough, no one's going to objectively be able to say, well, they're saying that as an individual, not as a representative of the company."[62]

Several helpful resources are available to collect industry best practices for developing an effective social media policy.[63]

Constantly monitor the social media landscape in real-time, but especially during a crisis. Your organization should be like a spider at the center of its web, able to detect every twitch and movement in its environment. Fortunately, many excellent tools exist that allow companies to detect emerging trends and evaluate the keywords, mentions, and conversations that arise and to understand the scope, urgency, and context of problems. In a larger sense, these tools also allow companies to be empathetic and sensitive to societal trends and can help identify key influencers leading critical conversations. (See Chapter 7 for a listing of social media monitoring companies.)

We close this chapter on social media with the insightful Brandon Borrman, formerly CCO of Twitter. We asked him about the future of crisis communications on social media. Buckle up.

> This is only going to get more difficult for communications people. When I started my career in the mid '90s, you had a media list and you had maybe 30, 40 people on it, and those were people you talk to. Suddenly, we should start talking to employees, too. Then social media started. Then, maybe we should start thinking about bloggers. What about those influential tweeters? The list

will continue growing, and legacy media will be just one subset of it. Figuring out how you engage the whole community that is shaping your reputation is going to be very difficult.

You're starting to also see things like Facebook's popularity waning a little bit, and new small groups and niches like Discord popping up and talking about your company. It may only be 40 or 50 people, but they may be your most influential customers. You have no idea what they are talking about. So as a communications person, you must start seeking these groups out and try to figure out where these important pockets are. The social media sphere is just going to get more and more diffuse as time goes on, because the internet is going to continue to get bigger and bigger.[64]

References

1. Plimsoll, S., and Thorpe, A., (2010, July), "Find and Target Customers in the Social Media Maze," *Marketing: Road to Recovery*, 10–11, Retrieved from ABI/INFORM Global (Document ID: 2109794771)
2. Ibid.
3. Winston, A. "Pepsi, United, and the Speed of Corporate Shame." *Harvard Business Review*. April 12, 2017. Retrieved online: August 19, 2022. https://hbr.org/2017/04/pepsi-united-and-the-speed-of-corporate-shame
4. Doyle, B. "TikTok Statistics – Updated Aug 2022." *Wallaroo Media*. August 13, 2022. Retrieved online: August 16, 2022. https://wallaroomedia.com/blog/social-media/tiktok-statistics/
5. Priday, R. "The Inside Story of the Great KFC Chicken Shortage of 2018." *Wired UK*. February 21, 2018. Retrieved online: August 13, 2022. www.wired.co.uk/article/kfc-chicken-crisis-shortage-supply-chain-logistics-experts
6. Ibid.
7. Brownsell, A. "KFC: A Very Fcking Clever Campaign." *Campaign*. November 21, 2018. Retrieved online: August 16, 2022. www.campaignlive.co.uk/article/kfc-fcking-clever-campaign/1498912
8. Longo, S. "KFC Chicken Shortage: Everything You Need to Know." *The Daily Mail*. February 20, 2018. Retrieved online: August 13, 2022. www.dailymail.co.uk/news/article-5414035/KFC-UK-Chicken-Shortage-Need-Know.html
9. McClusky, M. "The Viral Legend Who Cracked KFC's Hilarious Code Just Got the Most Glorious Reward." *Time*. November 8, 2017. Retrieved online: August 13, 2022. https://time.com/5015515/kfc-viral-tweet-reward
10. Longo. op. cit.
11. Brownsell. op. cit.
12. Ibid.
13. Bloch, A. "KFC Apologizes With a Full Page Ad in Today's Metro. A Masterclass in PR Crisis Management." February 23. 12:46 a.m. Tweet.
14. Brownsell. op. cit.
15. "From Chicken Crisis to Cannes: Lessons from KFC's Award-winning Campaign." *YouTube*. July 3, 2018. Retrieved online: August 14, 2022. www.youtube.com/watch?v=UMduI9bEV68

16. Ibid.
17. Ibid.
18. Jennings, H. "3 Tiers of a Social Media Crisis – And How to Manage Each One of Them." *PR News*. March 26, 2018. Retrieved online: August 16, 2022. www.prnewsonline.com/three-tiers-social-media-crisis
19. Ibid.
20. Ibid.
21. Specia, M. "Planning for the End of Elizabeth's Reign Began at the Beginning." *The New York Times*, September 8, 2022. Retrieved online: September 8, 2022. www.nytimes.com/2022/09/08/world/europe/london-bridge-what-happens-next-queen.html
22. Interview with Doron Levin, via Zoom. July 22, 2022
23. Boncheck M. and France, C. "How Leaders Can Keep Their Cool in a Crisis." *Harvard Business Review*. February 12, 2018. Retrieved online: August 13, 2022. https://hbr.org/2018/02/how-leaders-can-keep-their-cool-in-a-crisis
24. Interview with Brandon Borrman, via Zoom. July 29, 2022.
25. Ibid.
26. Interview with Alan Ohnsman, via Zoom. July 20, 2022.
27. Interview with Zenia Mucha, via Zoom. July 7, 2022.
28. Ibid.
29. Ibid.
30. Interview with Jayne O'Donnell, via Zoom. June 29, 2022.
31. Levin, op cit.
32. Ohnsman. op cit.
33. Ibid.
34. "Consumption of Tide Pods." *Wikipedia*. August 15, 2022. Retrieved online: August 20, 2022. https://en.wikipedia.org/wiki/Consumption_of_Tide_Pods
35. Ibid.
36. DelMonico, D. "So Help Me God, I'm Going to Eat One of Those Multicolored Detergent Pods." *The Onion*. December 8, 2015. Retrieved online: August 20, 2022. www.theonion.com/so-help-me-god-i-m-going-to-eat-one-of-those-multicolo-1819585017
37. "Tide Debuts New Sour Apple Detergent Pods." *The Onion*. July 11, 2017. Retrieved online: August 20, 2022. www.theonion.com/tide-debuts-new-sour-apple-detergent-pods-1819580060
38. "Ice Bucket Challenge." *Wikipedia*. August 12, 2022. Retrieved online: August 21, 2022. https://en.wikipedia.org/wiki/Ice_Bucket_Challenge#Predecessors
39. "List of Internet Challenges." *Wikipedia*. June 25, 2022. Retrieved online: August 21, 2022. https://en.wikipedia.org/wiki/List_of_Internet_challenges
40. Beyer, L. "Teens are Daring Each Other to Eat Tide Pods. We Don't Need to Tell You That's a Bad Idea." *The Washington Post*. January 17, 2018. Retrieved online: August 20, 2022. www.washingtonpost.com/news/to-your-health/wp/2018/01/13/teens-are-daring-each-other-to-eat-tide-pods-we-dont-need-to-tell-you-thats-a-bad-idea/
41. Ibid.
42. Rossman, S. "P&G Just Cannot Prevent the Tide Pod Challenge." *USA Today*. January 23, 2018. Retrieved online: August 20, 2022. www.usatoday.com/story/news/nation-now/2018/01/23/procter-gamble-ceo-safeguards-cant-prevent-tide-pod-challenge/1057105001/

43. Hirsch, L. "Tide Pods Are Being Mentioned Every 6 Seconds on Social Media." *CNBC.* January 23, 2018. Retrieved online: August 20, 2022. www.cnbc.com/2018/01/23/tide-pods-are-being-mentioned-every-6-seconds-on-social-media.html

44. Brunsman, B. "P&G CEO: Tide Pods Challenge 'No Laughing Matter.'" *Cincinnati Business Courier.* January 23, 2018. Retrieved online: August 20, 2022. www.bizjournals.com/cincinnati/news/2018/01/23/p-g-ceo-tide-pods-challenge-no-laughing-matter.html

45. Ibid.

46. Montgomery, B. "YouTube Is Taking Down Videos of The Tide Pod Challenge." *Buzzfeed.News.* January 18, 2018. Retrieved online: August 20, 2022. www.buzzfeednews.com/article/blakemontgomery/youtube-will-now-take-down-videos-of-the-tide-pod-challenge

47. Brunsman. op. cit.

48. Borrman. op. cit.

49. Ibid.

50. Ibid.

51. Mucha. op. cit.

52. Ibid.

53. Borrman. op. cit.

54. Ibid.

55. Ibid.

56. Ibid.

57. Ibid.

58. Interview with Ann Handley, via email. August 15, 2022.

59. Ibid.

60. Garrett, M. "During a Crisis, How Should Brands Behave on Social Media?" *Linkedin.* July 17, 2017. Retrieved online: August 22, 2022. www.linkedin.com/pulse/during-crisis-how-should-brands-behave-social-media-michelle/

61. Borrman. op cit.

62. Ibid.

63. Hirsch, S. "How to Create an Effective Social Media Policy," *Society for Human Resources Management,* March 18, 2021. Retrieved online: February 5, 2022. www.shrm.org/resourcesandtools/hr-topics/employee-relations/pages/how-to-create-an-effective-social-media-policy.aspx. See also Sehl, K. "How to Create Effective Social Media Guidelines for Your Business," *Hootsuite,* February 3, 2020. Retrieved online: February 1, 2022. https://blog.hootsuite.com/social-media-guidelines/

64. Borrman. op. cit.

Chapter 20

Best Practices in Crisis Communication

As Christmas Eve 2022 approached and millions of Americans prepared to board holiday flights, a massive winter storm known as a "bomb cyclone" swept in from the Pacific Northwest, intensified over the Great Lakes, and dropped severe blizzard conditions, powerful winds, and life-threatening cold on two-thirds of the country. In the last ten days of December, at every major airport, including Los Angeles, Denver, Chicago, Atlanta, and New York, all airlines were temporarily crippled by the storm, cancelling around 30,000 flights and stranding hundreds of thousands of passengers and crews for days, many without their baggage, during the busiest travel time of the year.[1]

As this perfect storm of weather and holiday travel exasperated so many passengers struggling toward their destinations, most airlines successfully fought back to restore normal operations in one to three days. Southwest Airlines, however, was a conspicuous outlier. In the days immediately before and after Christmas, Southwest cancelled 16,700 flights, more than all the other airlines combined, affecting an estimated two million customers and crew members.[2]

Families with young children were left stranded at airports for Christmas. Pilots and flight attendants slept on floors while waiting for their crew assignments. Mountains of luggage, many bags containing presents and necessities like medicine and car keys, piled up, with many bags sent ahead to destinations passengers never reached. Frustrated travelers waited in lines that snaked throughout terminals and were left on hold for hours.

On CNN, U.S. Secretary of Transportation Pete Buttigieg blasted Southwest's singular failure to get back on its feet, complaining, "The bottom line is that the rest of the aviation system has been on the road to recovery since the worst days of the storm." As for Southwest, with two-thirds of its flights cancelled, the Secretary declared, "Their system really has completely melted down," a label which branded the Southwest crisis and which was widely repeated by news media and on social media.[3]

Following what was a terrible experience for so many, the bewildered patrons of an airline beloved by many loyal fliers are now thinking twice about moving around the country on their favorite airline.

DOI: 10.4324/9781003322849-24

Hillary Chang, a frequent Southwest passenger whose luggage went missing in the maelstrom, told National Public Radio (NPR) that she had accumulated some points in the Southwest frequent flier program. Now, she says, "I've been thinking about it . . . I'm open to dating another airline."[4]

Southwest Airlines, founded by Rollin King and Herb Kelleher, began regional service from Dallas to San Antonio and Houston in 1971. Disrupting the airline industry status quo by offering lower fares, no schedule change fees, two free checked bags, a single economy class of service, and no reserved seats, Southwest focused on making flying less expensive, more customer-focused, and more fun.[5] Now among the top five largest airlines in the nation, Southwest is the world's largest low-cost carrier, carrying nearly 157 million passengers per year.[6]

How could such a storied and beloved brand experience such an epic failure? Just as importantly, how will it recover? The reasons for the year-end crisis are complex, and the answer you receive depends on whom you ask. Most airlines deploy a "hub and spoke" system, dispatching flights through major airports to reduce costs and provide on-site flexibility in terms of staffing and available aircraft. Southwest, however, predominantly uses a "point-to-point" system, which is leaner but much less flexible in terms of getting aircraft and flight crews where and when they are needed. By some accounts, Southwest was also using outdated computer systems to manage its crew rescheduling systems, and the high volume of last-minute flight cancellations overwhelmed the system and caused an increased reliance on time-consuming manual processes to reposition crews. Southwest denies that its systems were outdated, but the president of the union that represents Southwest pilots labeled the Christmas meltdown "catastrophic" and said neither he nor most pilots were surprised when it occurred.

"We're still using, not only IT from the '90s, but also processes [from] when our airline was a tenth of the size," he said. "And it's really just not scaled for an operation that we have today."[7]

In a December 27 video statement, in the thick of the crisis, Southwest CEO Bob Jordan said:

> The tools we use to recover from disruption serve us well, 99 percent of the time; but clearly, we need to double down on our already existing plans to upgrade systems for these extreme circumstances so that we never again face what's happening right now.[8]

Southwest's communications response was robust, in both legacy and social media, as it certainly needed to be:

• The airline apologized to customers at the onset of the storm, saying, "Our heartfelt apologies are just beginning," repeating its apologies from Bob Jordan and other high-ranking Southwest executives once the magnitude of the debacle became clear.

- Southwest's media website regularly updated its operational plan from the on-set of the storm and was transparent about the number of cancelled flights until the situation worsened, acknowledging it was no longer able to keep track.
- Once the end was in sight, Southwest published a commitment to return to normalcy by a specific date, which it did.
- An internal memo from Bob Jordan to employees was intentionally made public, candidly noting that "You know, we'll move forward with lessons learned here, as we always do. We have plans to invest in tools and technology and processes, but there will be immediate work to understand what happened."[9]
- Jordan has remained front and center, focused on customers and employees, issuing a detailed statement over his name that outlines Southwest's policies on reimbursement.
- Jordan's *The New York Times* interview on January 13 is a case study in effective crisis communication. He acknowledged, with empathy, "that we really messed up for a lot of customers" and expressed accountability for that. "At the end of the day," he said, "no matter how we got here, I'm responsible." Equally important, he laid out a clear path forward to assure that the issue would never happen again.[10]

By spring 2023, the bomb cyclone of December 2022 would be far from over for Southwest Airlines. The Department of Transportation launched a formal investigation. Estimated losses due to the meltdown are likely to exceed $1 billion, with individual and shareholder lawsuits potentially on the horizon.

An Evolving Discipline

In the nearly 100 years since corporate communication began to professionalize, seeking advice from outside counsel and organizing internal groups to manage the function, many people have written about what you should do in a crisis: How you should organize. What you should say. Actions you should take. But that advice, for the most part, has been based largely on their own, fairly narrow circumstances – what happened in one calamitous event for their company or organization.

The real reason you're reading this book is to determine what *you* should do in an unfolding crisis. How do you prepare? How do you respond? What's the best approach to assure you still have a business when this is over?

Corporate communicators, issues management specialists, and senior executives have called the authors of this book – with surprising regularity – and asked those very questions. Often the conversation begins with an inquiry about case studies. "Yes," we say, "we have each written case studies and have lived through a number of others. What sort of case are you interested in?" "Well, how about food cases?" the executive would say. "We have food cases. What's your interest?" A brief pause, then "How about contamination or recalls?"

That's the point at which this gets interesting. "Sure, we have cases on contamination. What do you need? Listeriosis? *E.coli*? Botulism? What sort of problem do you have?" Once we had narrowed the conversation to a particular kind of problem, our caller would invariably say, "Well, we're interested in how the issue played out for another firm and using their experience to guide us . . . to tell us what to do."

Of course, we're happy to share what we know and have experienced – that's one of the real joys of academic life and of providing counsel on corporate communications. But we're also quick to remind our caller that, while the cases we have may prove helpful in understanding the contamination process, issues involved with a large-scale recall, or problems associated with protecting the brand, every one of the case studies we've written, advised on, or lived through all *happened in the past* – some of it recent, much of it distant.

Spanish philosopher George Santayana in 1905 famously wrote, "Those who cannot remember the past are condemned to repeat it."[11] The more difficult truth is this: while history does repeat itself, it never occurs again *in quite the same way*. Each scenario is slightly different, each story has recurring elements but different outcomes. The technology involved is different, regulatory oversight has changed, and the capabilities of those involved are simply not the same.

Most 21st-century executives, especially in the G-8 nations, cannot bear the thought of a business problem that time and large sums of money will not solve. We've gotten good at responding to changing circumstances, but we're obligated to acknowledge just how rapidly change is happening in our businesses, our societies, and our ability to fix things when they go wrong. What worked for one may not work for another, and what worked once may not work again.

You may find it both interesting and helpful to read in detail about how James Burke and David Collins responded to a contamination crisis at Johnson & Johnson. Their widely available pain reliever Tylenol had been poisoned by a maniacal individual who was never caught.[12] In those days, everything from cold medicine to digestive aids were packaged in gelcaps that you could separate and empty, simply by pulling the container halves apart. That intruder in the suburbs of Chicago laced the acetaminophen in those gelcaps with potassium cyanide. Just one would be enough to kill an ordinary human being.[13] Before Burke and Collins and their team were able to complete the recall, Paula Prince – a 35-year-old United Airlines flight attendant – and six others were dead.[14]

Burke, Johnson & Johnson's CEO, and Collins, Chairman of McNeil Consumer Healthcare – the company that managed the Tylenol brand as a subsidiary of J&J – responded very quickly, recalling millions of bottles of the product from store shelves and launching a campaign to inform anyone who had purchased the product to return it to point-of-purchase or get rid of it. That cost the company more than $100 million and threatened to extinguish the brand permanently.[15]

According to *The New York Times,*

Marketers predicted that the Tylenol brand, which accounted for 17 percent of the company's net income in 1981, would never recover from the sabotage. But only two months later, Tylenol was headed back to the market, this time in tamper-proof packaging and bolstered by an extensive media campaign. A year later, its share of the $1.2 billion analgesic market, which had plunged to 7 percent from 37 percent following the poisoning, had climbed back to 30 percent.[16]

What set apart Johnson & Johnson's handling of the crisis from others? It placed consumers first by recalling 31 million bottles of Tylenol gelcaps from store shelves and offering replacement product in the safer tablet form free of charge. "Before [this], nobody ever recalled anything," said Albert Tortorella, a managing director at Burson-Marsteller Inc., the New York public relations firm that advised Johnson & Johnson. "Companies often fiddle while Rome burns."[17]

The real problem for our caller inquiring about product contamination is that this all happened in September 1982. Before the internet, email, or cell phones. How we gather information, verify that it's accurate, speak with colleagues in the company, and communicate to the media has all changed. None of it, in fact, is remotely the same as it was 40 years ago.

Beyond that, the way we package food and drugs has changed, thanks largely to the determination of J&J executives to make sure that horrible set of events never happened again. The sealed gelcap, the foil overlay on the pain reliever bottle, the shrink-wrap plastic around the screwcap, and the glue spot on the cardboard box are all there to assure consumers and alert everyone to possible tampering. Those innovations and much more are the result of a pharmaceutical company's response to a crisis that threatened human life and the existence of a very well-known brand.

The 21st century is a different time. We operate, organize, and think about crisis communication differently. Studying the Tylenol crisis and the actions Jim Burke and Dave Collins took will certainly be interesting and instructive. But it won't solve the next crisis, which is bound to be different in a number of material ways. What follows is a set of 10 ideas the authors have gathered from nearly a hundred years of combined experience in tracking, studying, managing, and living through crises of all sorts. This is a useful, time-tested set of best practices.

Get the Facts . . . Fast

Deal From an Informed Position

You cannot establish credibility or respect for your enterprise, your brand, or yourself unless you know what you're talking about.

Separate Fact From Rumor

The staunchly isolationist senator Hiram W. Johnson (R-CA) said in 1918, "The first casualty when war comes is the truth."[18] When crises erupt, you must know for certain what it true and what is not.

Document What You Know for Sure

In addition to documenting your source for every fact or comment you offer, you must also document how you know it's so. What's the source of your confidence?

Become the Source of Reliable Information

If what you say to the press, the public, elected officials, and key stakeholders turns out to be true, they will begin to trust you. The more trustworthy and reliable you become, the more frequently they will turn to you for comment, information, and guidance.

Keep the Information Flowing

Don't stop communicating, even if new developments are not particularly rapid. Keep taking questions, continue answering them to the best of your ability. Take those phone calls and keep the lines of communication open.

Determine the Real Problem

Short Term

Problems presenting themselves as a crisis are frequently not problems but symptoms. They are often the product or result of much deeper issues that will require your attention. The first question to ask is, "How did this occur" then, "What action will we need to take to solve this?"

Long Term

The more important issue, affecting far more stakeholders than the short-term concern, is, "How can we prevent this from happening again?" Consider the long-term, permanent solutions you'll need to implement.

Is This Your Problem or Does It Really Belong to Someone Else?

Because so little in any organization belongs entirely to the company or the enterprise, you will find it useful to examine problem root causes by ownership. If this really isn't your product, your process, or your service, there is a very good chance it's not your problem. Respond accordingly.

Put Someone in Charge

With Responsibility

The person appointed to take charge of the Crisis Communications Team during an emerging crisis must have full responsibility for everything his or her team does as well as accountability for the results.

With Authority

That same person must have full authority to hire outside help, request help from inside the organization, authorize expenditures, commandeer resources, and make public statements.

With Resources

The crisis response chief must also have all that he or she needs to get the job done, including people with proper skills and credentials, funding, office space, telecommunication, and other forms of equipment, muscle, and mind power.

Tell People Who It Is

An essential ingredient for success in managing a crisis is for the world-at-large to know exactly who is in charge. The identity and contact data for team members and support staff should be kept confidential, but all within the organization and those in the news media must know whom to speak to and how to find them.

Assemble a Team

Staff It With the Expertise Needed

In a true crisis, your team must reflect the ethos of the enterprise, the nature of the industry, and the expertise expected of your brand. Be sure to include the broad skill sets of marketing, communication, production, logistics, and the law. Additionally, you should include social media, customer relations, and human resources.

Deploy a Rapid Response Team

This would include a small, talented subset of the Crisis Communications Team to quickly gather facts and develop media statements for immediate review by key leadership and final approvers.

Make It Large Enough to Be Effective

Even if certain expertise is required for a short period of time, do not be reluctant to spend the time and money to find it. Encourage those on the team to talk with one another daily and explain to the chief communicator what they know in plain English.

Keep It Small Enough to Be Nimble

A team of experts and specialists should probably be somewhere between one and three dozen in size. More than that becomes unwieldy and smaller than a dozen will mean that key members are being asked to double-task.

Isolate Team Members From Other Day-to-Day Concerns

Make it clear to the major division chiefs within your organization that they cannot call on, direct, or use the services of your team members. Otherwise, they will never get anything done. New mobile phones, new office space, and a very clear set of instructions about their new roles may prove to be essential.

Ensure Required Resources Are Available

Your crisis team should include an administrative director whose job it is to ask all members what they need and then, in your name, provide it to them. No task should come to a complete halt for lack of resources, money, or mind power.

Develop a Strategy

For Resolving the Problem

The first priority of a crisis management team must be resolution of the problem at hand. Whether it's plugging an oil leak, putting out a fire, or removing suspect products from retail shelves, this is the most immediate concern of the organization.

For Dealing With Affected Parties

While the press, the public, and elected officials will be interested, they are not necessarily among those directly affected. If victims, families, businesses, or communities are experiencing some form of negative impact, your organization must address them quickly, effectively, and compassionately.

For Communicating

Everyone imaginable will want facts, answers, and a prognosis for the situation as quickly as possible. The crisis team must include an experienced, skilled senior communicator who can prepare statements for the media and for the C-suite on a continuing basis. If that person is not an accomplished writer, you'll have to find one who can assist with that, full-time, until the crisis is resolved.

For Tomorrow and the Long Term

Once the immediate problem is resolved and a permanent solution is on the horizon, a sense of relief will sweep through the organization and your Crisis Communications Team. The job is not finished, though, until you are able to identify, test, and implement a long-range, permanent solution. Your team, the organization leadership, and all affected must have a high-level of confidence in what you've devised for the long term.

Establish Goals

Define Your Objectives for the Near Term, Midterm, and Long Term

Setting objectives for the near term will provide you and your organization's leadership with a sense of control and – if you can achieve them – accomplishment. Bigger midterm goals show that the company is committed to staying with this until all problems are addressed. And, long-term goals must include important, large-scale accomplishments that everyone affected can agree to.

Measure, Measure, Measure

This is huge. Peter Drucker, philosophy professor and management theorist, wrote, "You can't manage what you can't measure."[19] It remains true that some activities, ideas, and processes are difficult to measure, but that doesn't mean you shouldn't try. This is one of the few ways you'll have to show that you're experiencing progress or improvement.

Don't Be Discouraged by Critics, Negative Press, or Short-Term Failures

No matter what happens, at least some people will be unhappy, loud, and intensely critical. The news media will have no trouble finding them and getting a quote. You cannot be discouraged by early failures and frustrations in the task of managing a crisis. Say what you know to be true, do your best to deliver results, and celebrate small victories along the way.

Centralize Communications

Limit the Number of Spokespersons

In a continuing crisis, you should rely on a strictly limited number of spokespersons who are knowledgeable, authoritative, responsive, and patient. The more public spokespersons you have, the greater the probability they'll begin saying things that contradict one another or offering information that's dated or untrue. You probably don't need more than three such corporate advocates. One of them has to be awake. All should speak and listen to one another at some point each day.

Consider All Markets

Local, Regional, National, International

A problem discovered in one location does not mean that the problem will not affect others. News moves rapidly in all languages across the nation and around the world, so your team must consider all markets you serve and any special interests or concerns those markets may have.

Consider All Stakeholders

Victims, Families, Employees, Management, Suppliers, Contractors

A stakeholder is someone with something to win or lose, depending on actions taken by management. Do not ignore any of them. Frequently, their interests will be in opposition to one another. Many will demand that you listen and respond to their interests first. Do your best to address every stakeholder's concerns. Be empathetic and focused when they speak.

Consider Customers, Clients, Investors, Creditors, Regulators, Elected Officials

Customers and clients, of course, are the economic lifeblood of any organization but so are investors and creditors. It's their money you're working with. Regulators and other officials will have an eye on seeing that those interests are protected.

Consider Your Allies

Emergency Services, Government and Elected Officials, Outside Experts, Public Interest Groups Businesses That Depend on You, and Communities You Operate in

You're not in this alone. Many others are hoping and praying that you succeed. Early in the game, it's your job to find them and – if needed – ask for their help. It's often surprising how many people are on your side and willing to provide *pro bono* assistance to help resolve the crisis you're experiencing.

References

1. Barbaro, M. "The Southwest Airlines Meltdown," *The Daily. The New York Times.* January 10, 2023. Retrieved online: February 1, 2023. https://www.nytimes.com/2023/01/10/podcasts/the-daily/the-southwest-airlines-meltdown.html
2. Chokshi, N. "Southwest Says Holiday Meltdown Will Cost It More Than $1 Billion." *The New York Times.* January 26, 2023. Retrieved online: February 2, 2023: Southwest Lost $220 Million Because of Holiday Meltdown – The New York Times (nytimes.com)
3. Brown, F., Kripps, K. and Neild, B. "Buttigieg Warns Southwest CEO He Will Hold Airline Accountable After 'Meltdown'," *CNN.* December 27, 2022. Retrieved online: February 2, 2023. https://www.cnn.com/travel/article/southwest-flight-cancellations-winter-storm-tuesday/index.
4. Domonoske, C. "5 Things to Know About the Southwest's Disastrous Meltdown," *National Public Radio.* December 30, 2022. Retrieved online: February 2, 2023.

https://www.npr.org/2022/12/30/1146377342/5-things-to-know-about-south-wests-disastrous-meltdown

5. Southwest Airlines. Retrieved online: February 2, 2023. https://www.southwest.com/about-southwest/#aboutUs

6. List of largest airlines in North America. *Wikipedia*. January 27, 2023. Retrieved online: February 23, 2023. https://en.wikipedia.org/wiki/List_of_largest_airlines_in_North_America

7. Domonoske. op. cit.

8. Video: Southwest Airlines CEO Bob Jordan Issues Update. SWAmedia.com. December 27, 2022. Retrieved online: February 3, 2023. https://swamedia.com/releases/release-7e05ea1637937dc7354128bee780ad75-video-southwest-airlines-ceo-bob-jordan-issues-statement

9. CEO Bob Jordan Looks Forward After Normal Operations Resume. SWAmedia.com. December 31, 2022. Retrieved online: February 3, 2023. https://swamedia.com/releases/release-7e05ea1637937dc7354128bee7a3fc35-ceo-bob-jordan-looks-forward-after-normal-operations-resume

10. Chokshi, N. "We just couldn't keep up with the volume," *The New York Times*. January 13, 2023. Retrieved online: February 3, 2023. https://www.nytimes.com/2023/01/13/business/southwest-airlines-bob-jordan.html

11. Santayana, George. *The Life of Reason: Introduction and Reason in Common Sense*. Amherst, NY: Prometheus Books, new edition 1998. Original published, 1905–1906. Retrieved online: January 8, 2010. www.amazon.com/Life-Reason-Great-Books-Philosophy/dp/1573922102/

12. Friedman, Emily. "James Lewis, Suspect in the 1982 Tylenol Killings Submitted DNA, Print Samples,"*ABC News*. January 8, 2010. Retrieved online: January 8, 2010. https://abcnews.go.com/WN/suspected-1982-tylenol-killer-james-lewis-subpoenaed-boston/story?id=9513004

13. Markel, Dr. Howard. "How the Tylenol Murders of 1982 Changed the Way We Consume Medication," *PBS News Hour*. September 29, 2014. Retrieved online: September 29, 2014. www.pbs.org/newshour/health/tylenol-murders-1982

14. Daniel, Leon. "Flight Attendant Paula Prince Saturday Became the Seventh Victim . . ." *United Press International*, October 2, 1982. Retrieved online: October 25, 2022. www.upi.com/Archives/1982/10/02/Flight-attendant-Paula-Prince-Saturday-became-the-seventh-victim/2195402379200/

15. Atkinson, Rick. "Waking Up to the New Tylenol Nightmare," *The Washington Post*, February 23, 1986. Retrieved online: www.washingtonpost.com/archive/politics/1986/02/23/waking-up-to-the-new-tylenol-nightmare/e7f7e6c8-0457-4a02-9006-e28336768297/

16. Rehak, Judith. "Tylenol Made a Hero of Johnson & Johnson: The Recall That Started Them All." *The New York Times,* March 23, 2002. Retrieved online: www.nytimes.com/2002/03/23/your-money/IHT-tylenol-made-a-hero-of-johnson-johnson-the-recall-that-started.html

17. Ibid.

18. *The Society of Editors*. Retrieved online: 27 February 2022. www.societyofeditors.org/soe_blog/the-first-casualty-of-war-is-the-truth/

19. MacKenzie, Gray. "If You Can't Measure It, You Can't Improve It." *GuavaBox*, February 2022. Retrieved online: https://guavabox.com/if-you-cant-measure-it-you-cant-improve-it/

Index

Printed in the United States
by Baker & Taylor Publisher Services